KLA 1612 POP

## POLITICIZED JUSTICE IN EMERGING DEMOCRACIES

Why are independent courts rarely found in emerging democracies? This book moves beyond familiar obstacles, such as an inhospitable legal legacy and formal institutions that expose judges to political pressure. It proposes a strategic pressure theory, which claims that, in emerging democracies, political competition eggs on rather than restrains power-hungry politicians. Incumbents who are losing their grip on power try to use the courts to hang on, which leads to the politicization of justice. The analysis uses four original datasets, containing 1,000 decisions by Russian and Ukrainian lower courts from 1998 to 2004 in two politically salient types of cases – electoral registration disputes and defamation lawsuits against media outlets – as well as data from interviews with judges, lawyers, litigants, and judicial administrators. The main finding is that justice is politicized in both countries, but in the more competitive regime (Ukraine) incumbents leaned more forcefully on the courts and obtained more favorable rulings.

Maria Popova is an Assistant Professor in the Department of Political Science at McGill University. She is the winner of the 2007 Edward S. Corwin Award from the American Political Science Association for best dissertation in the field of public law and the 2006 Sumner Dissertation Prize in the Department of Government at Harvard University. Her writings have been published in *Comparative Political Studies, Demokratizatsiya, Europe-Asia Studies, Journal of East European Law,* and *Konstitutsionnoe Pravo: Vostochnoevropeiskoe Obozrenie.*

# Politicized Justice in Emerging Democracies

## A STUDY OF COURTS IN RUSSIA AND UKRAINE

### MARIA POPOVA
McGill University

CAMBRIDGE
UNIVERSITY PRESS

CAMBRIDGE UNIVERSITY PRESS
Cambridge, New York, Melbourne, Madrid, Cape Town,
Singapore, São Paulo, Delhi, Mexico City

Cambridge University Press
32 Avenue of the Americas, New York, NY 10013-2473, USA

www.cambridge.org
Information on this title: www.cambridge.org/9781107014893

First published 2012

Printed in the United States of America

*A catalog record for this publication is available from the British Library.*

*Library of Congress Cataloging in Publication data*
Popova, Maria, 1975–
    Politicized justice in emerging democracies : a study of courts in Russia
    and Ukraine / Maria Popova.
        p.    cm.
    Includes bibliographical references and index.
    ISBN 978-1-107-01489-3 (hardback)
    1. Judicial independence – Ukraine.    2. Judicial independence – Russia
    Federation.    I. Title.
    KLA1612.P67    2012
    347.47′012–dc23        2011037804

ISBN 978-1-107-01489-3 Hardback

# Contents

v

# Figures

# Tables

# Acknowledgments

I had a large network of supporters during each stage of research and writing that produced this book. Most of all, I owe an incalculable debt to my dissertation committee: Timothy Colton, Yoshiko Herrera, Bear Braumoeller, and Peter Solomon. They not only helped me write an award-winning dissertation but also continued to support me as I set out to transform the dissertation into this book. My advisor, Tim Colton, allowed me to be stubborn and to feel like I was steering my own project, while he made sure I did not veer into any dead-ends. Yoshiko Herrera's always useful and detailed comments, unwavering support, and friendship were indispensable right from when I decided I wanted to write a dissertation on the rule of law to the very last stages of the book-writing process. Bear Braumoeller pushed me to streamline the argument and guided me closely in applying quantitative methods to analyze the data I collected. Peter Solomon shared his vast knowledge on Soviet and post-Soviet courts with me and helped both deepen and broaden my understanding of how these institutions work. He also put me in touch with many of his friends and collaborators in Russia and Ukraine and thus facilitated my field research tremendously. He has been a most generous mentor and has helped me become a member of the larger community of scholars working on the intersection of law and politics.

I would like to recognize the generosity of various Harvard institutions that funded my dissertation research – the Graduate School of Arts and Sciences, the Center for European Studies, the Davis Center for Russian and Eurasian Studies, and the Ukrainian Research Institute. In 2005–2006, I appreciated the hospitality of the Centre for European, Russian, and Eurasian Studies at the University of Toronto. In 2007–2010, my research and writing were supported by a McGill Startup Grant. McGill University's Department of Political Science has been my institutional home since 2007, and I am very grateful to be working in such a friendly and intellectually stimulating environment.

I did the field research for this book during half a dozen extended trips to Russia and Ukraine in 1999–2004. In Moscow, I benefited from the advice and assistance of Yevgenia Albats, Andrei Buzin, Olga Sidorovich, Boris Timoshenko, and Marat Umerov. I am also thankful to the Carnegie Moscow Center and the Center for Justice Assistance at the INDEM Foundation for graciously hosting me during several field trips. In Kyiv, Oksana Syroid, Assya Ivantcheva, Tatyana Goncharenko, Aleksandr Goncharenko, Andreas Umland, Mary Mycio, and Volodymir Kovtunets helped me meet people and track down elusive data on court cases. Assya Ivantcheva shared her gorgeous apartment with me, as well as many late-night talks about Ukrainian politics and life. Oksana Syroid and Tanya and Sasha Goncharenko became my good friends and made my research trips a delightful experience.

I am grateful to friends and colleagues whose comments, advice, and input have greatly improved this book: Martin Dimitrov, Yoshiko Herrera, Juliet Johnson, Diana Kapiszewski, Oxana Shevel, Peter Solomon, and Alexei Trochev. I am especially indebted to Peter Solomon, who commented on multiple drafts, to Juliet Johnson who helped me write an effective book prospectus and who has been my mentor at McGill, and to Oxana Shevel and Yoshiko Herrera, who shared their knowledge of the book-writing and publication process and answered late-night last-minute questions about anything and everything. I am grateful to the reviewers at *Comparative Political Studies*, who offered useful comments on my analysis of electoral registration cases and thus helped me to substantially revise and expand Chapter 4 of the book.[1] Participants in the 2006 Danyliw Research Seminar on Contemporary Ukraine at the University of Ottawa, the Law and Politics Program Speaker Series at Dartmouth College, and the Separation of Powers conference at the Kennan Institute at the Wilson Center provided useful feedback on parts of the analysis presented in this book. I am, of course, most indebted to the reviewers at Cambridge University Press for their close reading of the manuscript – their input and suggestions were invaluable. John Berger at Cambridge University Press was a wonderful editor who offered expert advice and graciously answered my, sometimes panicked, questions. Elizabeth Chrun, Andrew Faisman, and Noelle Peach compiled the index and diligently worked on the bibliography. Noelle also caught some typos that would have made parts of the text quite confusing. Any shortcomings and mistakes that remain, needless to say, are my own.

Finally, I am grateful to my family for believing in me unconditionally. I wish they could all see this book.

[1]  Maria Popova (2010), Political competition as an obstacle to judicial independence: Evidence from Russia and Ukraine, *Comparative Political Studies*, 43 (10), 1202–29.

# Introduction

"My legal team painstakingly prepared my documents. The District Election Commission had no choice but to register me as I followed the law to the t," my interlocutor explained and whipped out a thick pink legal file with documentation, ready to start proving his point. He did not look like the type of guy who follows the letter of the law very often. He was a former Soviet Army officer, who had made it in business during the messy post-Soviet transition. By his account, his efforts to reform his sector had won him many enemies among bureaucrats who then tried to "get rid of him" by sabotaging his business, putting him in jail, or worse. Even the political consultant whom he had hired from Kyiv to run his political campaign in a small, provincial single-mandate district, quit after only a few weeks, explaining that he had to look out for his family. Unfazed, my interviewee said he continued the campaign with the help of his former Army buddies. As the March 2002 campaign entered its final two-week stretch, polls showed that the Army officer turned entrepreneur had a realistic chance at winning a seat in Ukraine's parliament, the National Rada. That is when, in his words, *vlast'* (i.e., the regime) decided to remove him from the race. The district election commission that had registered him suddenly discovered a mistake in his property declaration and cancelled his registration. Over the next two weeks, his legal team appealed the decision all the way to the Supreme Court only to see the highest court dash his hopes of a parliamentary seat less than 24 hours before voting started.

"I knew all along that I stood no chance of winning in court against the regime, but the Army taught me to always stand up for myself," he said with a tinge of pathos in his voice. I sheepishly suggested that some oppositionists did win in court, so his chances at victory were not nil. He insisted that any victorious oppositionist must have bribed the judge and added that every judge had a price. I asked about the judge hearing his case. The answer took me on a short roller coaster of waxing and waning hope for the rule of law in

Ukraine. "He turned out to be an honest man," my interviewee started, "he told me that there was no point in taking my money to put me back on the ballot, because my victory would be short-lived. Apparently, he had heard that there was a direct order from Kyiv to take me out of the race, so even if I won at the district court, I would be deregistered by a higher court and eventually by the Supreme Court. A refreshingly honest guy, I tell you." The tough, ex-Army officer and current entrepreneur then spent the rest of the conversation showing me petitions and court decisions, explaining in detail his legal case, and trying to convince me that he had meticulously followed the law and deserved a place on the ballot. He also ruefully decried the lack of rule of law and independent courts in Ukraine. He complained that without them all the promised civil and political rights guaranteed by the Ukrainian Constitution were meaningless. He said he hoped to live to see the day when law trumps money and power. He also said that he would enthusiastically participate in another election, if he lived to see it.

As I left the gawdy, nouveau riche restaurant where our interview had taken place, I thought about a paradox that I grappled with often during my field research in Russia and Ukraine. Most post-Soviet citizens appeared to be supporters of the rule of law, not legal nihilists. They professed to want to live in a society governed by law, and they eagerly pursued their legal rights through the legal process. The explosion of litigation rates in virtually every single legal issue area in both Russia and Ukraine has been extensively researched and documented and demonstrates that my interview subjects were not exceptions. Yet, the rule of law was clearly in crisis in both Russia and Ukraine. I heard repeatedly about how politicians leaned on the courts often to obtain favorable rulings in cases that interested them. I also heard about judges, who either yielded to political pressure, or, purportedly, took bribes in order to resist it. In either case, very few people, including post-Soviet judges themselves, felt that the courts were independent from outside influence and decided cases only according to the letter of the law.

Why has the rule of law proven so hard to establish in postauthoritarian settings, despite what appears to be near universal consensus that it is the most desirable legal arrangement. Why are independent courts such a rarity outside of the old consolidated democracies of Western Europe, North America, and Asia? Specifically, what factors promote the development of independent courts and what factors undermine this process? These are the questions that this book seeks to address through systematic qualitative and quantitative analysis of the output of Russian and Ukrainian lower courts during the late 1990s and early 2000s. I collected extensive information on litigants in 800 defamation lawsuits against media outlets and 252 electoral registration disputes and used quantitative methods to calculate and compare the probability of victory in court for progovernment and opposition litigants. Both types of cases are politically salient and directly affect the provision of two central political and civil rights, enshrined in both the Russian and the Ukrainian post-Soviet constitutions – the right to stand in elections and the right to free speech. I also conducted interviews with judges, lawyers, litigants, and judicial administrators in both countries to probe the results of the statistical analysis and to examine the theoretical mechanisms that I identify.

Currently, two views dominate both the political science literature on judicial independence and the agenda of rule of law promoters at organizations, such as the World Bank, the U.S. Agency for International Development USAID, and the American Bar Association. An institutional theory posits that judicial independence results from the structural insulation of the courts from the other branches of government. In other words, the courts will be independent, if institutional safeguards are put in place, which make it impossible for politicians to interfere in judicial decision making. The second view holds that independent courts are the product of robust political competition. When incumbents are unsure about their chances of reelection, they offer or institute independent courts as insurance against persecution by future incumbents. In other words, politicians who expect to be out of power prefer to respect judicial independence today in order to increase the likelihood that the next incumbents will do the same.

This book presents and tests a third, competing theory of judicial independence, which I call the theory of *strategic pressure*. It applies to those regimes that are neither consolidated democracies nor consolidated autocracies, whether they are electoral democracies, hybrid regimes, or competitive authoritarian regimes. The theory posits that, in these regimes, political competition has the exact opposite effect on judicial independence that it purportedly has in consolidated democracies: It *hinders* rather than *promotes* the maintenance of independent courts. Specifically, political competition makes dependent courts more useful and more attractive to vulnerable incumbents. At the same time, intense political competition in these regimes does not seem to make it more costly for weak incumbents to exert pressure on the courts. Finally, political competition markedly increases the number of court cases whose outcomes matter to incumbents. As a result, weak incumbents (i.e., those who face stronger competition and a higher probability of losing the next election) are more likely to try to extract favorable judicial decisions in a greater number of cases. The consequences are the politicization of justice, the subordination of the courts to the executive, and the failure of the rule of law project.

The data presented in this book overwhelmingly support the predictions of the strategic pressure theory of judicial independence. In new democracies, where crucial democratic institutions such as a free press and an institutionalized party system are underdeveloped, electoral insecurity creates negative, rather than positive, incentives for incumbents. Rather than refrain from leaning on the courts and buttressing judicial independence, incumbents who face intense political competition and a realistic chance of losing power lean forcefully on the courts. Electorally insecure, weak incumbents interfere not only in high-profile cases that may be crucial to their survival in power, but also in many less salient, but politically consequential cases. Thus, political competition results in a politicization of justice and a reduction in independent judicial output.

The broader implication of this argument is not that political competition is bad for the rule of law and we should not welcome it. The suggestion is that the broader institutional context within which political competition takes place can determine its effects on the rule of law. Intense political competition and electoral uncertainty may create one set of incentives for politicians serving in consolidated democracies and a totally different set of incentives for politicians serving in new, emerging democracies. Thus, most broadly, this book's argument contributes to a vast and growing literature on the distinctive nature of regimes that hover in between consolidated democracy and consolidated authoritarianism. These regimes may mimic a lot of the accoutrements of a democracy, but in effect they operate very differently.

## WHY STUDY THE RULE OF LAW?

The rule of law has become synonymous with a desirable legal system, just as democracy is widely seen as the epitome of a desirable political regime. International organizations advocate strengthening the rule of law around the globe. During the 1990s alone, the World Bank, USAID, and other development institutions spent an estimated US$700 million on programs promoting judicial reform and the rule of law (Messick, 1999). In a rare display of consensus, political scientists are also virtually unanimous that the rule of law, defined as equal protection and responsibility under the law, is desirable.

First, the rule of law promotes justice by increasing the predictability of state action. The rule-of-law doctrine's emphasis on the equality of litigants means that the laws on the books get applied more consistently, which increases predictability. Liberals argue that predictability is justice enhancing because it expands individuals' autonomy vis-à-vis the state and grants them more choice to govern their lives (Hayek, 1975; Waldron, 1989; Raz, 1990; Shklar, 1986).

Communitarians agree that greater predictability equals more justice because it contributes to the stability and viability of communities to which individuals naturally belong (Selznik, 1996).

Second, the rule of law facilitates the consolidation of democracy by guaranteeing basic civic and political rights (e.g., Linz & Stepan, 1996; Diamond & Morlino, 2004; Howard & Carey, 2004; O'Donnell, 2004). For example, the freedom and fairness of elections and the freedom of the press can both be easily undermined by powerful incumbents in the absence of stable rule of law. In addition, the absence of the rule of law usually undermines popular trust in formal democratic institutions (Rose, 2001) and thus contributes to political instability and regime fragility.

Third, the rule of law has long been considered an important predictor of economic development. The idea that a fair judiciary is indispensable to economic growth goes back to Adam Smith. A slew of recent empirical studies have confirmed an association between the rule of law and the expansion of a country's economy (e.g., Knack & Keefer, 1995; Kaufmann, Kraay, & Zoido-Lobaton, 2000; Feld & Voigt, 2003). The mechanism through which the rule of law purportedly causes economic development focuses on long-term investment. A judiciary that applies the laws on the books equitably and predictably effectively protects property rights from encroachment either by the state or by fellow competitors. As a result, economic actors feel secure to make long-term investments, which in turn foster economic growth.

In short, it seems that if a country is to overcome political instability, establish a democratic regime, and achieve higher economic growth, it has to have the rule of law. Establishing the rule of law is easier said than done, however. Some of the Latin American countries have had functioning democratic regimes for over two decades, but most have yet to establish solid foundations for the rule of law. Among the challenges are enduring executive interference in Supreme Court or Constitutional Court decision making, legal impunity for politically powerful actors, and lawless areas where the law simply does not reach. These problems are not specific to Latin America either. Virtually all postauthoritarian regimes in Africa, Asia, and the post-Soviet region display serious shortcomings when it comes to the rule of law. Instead, they feature elites that instrumentally use the law to extend their tenure in power by amassing personal fortunes, boosting their supporters, and/or weakening opponents.

## JUDICIAL INDEPENDENCE AND THE RULE OF LAW

Why is it so hard to implement the rule of law where it has not existed before? Perhaps the biggest hurdle for postauthoritarian regimes is the absence of the main institutional prerequisite for the rule of law, namely an independent judiciary. Only independent courts are likely to maximize the equality of litigants before the law. In Chapter 1, I argue that courts are independent when they produce decisions that do not systematically reflect the preferences of extrajudicial actors. I conceptualize judicial independence as a relational concept, which implies that every time we talk about how independent courts are, we need to specify the potential source of dependence. For example, in some countries or in certain time periods, courts may be independent from politicians but dependent on organized crime. In this book, I focus on explaining the variation in judicial independence from incumbent politicians.

In postauthoritarian regimes, judicial independence from politicians is crucial not only for establishing the rule of law but also for building a stable democracy. The courts can be instrumental to the functioning of basic democratic institutions such as free and fair elections, a free press, and a competitive party system. The courts can either act as watchdogs that protect basic civil and political rights or become attack dogs that destroy any viable opposition at the behest of the incumbents. Independent courts can effectively constrain powerful political actors from imposing their preferences in any dispute where they have a stake. Dependent courts can facilitate or tighten incumbents' undemocratic grip on power.

## WHY DO SOME COUNTRIES HAVE INDEPENDENT COURTS AND OTHERS DO NOT?

Currently, political scientists attribute judicial independence to two main causal variables: structural insulation of the judiciary from the other branches of government and political competition. Institutional theories posit that structural safeguards make it impossible or too costly for politicians to interfere in judicial decision making (e.g., Fiss, 1993; Russell & O'Brien, 2001; Finkel 2004). Political competition or "insurance" theories hold that electoral uncertainty, which is high in competitive regimes, makes it beneficial for politicians to provide independent courts. Independent courts allow incumbents to minimize the risks of finding themselves at the receiving end of politicized justice when they are voted out of office (Ramseyer, 1994; Magalhães, 1999; Ginsburg, 2003; Stephenson, 2003; Finkel 2005), to monitor bureaucrats through the courts (McCubbins & Schwartz, 1984), and to deflect blame for unpopular policies to the independent judiciary (Shetreet, 1984; Salzberger, 1993; Whittington, 1999).

The majority of the theorizing about judicial independence has focused on constitutional adjudication and, consequently, on the behavior of the highest courts (Whittington, 1999; Ginsburg, 2003; Chavez, 2004; Helmke 2005; Finkel, 2005; Vanberg, 2005; Moustafa, 2007; Trochev, 2008; etc.)[1]. However, the output of the lower courts seems to be just as important, if not even more important, to the overall level of the rule of law in the country. Lower courts hear the vast majority of cases. They are also the first point of contact between citizens and the justice system, and thus their behavior greatly affects citizens' perception of the level of the rule of law in their country. This perception is in turn important because it affects citizens' future decisions as to whether to take their disputes to court or to look for alternative ways of resolving them. We cannot assume that theories that explain Supreme Court output would also account for lower court behavior. After all, there are significant differences not only in the number of actors but also in the status between the higher and the lower court judges. Finally, some of the most influential theories of the rule of law and independent courts focus on judicial behavior in contract enforcement (Landes & Posner, 1975; North & Weingast, 1989; Weingast, 1997). However, the level of judicial independence from politicians may vary significantly across legal issue area within one country during the same time period. For example, in post-authoritarian regimes, economic disputes might be less important to incumbent power holders, than disputes related to the mechanism of attaining and holding on to power.

This book aims to fill these gaps in the literature by analyzing lower court behavior beyond the area of property rights enforcement. It considers the determinants of judicial independence from incumbents in politically salient legal issue areas. It focuses on the dynamic relationship between political incumbents and the courts in regimes that are neither consolidated democracies nor consolidated authoritarian regimes. This large, and growing, set of polities is characterized by an often-volatile combination of formal democratic institutions and leftover, informal authoritarian institutions and practices. For example, these regimes routinely hold elections to select the incumbents in the executive and legislative branches, but often lack some or most of the informal institutions that guarantee fair contestation and full participation. In addition, uncertainty is pervasive in such regimes, as old institutions crumble and old elites weaken, but new institutions and elites are of questionable strength and durability.[2] As a result, politicians in these regimes often have shorter time-horizons – they either (1) cannot be sure that they can plan to be in politics for the long haul or (2) think they could remain in power indefinitely, even if

---

[1]   Notable exceptions are Ramseyer (1997) and Hilbink (2005).
[2]   On the pervasive uncertainty of transitional settings, see, for example, O'Donnel and Schmitter (1986), Bunce (1993), Crescenzi (1999), and McFaul (1999).

elections take place, by manipulating the levers of power. Chapter 2 discusses the negative consequences of mixed institutions and high uncertainty on the rule-of-law project in these regimes.[3] It advances the argument that political incumbents, who care only about the present and the immediate future, choose to subordinate the courts more often than their counterparts in consolidated democracies, who have the relative luxury of engaging in longer-term planning of their political careers and legacies. In addition, the costs of pressuring the courts in the context of leftover authoritarian informal institutions and practices are lower on average, compared to the costs in consolidated democracies. Consequently, subservient courts are the norm rather than the exception in the regimes that are neither consolidated democracies nor consolidated authoritarianisms.

The main theoretical contribution of this book is the strategic pressure theory, which focuses on the relationship between political competition and independent courts in emerging democracies. The theory posits that intensifying political competition only further reduces the level of judicial independence because it increases the benefits that weak incumbents get from dependent courts and expands the set of cases that become politicized. The benefits of exerting pressure are larger because weak incumbents can significantly boost their chances of reelection through favorable court decisions. In addition, vulnerable incumbents not only insist on winning each case they are involved in but also try to exert pressure in all cases in which their competitors have a stake in order to weaken the competitors or simply to signal strength and thus prevent the opposition from recruiting supporters. Lower court judges, who face a collective action problem with resisting this pressure, end up systematically favoring the incumbents in all disputes. Thus, the end result of intense

---

[3] Finding a short term to describe all regimes that are neither consolidated democracies nor consolidated authoritarian regimes has proven to be very challenging. This is not a coherent regime type, and scholars have identified over 550 different configurations that populate this portion of the regime spectrum (Collier & Levitsky, 1997). In the title of the book and, intermittently in the book, I use the "emerging democracy" term. The term is very often used in news coverage of postauthoritarian countries, but it is less often used in scholarly accounts, perhaps because it implies that any regime purportedly transitioning to democracy is necessarily heading toward the ultimate consolidation of a democratic regime. This latter has been exposed as an erroneous and overly optimistic assumption (Bunce, 1995; Carothers, 2002), and I do not seek to revive it. With this choice, however, I partly aim to get away from the scholarly debate about the (possible) distinctions between some of the other more popular terms such as "electoral democracy," "hybrid regime," "competitive authoritarianism," or "diminished democracy." As I emphasize in this paragraph and elaborate in Chapter 2, the two regime characteristics that are crucial to my analysis are the mixed democratic/authoritarian institutional landscape and the high level of uncertainty. I do not want, however, to introduce yet another regime term to an already overcrowded field, so I have opted for "emerging democracy."

political competition is an even lower level of judicial independence and, consequently, the failure of the rule of law project.

## JUDICIAL (IN)DEPENDENCE IN RUSSIA AND UKRAINE

December 3, 2004, was a coming-out party of sorts for the Ukrainian Supreme Court. In a defiant move against the incumbent Kuchma regime, twenty judges from the Supreme Court's Civil Collegium cancelled the decision of the Central Election Commission, which had declared President Kuchma's chosen successor, Viktor Yanukovych, the winner of the November 21 presidential election runoff. In the pithy, two-page decision, the Supreme Court argued that electoral law violations during the campaign and on election day (November 21, 2004) were so significant and pervasive that they made it impossible to determine with certainty the true outcome of the free vote. The ruling also ordered that a rerun of the runoff and scheduled it for December 26.[4] Embattled opposition candidate Viktor Yushchenko, his political allies, and the millions of supporters who had been protesting peacefully for over two weeks in Kyiv's Independence Square won a resounding victory. The court decision was, without a doubt, the climax of the Orange Revolution. It has been hailed as a rare triumph for the rule of law in the post-Soviet region and a demonstration of the Ukrainian judiciary's growing independence from politicians.

On May 31, 2005, it was Moscow's Meshchanskii district court's turn to enter news headlines around the world. A three-judge panel convicted Russia's wealthiest man, Mikhail Khodorkovsky, on charges of fraud and tax evasion, sentenced him to 9 years behind bars, and ordered him to pay the equivalent of US$613 million in taxes and fines. Once imprisoned, Khodorkovsky saw a series of court decisions dismember his multibillion-dollar company, Yukos. In February 2007, the Russian prosecution office opened a new criminal case against Khodorkovsky, and in 2010, Judge Viktor Danilkin from Moscow's Khamovnicheskii district court convicted Khodorkovsky again and sentenced him, this time, to a 14-year prison term. Khodorkovsky will not be a free man anytime soon. The oil tycoon himself, his defense, human rights advocates, opposition figures, and even former Russian judges have claimed that the numerous criminal cases against Khodorkovsky, his company Yukos, and other Yukos's employees were decided in the Kremlin rather than in court. Most in

---

4  The full text of the Supreme Court decision can be found in English, here: http://www.skubi. net/ukraine/findings.html and in Ukrainian, here: http://www.scourt.gov.ua/clients/vs.nsf/o/2A 1C4C7D8C6241CBC3256F9D00228DA5?OpenDocument

Russia and abroad share this opinion, and Khodorkovsky has become Russia's most visible modern-day political prisoner. Indeed, the selective prosecution of disloyal oligarchs, who defied the Putin administration's informal ban on meddling in politics, has generated talk about Russia's catastrophic failure at building a rule-of-law-based postcommunist state.

These rulings showcase the involvement of post-Soviet courts in the political process. However, does the contrast between Russia and Ukraine hold if we move beyond these high-profile cases? Has the Russian judiciary consistently been more dependent on incumbent politicians than the Ukrainian judiciary? Has judicial decision making been more politicized in Russia than in Ukraine? Have Ukrainian litigants consistently enjoyed greater equality under the law than Russian litigants? Has Ukraine indeed gone unambiguously further in establishing the rule of law than Russia? Apart from testing the theories on judicial independence, the book provides answers to important empirical questions about the nature of the Russian and the Ukrainian post-Soviet regimes in the period under study. Have Russian or Ukrainian parliamentary elections been fairer or, perhaps more accurately put, less manipulated? Are the Russian or the Ukrainian courts more vulnerable to pressure from politically powerful actors? Are the Russian or the Ukrainian media more often subjected to legal harassment?

To solve these empirical puzzles, this book presents a systematic examination of a large set of politically salient cases, decided by Russian and Ukrainian district courts during the 1998–2004 period. During this period, although both Russia and Ukraine routinely held elections, they had yet to consolidate either a democratic or an authoritarian regime. The analysis presented in this book argues that contrary to journalistic coverage and popular expectations, Ukraine fared worse than Russia at judicial independence. This is not to say that Russia had effectively implemented the rule of law by developing an independent judiciary. Rather, the evidence emphasizes that the rule-of-law project only suffered rather than benefited from the intense political competition that has been the norm in post-Soviet Ukraine.

The empirical chapters on electoral and defamation cases also aim to make a methodological contribution to the comparative study of courts. Currently, the literature uses three main measures – reputational indices, structural measures, and government batting averages at the Supreme Court. Reputational indices are useful for conducting large-N tests on the universe of countries, but the large standard errors associated with each country estimate make it hard to compare similar countries to each other. For example, the most that the reputational indices show is that the Western European democracies have more independent judiciaries than their Eastern European neighbors. In fact,

Russia and Ukraine receive virtually identical scores on the World Governance Indicators (WGI) index.[5]

Structural measures such as an institutional description of the judiciary are also notoriously unreliable because they ignore informal practices that may render the institutional safeguards useless (Clark, 1975). The high score that Argentina receives on each structural measure of judicial independence exemplifies the problem with structural indices, because the Argentine Supreme Court purportedly regularly yields to executive pressure (Helmke, 2002; Chavez, 2004; Finkel, 2004; Dix, 2005). Finally, simple counts of how often the government wins in court ignore the substantive difference between a government that puts pressure on the courts in order to secure favorable outcomes and a government that does a good job of complying with its own laws.

The book develops a quantitative measure of judicial independence based on the probability of success in court for different types of litigants. The measure stems from the simple assumption that an independent court would adjudicate cases by considering their merits under the law, rather than the characteristics of the litigant, associated with the case. Conversely, dependent courts would be guided in their decision making by the characteristics of the litigants. For example, if courts are dependent on incumbent politicians, litigants who are closely associated with the incumbent regime would have a higher probability of wining their cases (i.e., they would win more often) than litigants who lack connections to the regime or are connected to the opposition. Even more simply put, independent courts are unbiased, dependent courts are biased in favor of those they are dependent on. I apply this new measure to gauge the difference in the level of judicial independence in Russia and Ukraine. This measure that is calculated directly from actual trial outcomes can capture small differences in levels of judicial independence and therefore allows reliable comparisons of similar countries and within countries over time.

## ROADMAP

The book starts out with a definitional discussion of judicial independence. Chapter 1 draws on both the normative and positive literature on judicial

---

[5] The average rule-of-law scores for Russia and Ukraine over the 12 years that the Kaufmann team has been producing the World Governance Indicators (1996–2008) are –.89 and –.77, respectively. The .12 difference between the two countries is well within the standard error for each estimate. For the period, covered in this book (1998–2004), the scores are completely undistinguishable in statistical terms – –.91 for Russia and –.89 for Ukraine (Kaufmann et al., 2010).

independence and argues that judicial independence should be conceptualized in terms of overall judicial output (i.e., the full set of decisions that courts deliver in an issue area or time period of interest). This definition of the term competes with two other conceptualizations that view judicial independence as a feature of judicial institutions and as a type of behavior of individual judges. This chapter argues that a judicial output conceptualization is preferable because it is most closely tied to the tenets of the rule-of-law doctrine. And it is precisely the purported link to the rule of law that makes judicial independence desirable and worth studying. Once I have defined what judicial independence is, I discuss the factors that may influence its variation across countries or over time. Chapter 2 presents the *strategic pressure* theory of judicial independence.

Chapter 3 explains the research design of the two-country comparison, which aims to test the *strategic pressure* theory against the traditional theories of judicial independence. The chapter argues that a focused comparison of Russia and Ukraine can help us evaluate the predictive power of each theory. The two countries share a common Soviet and pre-Soviet historical legacy, virtually identical post-Soviet political institutions, and a similar type of economy and level of economic development; nevertheless, they diverge on two variables that are seen as crucial for judicial independence, namely the intensity of political competition and the structural insulation of the judiciary from the other branches of government. Chapter 3 also introduces the new trial outcome measure of judicial independence. I list four steps through which this measure can be implemented. Finally, the chapter describes the quantitative data sets that I put together during my field research in Russia and Ukraine.

The two chapters that follow demonstrate how I apply the measure to determine the level of judicial independence in Russia and Ukraine in two politically salient issue areas, namely defamation lawsuits against media outlets and electoral registration disputes. Chapter 4 presents the analysis of electoral registration disputes associated with two parliamentary campaigns in Russia and Ukraine during the 2002–2003 period. The analysis suggests that the systematic advantage that pro-Kuchma plaintiffs enjoyed in court during the 2002 Rada campaign was at least twice as big as the advantage that pro-Putin plaintiffs benefited from during the 2003 Duma election. Chapter 5 presents the analysis of defamation lawsuits in both countries and again judicial independence in 1998–2003 appears to be lower in Ukraine than in Russia. In Ukraine, plaintiffs affiliated with the government not only won more often than everybody else, but also received significantly higher moral compensation awards.

The predictions of the strategic pressure theory of judicial independence, thus, appear to be borne out by the analysis in both quantitative analysis chapters on Russia and Ukraine. Chapters 6 and 7 use qualitative data from interviews with judges, lawyers, politicians, judicial administration officials, journalists, and litigants to show that the mechanisms of the strategic pressure theory account for the differences uncovered by the systematic analysis of trial outcomes. More specifically, Chapter 6 discusses a set of informal practices, common to Russia and Ukraine, that equip incumbent politicians with tools for circumventing the formal institutions that have been adopted in both countries to guarantee judicial independence. Chapter 7 presents evidence that, in the period under study, Russian politicians did not impose their preferences on judicial output as much as Ukrainian politicians did, not because they *could not* accomplish it, but because they *would not* bother with it. The qualitative data reveals that Ukrainian judges systematically favored government-affiliated litigants, precisely in response to pressure by incumbents who sought to weaken the opposition which threatened their hold on power.

The concluding chapter discusses the implications of post-2004 developments in Russia and Ukraine for the strategic pressure theory. It reviews some of the high-profile examples of the interaction between courts and political incumbents, such as the Khodorkovsky and Yukos prosecutions in Russia and the executive–judicial confrontation that has characterized post-Orange Ukrainian politics. Finally, it suggests ways in which we could use the arguments in this book to study variation in judicial independence across regime types, rather than within one regime type. In other words, why are independent courts the norm in old consolidated democracies and a rarity in new ones?

# 1

# What Is Judicial Independence?

There are many definitions of judicial independence. This chapter explains why I use only one of them – an independent judiciary delivers decisions that do not *consistently* reflect the preferences of a particular group of actors. The emphasis is on consistently because each decision will reflect somebody's preferences – the winner's. The key is that when courts are independent, no one can expect to win all the cases that they would like to win. The chapter also proposes that we should be aware that independent judicial output can result either when actors are unwilling or incapable of imposing their preferences in court.

## INSTITUTIONAL JUDICIAL INDEPENDENCE

In institutional terms, judicial independence refers to the insulation or autonomy of the judiciary from the other branches of government or from the public (Fiss, 1993; Ferejohn, 1999; Russell & O'Brien, 2001; Chavez, 2004; Finkel, 2004). Institutional judicial independence is higher when there are more structural safeguards against interference by nonjudicial actors in judicial decision making. Institutional shields include life tenure guarantees for judges, judicial control over appointment, promotion and dismissal, as well as the drafting and administration of the judiciary's budget. Institutional insulation definitions of judicial independence are particularly prevalent in policy analysis of levels of the rule of law around the world. For example, in its annual reports on the East European states' progress toward meeting the accession criteria, the EU has consistently criticized certain candidate states for providing institutional opportunities for executive interference in judicial affairs, such as vesting appointment powers with a political actor, rather than a corporate judicial body, such as a Judicial Council (Open Society Institute, 2001; ABA/CEELI, 2002a).

Focusing on institutional guarantees against undue influence on judicial decision making may seem practical because identifying these structural shields is a fairly straightforward measurement task. However, as Ferejohn (1999) points out, institutional judicial independence is not intrinsically valuable (p. 353). The desirability of independent courts hinges squarely on the assumption that the institutional shields prevent external actors from influencing judicial output, which in turn ensures equal responsibility and protection under the law (i.e., rule of law) and provides stable protection of property rights (i.e., promotes economic growth).

However, there is mounting empirical evidence from around the world that makes this assumption problematic. Clark (1975) devises a "judicial effectiveness score," which measures the institutional independence of Latin American Supreme Courts. His measure includes indicators such as tenure guarantees, method of appointment and removal, and salary guarantees for each court. However, he is surprised to find that courts generally perceived as less independent (the Argentinean and the Brazilian ones) score much higher than seemingly more independent ones (such as the Costa Rican one). Hilbink (2007) and Helmke and Rosenbluth (2009) also note that during the tenure of the Latin American military dictatorships (Chile, Brazil, and Argentina are the main cases), institutionally independent judiciaries failed to constrain the military juntas and protect human rights that were officially guaranteed by the countries' constitutions. In the Asian context, Ramseyer and Rosenbluth (1993), Ramseyer and Rasmussen (1997), and O'Brien and Ohkoshi (2001) have shown that despite the standard institutional safeguards against judicial dependence on the executive, Japanese judges are rather deferential toward incumbent politicians. Finally, in the European context, Guarnieri (2001) argues that the institutional autonomy of the Italian judiciary from the executive has led to judicial bias in favor of the political opposition and undue influence of the media and the mafia on individual judges. Smithey and Ishiyama (2000) build a "judicial power" indicator for postcommunist high courts, which also suggests that institutional independence does not co-vary with behavioral independence. According to their index, which includes variables such as judges' terms relative to those of other political actors, conditions for judicial removal, and number of actors involved in the selection of judges, Poland, Estonia, the Czech Republic, Hungary, and Slovenia have much weaker courts than Armenia, Romania, Bulgaria, and Moldova. Judicial assessments conducted by the EU, the World Bank, and the Open Society Institute, however, suggest that the courts in the first group of countries exhibit much more independent behavior than their counterparts in the second group. Herron and Randazzo (2003) test the hypothesis that postcommunist high courts that are institutionally more insulated from the executive will be more likely to exhibit independent behavior and find that formal independence is a significant but *negative* predictor of independent behavior.

One way to interpret this evidence is to conclude following Kornhauser (2002) that judicial independence is a useless concept, which should be abandoned, because we cannot show that it is either necessary or sufficient for the rule of law, economic prosperity, or good governance – the inherently desirable ends, which justify the need to promote and study judicial independence in the first place. Alternatively, this evidence could simply convince us that we should stop using the institutional setup of the judiciary as a measure for its independence. Rather the institutional configuration of the judiciary should be treated as an independent variable in the analysis of judicial independence. In other words, institutional set up could be used to try to explain why some courts are independent and others are not.

## BEHAVIORAL JUDICIAL INDEPENDENCE

An alternative approach to institutional definitions is a judicial behavior conceptualization of judicial independence. If judicial behavior is the focus of interest, then the relevant unit of analysis becomes the individual judge (e.g., Becker, 1970; Salzberger, 1993; Ramseyer, 1994, 1997; Ramseyer & Rasmusen, 2001a, 2001b). We could compare judiciaries according to the percentage of judges who generally adjudicate cases independently. Becker (1970), in an often-quoted definition, argues that independent judges are those who believe that they can and do decide cases consistently with their interpretation of the law rather than that of any other actor. In particular, independent judges follow this strategy even when a decision averse to the desires of other power holders could possibly result in retribution either on the judges personally or on the power of their court. According to this definition, a country has high judicial independence if a large percentage of its judges both feel independent and act independently[1].

The first drawback of the behavioral definition stems from the tension between feelings of independence and independent actions. It seems that the two things do not necessarily go together. In particular, how would we classify cases, in which judges do not feel independent, that is they know that ruling

---

[1]  How large is large is an important question. However, it hardly seems possible to come up with a threshold that would not be arbitrary. Therefore, this definition is more appropriate for comparative studies. For example, we could ask whether a larger proportion of judges in country A or in country B are independent.

against the regime could and probably would lead to retribution, either against them or against the court, but they act independently nonetheless? What is the level of judicial independence in these cases?

Consider the historic Orange Revolution case, in which the Ukrainian Supreme Court canceled the results of the presidential election runoff and ordered a rerun. Retribution from the incumbent Kuchma regime, whose selected candidate, Viktor Yanukovych would have become president, had the Supreme Court not canceled the Central Election Commission decision, was certainly possible. In fact, a judge from the Supreme Court explained that his colleagues were acutely aware that the Kuchma regime would try to coerce or coax them into delivering a pro-Yanukovych decision. As a result, the twenty judges hearing the case decided to isolate themselves completely from the outside world during deliberations in order to thwart a possible divide-and-rule strategy by the regime, in which individual judges may have been targeted for pressure (A. V., 2004). In other words, the judges clearly did not feel independent from the regime, but they did rule against it. Does the ruling indicate behavioral judicial independence or not?

In addition, reliable data on how judges feel seems elusive. Presumably, we could use surveys to get judges to tell us whether they feel independent or not, but even sincere judges themselves might not be able to distinguish between their *true* interpretation of the law and the myriad of influences from a variety of sources that might affect their judgment. Finally, we would have to come up with an inherently arbitrary threshold to distinguish between an independent judge and a dependent judge. Should judges who feel or rule independently 51 percent of the time qualify as independent judges?

Even if we could reliably measure behavioral judicial independence, we run into a normative problem. Behavioral judicial independence might not be desirable at all from a rule of law perspective. Judges, like the rest of us, have complex personalities and diverse ideologies. One possibility is that given complete decisional independence, they may completely disregard the law and impose their ideological preferences on the rest of society. As the attitudinal model of decision making at the U.S. Supreme Court has shown, judges' personal ideology plays a significant role in their decision making process (Segal & Spaeth, 1993). It seems that in a system characterized by highly independent judges, equal responsibility and protection under the law can no longer be universally guaranteed because the outcome of individual cases would depend greatly on the personality and biases of the presiding judge. Most scholars in fact agree that granting sweeping decisional independence to individual judges is undesirable, because as fallible human beings they should not be fully unaccountable for their decisions (Burbank & Friedman, 2002).

## DECISIONAL JUDICIAL INDEPENDENCE

Decisional judicial independence exists if no actor can *consistently* secure judgments that are in line with his or her preferences. Quite a few studies conceptualize judicial independence as a feature of judicial output (Landes & Posner, 1975; Shapiro, 1981; Rosenberg, 1992; Hanssen, 2004). For example, Shapiro's often-cited definition of judicial independence as the "inability of government to influence the outcome of any individual case" points to individual cases as the appropriate unit of analysis (Shapiro, 1981, p. 8). Rosenberg also suggests looking at individual decisions to see whether they reflect the preferences of elected officials (Rosenberg, 1992, p. 373).

"Consistently" is the key word in the definition. It means that we need to look at the outcomes of multiple cases involving a given actor in order to determine reliably whether the courts are independent from that actor or not. It seems inherently impossible to determine on an individual case basis whether a ruling reflects the judge's own interpretation of the law or someone else's. Each case has a winner and a loser, and we have no way of knowing whether the judge sides with the winner due to a good faith belief that the winner's case was stronger or out of a fear of retribution. Power differences between the litigants might help to clarify things somewhat. For example, when ordinary citizens win cases against powerful state agencies, it is unlikely that the judge was dependent on the citizen. However, powerful state actors surely have meritorious cases too, so a victory by such actors does not automatically mean that the court lacks independence. Also, how do we interpret the outcomes of individual cases, where both litigants are potential principals on whom the court could be dependent?

To go back to the Orange Revolution case – the Ukrainian Supreme Court judges had to choose whether to side with the million-strong crowd gathered under their windows or with a regime that had shown readiness to go after judges who rule against it[2]. Both actors, at the moment that the judges were deliberating, had significant, albeit different, sources of power vis-à-vis the court. Or, what should we make of the decision in a defamation case, which pits a powerful incumbent politician against a newspaper, owned by a politically active oligarch. Both Russian and Ukrainian courts heard numerous cases like that where we would not be able to glean the level of judicial independence from just looking at the outcome of an individual case.

---

[2]  Chapter 7 discusses the repercussions suffered by judges who ruled against the preferences of the Kuchma regime.

This caveat can be overcome by systematic analysis of many, similar cases. I propose that we should define decisional judicial independence in terms of the number and the identity of the actors who do *not* exercise power over the adjudication process, as well as in terms of the magnitude of the power of the actors who do manage to impose their preferences. According to this definition, judicial independence would be low if pressure is exerted routinely in a vast majority of cases and multiple actors can impose their preferences over judicial outcomes. Conversely, judicial independence would be high if fewer actors have power over the outcome and only in a few cases.

Decisional judicial independence seems preferable to behavioral and institutional definitions because it is certainly a necessary component of the rule of law. The emphasis of the rule of law doctrine on equal protection and responsibility for all under publicly promulgated laws essentially calls for establishing a legal system that would guarantee that the preferences embodied in publicly promulgated laws would be consistently imposed on individual case outcomes. In addition, if no one actor can consistently impose his or her preferences on the court, this would be an indication that judicial output reflects the "true" preferences of the law.

## INDEPENDENT FROM WHOM? JUDICIAL INDEPENDENCE FROM DIFFERENT PRINCIPALS

However it is defined, judicial independence is a relational concept so we should always specify the potential source of dependence (Russell & O'Brien, 2001). More normative studies should explicitly address the question of which type of judicial independence is most desirable – independence from politicians, from the public, from interest groups, from the presiding judge's personal ideology, from the judges sitting at the higher courts, from litigants, and so on. The emphasis in many judicial independence definitions on minimizing meddling by politicians in judicial decision making suggests that independence from politicians is at the top of the desirability list. In addition, scholars have pointed to the drawbacks of judicial dependence on public opinion or on individual litigants (Shapiro, 1981; Burbank & Friedman, 2002).

Once we recognize this additional dimension of variation, the next question that arises is whether and how independence from different external actors (i.e., different principals) might vary within the same judicial system at any given point in time. We should investigate whether different types of independence always go together, in which case we can talk about a general level of judicial independence. Or there might be a trade-off – maximizing

independence from one actor may automatically open the door for dependence on another actor. For example, we could imagine a judiciary that is
simultaneously highly independent from politicians (i.e., politicians cannot
consistently impose their preferences on judicial output) and highly dependent vis-à-vis organized crime (i.e., rich mobsters can get favorable rulings in
most or all cases that interest them).

In addition, both the degree and the source of judicial dependence may
vary across different legal issue areas within the same judicial system. By a
legal issue area, I mean the universe of cases litigated with reference to a
specific law or group of laws. The area could be as narrow as defamation law
involving media outlets as defendants or litigation arising from privatization
deals, or as wide as criminal law or civil law. The crucial point is that different issue areas have a different set of actors with preferences about judicial
outcomes. For example, the executive might not have strong enough preferences to attempt to secure favorable judicial decisions in disputes that are not
politically salient.

## CAPACITY VS. WILLINGNESS CONCEPTUALIZATION
## OF JUDICIAL INDEPENDENCE

The last example raises the question: Should we always define judicial output
that does not systematically reflect the preferences of a given principal as judicial independence? Does it matter whether the principal *cannot* or *would not*
impose his or her preferences on the outcomes of cases that interest him or
her? If the principal seems unwilling to interfere in judicial decision making,
does it matter whether the restraint is due to strong belief in the rule of law
doctrine or to a self-interested rational calculation that interference would be
too costly? I argue that the definition of judicial independence should incorporate all three scenarios, but scholars should be cognizant of the distinctions
between them.

Most studies of judicial independence do not touch upon this issue at
all. Some scholars talk about the government's *inability*, rather than *unwill-
ingness* to influence judicial decision making (Shapiro, 1981; Russell &
O'Brien, 2001; Chavez, 2004). Others discuss circumstances under which
politicians *provide* or *offer* independent courts, which implies that politicians
in such cases refrain from pressuring the courts to deliver favorable rulings
(Salzberger, 1993; Ramseyer, 1997; Hirschl, 2000; Stephenson, 2003). Often
times, though, the implications seem to be the unintended result of particular word choice, rather than explicit assumptions or intentional definitional
choices.

The distinction may be consequential, however, so it deserves some attention. For the purposes of clarity, I will discuss politicians, who are probably the principal whose influence on the courts is most consequential for the rule of law. In the *capacity* conceptualization, we can categorize judicial output as independent only when politicians simply *cannot* influence judicial output even if they tried. The *willingness* conceptualization views judicial independence as the result of a conscious choice by politicians to not interfere in judicial decision making; they have the capacity to influence judicial output but refrain from exercising this power. The willingness conceptualization itself can be divided in two scenarios. First, politicians may be unwilling to lean on the courts as a result of a strategic calculation that it is not in their best interest to try exerting pressure – either because the potential costs of doing it are too high or because the potential benefits of doing it are insignificant. Alternatively, politicians may be unwilling to pressure the courts for ideological reasons (i.e., they may espouse a strong belief in the rule of law and judicial independence and as a result would not even consider pressuring the courts).

The three conceptualizations can be hard to distinguish observationally. Even when politicians tout their staunch commitment to independent courts and, indeed, refrain from attacking the courts to get their way, we cannot be sure of their sincerity. It could be that they forego applying pressure because it is too costly or not beneficial enough. Surveys about politicians' attitudes and commitment to the rule of law are unlikely to be productive. The billions of dollars spent around the world on rule-of-law promotion have probably ensured that virtually any politician around the world knows the "right" answer to questions about judicial independence and the rule of law.

The distinction between capacity and willingness is also tricky to observe. When politicians make obvious attempts to pressure the courts, but judicial output does not reflect their preferences, it is clear that the principals simply *cannot* impose their will on the courts. But such failed attempts at interference are not likely to be sustained practice and we rarely see them. Politicians at some point either figure out a more effective way to pressure the courts or give up trying to interfere. When politicians do not engage in obvious influence peddling, determining whether the restraint is due to a realization that pressure would be futile or to a calculation that the costs of interference are too high might be quite hard. Rather than look at the actual judicial output, we would then need to look closely at the behavior of politicians and at the existence of informal or formal institutional channels, through which they could affect judicial decision making. For example, throughout its EU accession process, the Czech Republic was repeatedly criticized for formal institutions, which facilitate *potential* executive pressure on the courts. The EU monitoring reports, however, never provided evidence or even claimed that the executive actually took advantage of these potential institutional channels. Thus, this seems like a scenario, which allows us to distinguish observationally between judicial independence due to lack of willingness, rather than lack of capacity by politicians to subordinate the courts.

At first glance, the distinction between willingness and capacity seems irrelevant to the relationship between judicial independence and the rule of law and the desirable phenomena that follow. Whether politicians do not interfere because they cannot or because it is too costly to them, the politicians would not be receiving preferential treatment. As a result, all actors involved in the adjudication process will expect litigant equality. Therefore, we would conclude that in both cases the courts are de facto independent and the rule-of-law doctrine is in place.

Within the willingness conceptualization, however, the distinction between "unwilling because of high costs" and "unwilling because of low benefits" seems normatively important. The second scenario seems normatively "inferior" and may create different expectations for all participants in the adjudication process. It is debatable whether we could call the courts independent if the only reason for noninterference by the principal is the lack of motivation on the principal's part. Consider the following analogy – in this situation the politicians have the courts on an invisible leash; unless they pull it, no one knows how long it is or whether it is even there. In other words, unless politicians choose to exercise their influence on the courts, the courts (and any other actor, for that matter, including the politicians) have no idea how strong that influence is and whether it would get them consistently favorable rulings.

Epistemological conundrums aside, the more important issue is whether this scenario is as likely as the others to promote the rule of law. First, judicial independence that stems from politicians' apathy appears to be less sustainable in the long run because it is dependent entirely on the incumbents' decision to impose their preferences or not. In addition, this type of judicial independence might make a smaller contribution to economic growth because presumably societal actors would realize that the judiciary's ability to withstand pressure has not been tested and this realization might reduce long-term investment. Finally, the fact that neither the courts nor other societal actors are sure of the boundaries of how much judicial independence the politicians would tolerate probably decreases the level of predictability of state action.

Others may argue that even this diminished form of judicial independence is conducive to the rule-of-law project. Independent judicial output which does not systematically reflect the preferences of any principal boosts both the real and the perceived equality of litigants. And equality under the law is what it is – a central component of the rule of law – regardless of how it comes about. I leave the normative issue to be debated by normative theorists. The details of the Russian case will illustrate in the following chapters that we should be aware of the conceptual difference between judicial independence provided *by* the principal and judicial independence wrested *from* the principal. Clearly, all three types of judicial independence deserve scholarly attention.

## JUDICIAL INDEPENDENCE AT DIFFERENT LEVELS OF ABSTRACTION

A final definitional conundrum is whether the concept of judicial independence should refer to unencumbered decision making at the level of the case or at the level of the rule.[3] Scheppele (2002) makes a convincing case that it is hard to distinguish conceptually between judges taking orders in specific cases and strictly following a rule that is so straightforward and so detailed that it predetermines the outcomes of specific cases. In other words, politicians can impose their preferences on judicial output either through "telephone law" when they just call up the judge and demand a specific ruling, or by passing laws that if followed would maximize the politicians' utility. I argue, however, that the rule of law requires decisional judicial independence at the level of the case, but not necessarily at the level of the rule.

The legal saga involving Italian premier Silvio Berlusconi illustrates the conceptual blurring that Scheppele describes. Before becoming the head of government, Italy's most powerful tycoon was facing criminal prosecution for false accounting, money laundering, bribery, and tax fraud. During his term in office, his parliamentary faction managed to pass amendments to the criminal code, which decreased the statute of limitations on false accounting and granted the prime minister immunity from prosecution while in office. These measures resulted in the dismissal of some charges and the postponement of others. Other measures, however, such as a proposed amendment to the

---

[3] Kim Lane Scheppele who introduces this distinction actually talks about a third level as well, which is the level of the principle. Scheppele argues that the rule of law requires judges to be *dependent* at the level of the principle. This means that judicial output should consistently reflect the "preferences" enshrined in the constitution in the form of certain overarching principles (Scheppele, 2002, p. 244).

rules regarding the admissibility of documents obtained from other countries did not pass despite the efforts of Berlusconi's faction to push them through parliament (Economist Intelligence Unit, 2002). Scheppele basically questions whether there is a fundamental difference between these events and the Soviet experience with "telephone law" in which some judges received direct instructions from the executive on how to adjudicate specific cases.

I argue that the two scenarios are different from the standpoint of the rule-of-law doctrine. "Telephone law" would benefit only Berlusconi, whereas the selective amendments to the criminal code would now benefit all fraud perpetrators. It may seem that the second scenario is even less desirable than the first because it would let more criminals off the hook and contribute to a long-term increase in levels of accounting fraud. However, only the first scenario violates the rule of law's emphasis on equal responsibility and protection under the law because it gives an advantage in court to one litigant. The second scenario is in line with the tenets of the rule-of-law doctrine because it increases litigant equality under the law.

Another difference is that promulgating laws in a politically competitive environment is costly in terms of time and efforts. Ad hoc interference in specific cases, on the other hand, especially if it is an informally established prerogative of the incumbents, requires virtually no political resources and has no time lag, so it is a much more effective tool for imposing the politicians preferences on individual trial outcomes. We should then expect that dependence at the level of the case would affect a much larger set of cases than dependence at the level of the rule. Since I argue that we should measure decisional judicial independence through the percentage of cases adjudicated independently from a given actor, then dependence on politicians at the level of the case would result in a much lower level of judicial independence than dependence on politicians at the level of the rule.

## CONCLUSION

This chapter argues that the definition of judicial independence should stem from the link between judicial independence and the rule of law. It also argues that decisional judicial independence is necessary for the rule of law, and institutional and behavioral judicial independence are not. Therefore, the book seeks to explain variation in decisional judicial independence, which is defined as judicial output, which does not systematically reflect the preferences of non judicial actors. Under this conceptualization, courts are independent from a given actor if this actor does not consistently impose his or her preferences on trial outcomes. The definition also suggests that analyses of judicial independence should identify the principal whose real or potential influence on the courts is the focus of study. Finally, studies should also specify whether independent judicial output results because politicians (1) lack the capacity to interfere in court decision making; (2) rationally conclude that it is not in their interest to interfere; or (3) espouse a strong ideological commitment to independent courts.

**2**

# Judges and Politicians: Theories about the Origins of Judicial Independence

Since judicial independence is a prerequisite for the rule of law, and the rule of law promotes successful political and economic reforms, it is extremely important to know how judicial independence can be established where it has not existed before. In new competitive regimes, which are the focus of this book, incumbent politicians and their coterie may prevent the emergence of an independent judiciary that constrains their behavior. Thus, any account of the origins of the rule of law must examine the relationship between incumbent political elites and the courts.

The literature currently offers two main answers about how we get independent courts. Institutional theories claim that structural insulation of the judiciary (i.e., the existence of formal institutional safeguards) can prevent political interference in judicial decision making. Strategic actor theories argue that independent courts are a by-product of electoral competition – either political incumbents refrain from attempting to pressure the courts, when they face a realistic chance of losing the next election or judges resist any attempts at interference with their decision-making process when they anticipate a turnover in executive/legislative power. The first part of this chapter describes the claims and mechanisms of these theories in greater detail. The second part of the chapter lays out a new strategic actor theory, which I call a *theory of strategic pressure*. The theory posits that in regimes that are neither consolidated democracies, nor consolidated authoritarian regimes, political competition actually reduces, rather than increases judicial independence. Simply put, weak incumbents need subservient courts more than strong incumbents. The chapter concludes by explaining why the strategic pressure theory applies only to these intermediate cases on the democracy-autocracy regime spectrum and how it could help us understand why independent courts are such a rarity outside Western Europe and North America.

## STRUCTURAL INSULATION THEORIES OF JUDICIAL INDEPENDENCE: HOW TO MAKE IT IMPOSSIBLE FOR POLITICIANS TO PRESSURE THE COURTS

Accounts of politicians' inability to pressure the courts into delivering favorable rulings often attribute causal power to institutional configurations. U.S. legal scholars tend to believe that judicial independence is the direct and inevitable result of constitutional guarantees. The U.S. Constitution insulates judges from the political process through constitutional guarantees of life appointments and salaries that may not be diminished during their terms of office, and these provisions basically make it impossible for incumbent politicians to pressure sitting judges (Brutus, 1788; Kaufman, 1980). In addition, constitutional guarantees can prevent the executive or the legislature from altering the structure of the judiciary in self-serving ways (Russell & O'Brien, 2001).

Institutional solutions need not be constitutionally enshrined, however. The U.K., Israel and New Zealand, for example, do not have written constitutions, yet boast independent judiciaries (e.g., Shetreet, 1984; Salzberger & Fenn, 1999; Maitra & Smyth, 2004). The important thing is that the judiciary is structurally insulated from the other branches of power – that way incumbent politicians simply do not have leverage over the sitting judges and thus cannot influence the decisions they take (Fiss, 1993). Structural insulation usually refers to judges having security of tenure and control over the judiciary's budget. Security of tenure means that the judiciary itself controls the process of appointing, remunerating, promoting, disciplining, demoting, and removing judges (Tate & Vallinder, 1995; Domingo, 2000; Russell & O'Brien, 2001; Helmke, 2002). These powers can also be vested in a separate institution (e.g., a Supreme Judicial Council) with a budget and appointment procedures outside the executive's exclusive influence (Guarnieri, 2001). Finally, a professional court administration is also believed to foster judicial independence because it separates judges from mundane micromanagement tasks (Hall, Stromsen & Hoffman, 2003).

As I mentioned in Chapter 1, however, empirical tests of the link between structural insulation and judicial independence lean toward refuting the relationship. Moreover, inconclusive or contradictory empirical tests may be the lesser problem. The main shortcoming of theories that attribute independent judicial output to institutional safeguards against interference is that they underestimate the importance of informal institutions and behavioral regularities. Given *the right combination of incentives*, informal institutions can trump formal ones (Helmke & Levitsky, 2004). In other words, if the incentive to interfere in judicial decision making is strong enough, politicians can exert pressure on the courts through informal channels, no matter what the institutional configuration of the judiciary is. Numerous studies of Latin American judicial politics have discussed the ineffectiveness of security of tenure guarantees (e.g., Rosenn, 1987; Helmke 2002; Chavez 2004; Dix 2005; Kapiszewski 2007; Finkel 2008). Despite having all the institutional safeguards on paper, Supreme Court justices have regularly been coerced into siding with the executive or resigning. In the postcommunist states, a strong tradition of ex parte communication between judges and litigants and discussion of cases between judges and politicians (often referred to as "telephone law") has also undermined newly established insulated institutions (Solomon & Foglesong, 2000; Ledeneva, 2008).

Weaker versions of the institutional theory posit that more insulated formal institutions are simply more auspicious to decisional judicial independence than others (Russell & O'Brien, 2001; Chavez, 2004; Rios Figueroa, 2006; Finkel; 2008; Woods & Hilbink, 2009). This may well be the case, but it is then important to keep in mind that the formal institutions are an intervening, rather than a causal variable. Institutions do not appear spontaneously, they have to be created or adopted. So to fully understand the sources of judicial independence, we would need to know why some countries have the "right" kind of formal institutions, while others have the "wrong" kind. Whether the formal institutional setup of the judiciary is constitutionally enshrined or adopted through ordinary legislation, it is always the product of the actions of politicians (either in the legislature or in the executive), so the question becomes: Under what circumstances do politicians decide to offer/introduce independent courts? Currently, the succinct answer is "under intense political competition." An elaboration follows.

## STRATEGIC ACTOR THEORIES OF JUDICIAL INDEPENDENCE: WHEN DO POLITICIANS OFFER INDEPENDENT COURTS?

A large literature looks at the motivations of politicians who consider whether to lean on the courts or to leave them to reach decisions without interference. Some accounts emphasize the benefits that independent courts can bring to incumbents, such as greater policy stability as independent courts prevent incumbents from capriciously changing those policies of their predecessors that do not meet their short-term political interests (e.g., Landes & Posner, 1975; North & Weingast, 1989; Ramseyer, 1994; Stephenson, 2003; Hanssen, 2004; Inclan, 2009) and a blame deflection mechanism through which politicians can unload politically thorny issues onto the courts (Shetreet, 1984;

Salzberger, 1993). Other accounts focus on the main costs of applying pressure on the courts, such as public backlash against attempts to interfere in judicial decision making (Ferejohn, 1999; Vanberg, 2001; Whittington, 2003) and coalition-building resources needed in order to implement an attack on the judiciary (Gely & Spiller, 1990, 1992; Whittington, 2003).

Perhaps most importantly, a growing group of theories, dubbed *political insurance theories*, look at both sides of the cost-benefit calculus and claim that independent courts are an important insurance policy for politicians who may lose power. Politicians in danger of losing office may fear finding themselves on the receiving end of politicized justice once they are out of power. If this fear is strong enough, it may also cause politicians to refrain from leaning on the courts and to adopt measures (such as strengthening constitutional review) to boost judicial independence. This logic implies that intense political competition, which boosts electoral uncertainty, should encourage incumbents to provide independent courts as an insurance policy against future persecution by the next incumbent. More broadly, incumbents who provide independent courts ensure themselves against being completely powerless once they have let go of their control of the executive and the legislative branch (Ginsburg, 2003; Chavez, 2004; Finkel, 2008, etc.).

Ramseyer (1994; Ramseyer & Rasmusen, 2003) argues that precisely this logic explains the low level of judicial independence in Japan – the LDP did not fear finding themselves in opposition, so they did not feel the need to offer independent courts. Ginsburg (2003), who actually coined the term *political insurance theory*, has argued that the insurance calculus explains the emergence of constitutional review in East Asia. Hirschl's (2000) *hegemonic preservation* thesis makes a similar claim, though his emphasis is on judicial empowerment, rather than on independence. The claim is that politicians adopt institutions that constrain their power in order to entrench their own policies and rules and ensure their continuation beyond their tenure in power. The key causal variable again is political competition (and more specifically, the electoral uncertainty that it triggers).

The insurance hypothesis has, perhaps, become the conventional wisdom argument on the genesis of independent courts in postauthoritarian settings. Case studies on judicial reform dynamics Latin America, Southern Europe, Eastern Europe, and Asia have all pointed to the insurance calculus (Magalhaes, 1999; Skaar, 2003; Chavez, 2004; Dix, 2005; Finkel, 2008).

It is important to note, however, that the majority of the political insurance theories focus on constitutional review and on the relationship between politicians and the high courts.[1] These theories also explain politicians' decision and motivations in implementing institutional changes that *are expected* to boost judicial independence, by closing some channels for political interference in judicial decision making. Thus, these theories do not have an explicit prediction about how lower courts decide routine cases that are of great interest to incumbent politicians, which is the focus of this study. It is possible that weak incumbents could adopt judicial reforms that appear to strengthen and insulate the judiciary just to feign commitment to the rule of law. Instead, behind the scenes, they could well be continuing to hound the courts for friendly rulings, using informal methods and practices.

The insurance theories are very useful for this study because they provide a plausible hypothesis and raise an important question. If intense political competition has been shown to motivate incumbents to take institutional steps to boost judicial independence (at least at the high court level), does it also motivate incumbents to refrain from pressuring the lower courts during the adjudication of highly salient, but not constitutional, cases? Constitutional cases differ in a very important way from ordinary trial outcomes, in which ordinary legislation is applied to the specific circumstances of a given case. Constitutional cases put constraints on future behavior by politicians, and they are also binding on future adjudication of cases. Thus, they are mainly prospective. Court decisions reached by the lower courts are much less prospective and are grounded in current concerns, especially in civil law countries. The official absence of a precedent doctrine (stare decisis) in civil law countries effectively means that individual trial outcomes in lower court cases have very weak implications beyond the specific circumstances of the individual case. Thus, they hardly constrain future political incumbents. Given this important difference, it bears checking whether the political insurance calculus applies to the behavior of incumbent politicians faced with a credible threat of losing power. Later in this chapter, and in the rest of the book, I argue that it does not, at least in new competitive regimes that are not yet consolidated democracies.

## STRATEGIC ACTOR THEORIES OF JUDICIAL INDEPENDENCE: WHEN DO JUDGES RESIST PRESSURE FROM POLITICIANS?

It seems odd to discuss independent courts without discussing the behavior of judges. Perhaps judicial independence can result also when judges simply

---

[1] Only Ramseyer (1994, 2003) looks at the independence of lower court judges from political incumbents.

refuse to yield to pressure from politicians. Widner (2001) offers one theory of judicial independence, which focuses on the behavior of judges, rather than politicians. Widner argues that judicial independence emerged in Eastern and Southern Africa despite economically and politically inauspicious circumstances, because high court judges took up the issue and demanded decisional autonomy from politicians. In addition to simply asserting their independence, activist judges like Tanzanian Chief Justice Francis Nyalali attempted to build up popular support for the judiciary in order to increase the costs associated with applying pressure on the judiciary. Scheppele (1999) also suggests that the ability of the Hungarian Constitutional Court to exercise judicial review independently and confidently was in large part a function of the personal leadership of Chief Justice Laszlo Solyom.

These judicial assertiveness theories raise a question about the circumstances under which judges would be so committed to the principle of judicial independence that they would be willing to reject the carrots and bear the sticks that the politicians can use in order to impose their preferences. In fact, given the almost universal view of judicial independence as desirable, if it emerged as a direct result of high court justices' efforts, judicial independence should be ubiquitous, especially in postauthoritarian regimes. Empirical studies, of course, show that this is far from the case. Helmke (2002) offers one answer to the question of when judges would stand up to pressure from politicians. In contrast to the dignified guarantors of the rule of law in Widner's and Scheppele's accounts, the high court justices in Helmke's account are more akin to rats abandoning a sinking ship. Like the political insurance theories, Helmke's strategic defection theory posits that intense electoral competition triggers high court output that does not closely reflect the preferences of incumbent politicians. Helmke argues that when incumbents are weak and on their way out of office, justices have a strategic incentive to resist pressure, and thus produce judicial output that is markedly at odds with the preferences of the incumbents. Justices fear retribution from the next government and therefore disassociate themselves from the incumbents by ruling against them. Helmke (2002) provides empirical support for her theory on the basis of longitudinal analysis of the output of the Argentine Supreme Court. The decisions of the Georgian, Ukrainian, and Kyrgyz Supreme Courts to side with the opposition during the "colored revolutions" of 2003–5 despite considerable pressure from the incumbents corroborate the strategic defection theory and suggest that it is generalizable beyond Latin America.

Helmke's theory is an important contender in explaining judicial independence at the highest levels of the judiciary. Can we extrapolate from it, however, and use it to also explain the behavior of lower court judges in applying ordinary legislation, rather than engaging in constitutional interpretation? I argue that we should not for a couple of reasons. First, the judicial actors in Helmke's account should indeed be afraid of retribution by future incumbents because their decisions are prospective and will have very direct implications for future incumbents. Thus, when they come to power, future incumbents have an incentive to punish disloyal judges that goes beyond simple revenge (which may, of course, be a motivating factor). By contrast, the lower court decisions that I am considering affect future incumbents only indirectly. They might be detrimental to their interests while the future incumbents are still just oppositionists, and they may well prevent the oppositionists from coming to power. But if the oppositionists nonetheless make it into power, these decisions are no longer relevant. If they punish the judges for having taken them, it would be an act of pure retrospective revenge, rather than an act in line with their then current interests. Finally, lower court judges may be more afraid than high court justices of current incumbents than of future incumbents. Lower court judges considering defection would probably face a collective action problem due to information uncertainty – if they are the only ones who have estimated the incumbents as weak, they would bear the brunt of the incumbents' punishment.

In short, Helmke's theory informs this analysis, because like the political insurance theories, the strategic defection theory suggests that the intensity of political competition is an important factor that affects the relationship. In addition, the strategic defection theory contributes greatly to our understanding of the complexity of judicial behavior. Like, Helmke, I also find that judges are self-interested actors who decide whether to yield to political pressure or resist it by assessing how a particular action would affect their own careers. This is in sharp contrast to the myth of judges, ideologically committed to protecting and implementing the rule of law. However, I argue that the strategic defection calculus is not directly applicable to the circumstances that I am analyzing – decision making by lower courts in politically salient, but not constitutional cases.

## JUDICIAL INDEPENDENCE AND REGIME TYPE: WHY ARE INDEPENDENT COURTS A RARITY OUTSIDE OF THE WORLD'S CONSOLIDATED DEMOCRACIES?

Existing theoretical accounts of judicial independence, which link political competition and electoral uncertainty to the provision of independent courts, rarely explicitly consider the effects of the regime context within which political competition takes place. By regime context, I specifically mean the many differences between old consolidated democracies and new unconsolidated democracies. In addition, amidst all the talk about the costs and benefits of independent courts, the benefits that incumbents reap from a subservient judiciary are curiously absent from most theoretical accounts. This might be because these benefits are quite obvious – having a subservient court means you do not lose individual cases, and that is a benefit for all incumbents. However, failing to discuss these benefits is tantamount to assuming that they are a constant rather than a variable. Such an assumption seems unwarranted. The benefits of dependent courts should vary in response to different causal factors, just as the benefits and costs of independent courts vary. This section addresses both issues.

By consolidated democracies, I mean regimes where democracy and its rules are widely perceived to be "the only game in town" (Linz & Stepan, 1996). Both the elites and the public expect elections to take place regularly into the foreseeable future. There are no viable antisystemic political actors and civilian control over the military is effective and unchallenged. The main political actors accept that they will be involved in an incumbent-opposition relationship into the foreseeable future. All civil and political rights crucial to the functioning of a democratic regime are respected and made meaningful by the existence of appropriate institutions. For example, voting rights are guaranteed as campaign laws are applied strictly yet impartially and vote buying and electoral fraud are nonexistent or minimal; electoral participation rights are meaningful because there is a developed and stable party system (i.e., most parties have extensive networks of grass-roots organizations and compete in successive elections); free speech rights are epitomized by a vibrant independent press. Consolidated democracies display lower levels of uncertainty, which results in risk-averse behavior by politicians and long time horizons.

By contrast, emerging democracies, where democratic institutions have been around for much shorter periods of time, are distinct from consolidated democracies. Not all emerging democracies are, of course, the same. They can be quite different from each other, as they build democratic institutions in distinct order and at varying pace. As a result, many different monickers have been used to describe the regimes that have emerged from the latest democratization waves. In the 1990s, scholars counted more than 550 different "diminished" types of democracies, regimes that displayed some democratic institutions, but not others (Collier & Levitsky, 1997). Some of these regimes meet the procedural minima for democracy, but lack most of the institutions that guarantee fair contestation and full participation (Diamond, 1996, 2002). For example, electoral fraud and vote buying may be rampant and hollow out the meaning of free elections. Influence peddling and corruption may pervade the party system. Parties come and go, resulting in high levels of electoral volatility. Parties may lack a strong basis in society, so in effect they may not serve their democratic purpose of aggregating societal interests and representing them in government. The press may be more of a PR organ of powerful interests than an arena for the exercise of free speech. Many such *unconsolidated* regimes function in a seemingly ad hoc manner. Each election may well be the last. The possibility of democratic breakdown constantly lurks in the background either in the form of a military coup or the ascension of an antisystemic figure to the highest elected office. The main political actors have deep-rooted mistrust in each other. Public trust and support for democracy are often also low (Schmitter, 1994).

There are two characteristics that all of these new competitive regimes (or "emerging democracies") share and that I argue reverse the effect that political competition has on the relationship between politicians and courts. The first characteristic is a mixed institutional environment – new, democratic formal institutions coexist with old, authoritarian-era institutions and informal practices. The literature on the topic is vast, and it has addressed questions about the interaction of the new and old institutions and the results that it produces. For example, how do differences in bureaucratic and cultural legacies affect the type of party system that emerges during a democratic transition (Kitschelt, 1995; Rose, 2001; Hale, 2006, etc.)? Or do voters in new democracies behave similarly or, radically differently, to voters in consolidated democracies (Colton, 2000; Tucker, 2006, etc.)? What happens when formal institutions of democratic representation function in the context of a weak civil society (e.g., Howard, 2003)? Most would probably agree that the mixed institutional environment does make politics in emerging democracies fundamentally different from politics in consolidated democracies, where democracy has been the only game in town for a while.

The second characteristic of the regimes that occupy the spectrum between consolidated democracy and consolidated authoritarianism is the ubiquitous and high level of uncertainty (see, e.g., O'Donnel & Schmitter, 1986; Mainwaring, O'Donnell & Valenzuela, 1992; Bunce, 1993, etc.) This uncertainty, however, goes beyond the "bounded" uncertainty in consolidated democracies, where the outcome of each election is unknown until all the ballots are counted. Rather, it is a much more pervasive, "unbounded" uncertainty, where actors simply do not know whether the regime in its current institutional form would persist in the near or distant future (Schedler, 1998). For example, actors do not know what the rules of competition are going to be like tomorrow, whether the person who garners the most votes would actually be declared the winner of the election, or whether the amount of freedom of the press or freedom of association will be similar from one incumbent administration to the next. This type of "unbounded" and pervasive uncertainty shortens the time horizons of all actors who participate in the politics of a new democratic regime. In other words, actors care much more about the present than about the near future and even less about the distant future. As I will argue later, the shorter time horizons have a profound effect on the behavior of politicians vis-à-vis the courts.

Whatever conceptualization or classification of regimes we use, it is hardly controversial to note that independent courts are the norm in Western Europe, North America, and Australia (i.e., the old consolidated democracies), and they are a rarity outside this region (i.e., in the emerging democracies) (Howard & Carey, 2004). Weak incumbents in consolidated democracies surely also prefer to remain in office and could thus benefit from subservient courts. Why does it seem then that incumbents in consolidated democracies very rarely (if ever) lean on the courts to obtain favorable rulings, whereas in other competitive regimes extrajudicial interference appears to take place more frequently?

Existing political competition theories of judicial independence emphasize electoral uncertainty, but they do not ask whether weak incumbents in old consolidated democracies view a potential loss of power differently than weak incumbents in emerging democracies. If incumbents in emerging democracies have different time horizons and operate in a different institutional context, should we not expect them to engage in a fundamentally different cost-benefit analysis when they decide whether to lean on the courts or not?

I argue that in regimes that are neither consolidated democracies yet, nor consolidated autocracies, the costs of pressuring the courts are lower but the benefits of pressure are higher. At the same time, some of the benefits that incumbents in consolidated democracies purportedly reap from independent courts do not apply in emerging democracies. In other words, in emerging democracies, subservient courts are the norm, rather than the exception, because courts are more valuable to incumbents, *and* incumbents have an easier time imposing their preferences. Table 2.1 summarizes these differences between consolidated and electoral democracies.

The costs of pressuring the courts are lower in emerging democracies because incumbents have access to existing mechanisms for pressuring the judiciary, inherited from the authoritarian regime. Even if sweeping institutional reforms of the judiciary take place at the outset of the transition away from authoritarianism, informal channels for pressuring judges are tougher to root out (Solomon & Foglesong, 2000). The persistence of these informal channels lowers the costs of implementing an attack on judicial independence.

TABLE 2.1. *Cost-benefit analysis by incumbent politicians in different regimes*

|  | Consolidated democracies | Emerging democracies |
| --- | --- | --- |
| Costs of pressuring the courts | High | Low |
| Benefits of pressuring the courts | Low | High |
| Benefits from independent courts | High | Low |

In addition, incumbents in newly competitive regimes are probably less fearful of public backlash than incumbents in consolidated democracies. It is likely that postauthoritarian citizens are more accustomed to political interference in judicial affairs than their counterparts in consolidated democracies. However, even if postauthoritarian publics happen to have a lower threshold of tolerance for politicians who attempt to influence judicial output, there is a prior condition for public backlash to result: The electorate should be able to detect the attacks to react to them (Vanberg, 2001).

An active and inquisitive press is crucial to the level of transparency. Yet in postauthoritarian settings, the media are, almost by definition, less experienced in investigative journalism than the media in consolidated democracies (see, e.g., Chua, 2002; Waisbord, 2002; Hughes & Lawson, 2005). In addition, the postauthoritarian media are often themselves the subject of attacks, so they might not cover the incumbents' transgressions as vigorously as the media in consolidated democracies because of self-censorship (see, e.g., Rodan, 1998; Amayreh, 1999; Simon, 2004). Oligarchic domination of the media market can further decrease the level of transparency (see, e.g., Simon, 2004; Hughes & Lawson, 2005;). Finally, postauthoritarian publics often distrust the media, which also hinders their ability to expose attacks on judicial independence (see Fossato, 2001).

I argue that the benefits of a subservient judiciary are higher in emerging than in consolidated democracies. This is because under institutionalization of the party system and high electoral volatility are endemic in electoral democracies (Mainwaring & Zoco, 2007). When parties lack well-developed grass-roots organizations, stable financing, and a party label that transcends the name recognition of the leader, a few court decisions can inflict dramatic damage. For example, one court through one single trial during a crucial moment can destroy even major oligarchic structures and thus severely undercut a party's campaign. By contrast, it would be much harder (more costly and more time-consuming) for the courts to systematically persecute the hundreds of individuals and companies who finance established parties in consolidated democracies. Similarly, closing down a party newspaper will have much greater impact on that party's popular approval rating if the newspaper is the only channel for communicating with its supporters. The same court decision will have a smaller effect on established parties that have a dense network of grass-roots organizations through which to energize their base. Many parties in new democracies are little more than vehicles for their leaders to participate in parliamentary elections. Thus, a court decision to remove the party leader from the ballot could destroy the whole party.

Finally, the benefits of independent courts, identified by the literature on judicial independence in consolidated democracies, should be generally lower in emerging democracies. For example, the intertemporal policy control calculus does not work well in the high-uncertainty environment of emerging democracies. The decision to favor increasing future policy control over maximizing current policy control assumes that incumbents care about the future and expect to be in politics for the long haul. However, in emerging democracies, where the rules of the game are not firmly established, incumbents will be more likely to prefer to use the courts to strengthen their position and thus avoid yielding power altogether. For them, the trade-off between current and future policy control may be a moot point.

In addition, it is equally unwarranted to assume that interest groups in emerging democracies would value policy stability over the short-term benefits of short-lived policies as interest groups in consolidated democracies supposedly do. In fact, if Hellman (1998) is correct about the power of the initial winners of the postcommunist transformation, presupposing that interest groups in postauthoritarian settings would value long-term policy stability is simply empirically wrong (Hellman, 1998). Thus, the mechanism identified by Landes and Posner (1975), in which interest groups basically encourage politicians to provide independent courts by paying more for current policy proposals, does not apply to emerging democracies.

A benefit of independent courts, which seems more relevant to emerging rather than to consolidated democracies, is protection from selective prosecution. This benefit also depends on an intertemporal calculus, but instead of policy control, incumbents give up current opportunities to harass opponents through the courts, in exchange for insurance that they will not become the subject of harassment once they find themselves in opposition. However, the same caveat applies as in the policy stability hypothesis – incumbents have to expect to be in politics for the long haul to credibly commit to such an arrangement. The deep-seated mistrust of other political actors, which characterizes many emerging democracies, however, undermines the likelihood of credible commitment. Moreover, alternative methods for obtaining immunity from prosecution, beside independent courts, often exist. For example, incumbents can collect enough compromising material on the opposition, which can serve as a guarantee against prosecution once they are out of office (see Darden, 2001).

Testing to see whether these propositions specifically account for the obvious contrast between the prevalence of independent courts in the old democracies and their scarcity beyond that regime group is beyond the scope of this book. It would require a comparison between an old consolidated democracy and a new electoral regime, like those in Russia and Ukraine. However, this regime context provides an explanation as to why political competition and electoral uncertainty affect incumbents in emerging democracies in very different ways than they do incumbents in consolidated democracies.

## POLITICAL COMPETITION AND JUDICIAL INDEPENDENCE IN EMERGING DEMOCRACIES – A STRATEGIC PRESSURE THEORY

Contrary to the conventional wisdom, I argue that in newly competitive regimes, political competition magnifies the benefits of subservient courts to incumbents, thus reducing rather than increasing judicial independence. According to this theory of strategic pressure, political competition fosters the politicization of justice and dependent courts through three distinct mechanisms.

*Mechanism 1:* Intense political competition dramatically increases the benefits that incumbents in emerging democracies can derive from pressuring the courts and as a result creates a strong incentive for incumbents to pressure the judiciary.

When incumbents are weak, they can use subservient courts as campaign instruments to maximize their reelection odds by securing favorable rulings in politically salient issue areas, such as campaign finance, electoral registration, redistricting, or polling station organization. Moreover, weak incumbents can boost their chances of retaining power by using dependent courts as a weapon against their main competitors. For example, a subservient judiciary can severely undermine the opposition by prosecuting its financial backers for tax evasion or fraud, siding with municipal authorities to deny meeting permits for opposition rallies or prosecuting opposition activists on trumped up hooliganism or vandalism charges.

By contrast, strong incumbents do not need subservient courts as much as weak incumbents do. If they are electorally secure (i.e., their position in power is not threatened by an electorally viable opposition), they do not need to use the courts to fight off the opposition's advance. Moreover, strong incumbents in emerging democracies (and this is probably even more true in authoritarian regimes) may have other instruments at their disposal to achieve their policy or political goals, apart from subservient courts. A court decision that does not conform to their preferences can be "fixed" or circumvented through other means. For example, instead of fighting electoral registration battles in the courts tooth and nail, the Putin regime (even more electorally secure after the 2003 Duma elections) changed the whole party registration system through legislation and effectively killed the democratic parties – Yabloko and Union of Right Forces (SPS)– in time for the 2007 elections.[2]

Finally, political competition, manifested in significant ideological distance between the incumbents and the opposition, should boost the incumbents' desire to hold on to power. After all, if future cooperation between the incumbents and the opposition is not in the realm of possibility, then incumbents should be less willing to cede power. This dynamic also creates an incentive for incumbents to pressure the courts as a way of increasing the probability of remaining in power.

*Mechanism 2:* In emerging democracies, political competition does not increase the costs associated with pressuring the courts.

The political resources incumbents need to expend to implement an attack on judicial independence are unrelated to electoral uncertainty. If an attack is construed as passing legislation aimed at curtailing the insulation of the judiciary from the other branches, then weak incumbents would indeed have a harder time implementing or credibly threatening the judiciary with such an attack. However, incumbents can effectively influence judicial output (especially at the district court, rather than the Supreme Court level) through informal and ad hoc measures, such as budget cuts, insufficient appropriations, withholding of benefits that judges are entitled to by law, and simply failing to comply with individual rulings (Solomon & Foglesong, 2000). The police and the tax authorities, who are usually controlled by the executive, can also

---

[2]  It is important to note that the courts are less useful to strong incumbents in emerging democracies only in comparison with weak incumbents in other such regimes, not in comparison with any incumbent in an old consolidated democracy. In comparison with incumbents in old consolidated democracies, strong incumbents in emerging democracies still can draw potentially higher benefits from subservient courts. To continue with the electoral registration example, Russia's underinstitutionalized party system makes it possible for Russian incumbents to destroy individual parties by "decapitating" them through deregistration. The Liberal Democratic Party of Russia (LDPR) without Zhirinovsky is finished, whereas Labor without Blair or the Social Democratic Party of Germany (SPD) without Schröder can clearly survive.

be used to harass individual judges. These are some examples of legal infor-mal mechanisms through which the executive can coerce the judiciary into delivering favorable rulings. Threats and violence can also work quite effec-tively. None of these mechanisms requires building broad consensus among the political elites, so intense political competition is not likely to make them more costly.

*Mechanism 3:* In emerging democracies, political competition produces a *politicization of justice* effect.

The term "politicization of justice" is meant to be the antonym of the "judicialization of politics" concept. The judicialization of politics literature, which examines (and largely criticizes) the trend toward the insertion of the courts in the thick and thin of political life focuses exclusively on consolidated democracies. That literature raises a concern about judges becoming too pow-erful and usurping responsibilities that should belong to elected politicians. In other words, the issue in consolidated democracies is too much judicial inde-pendence, rather than too little (Stone Sweet, 2000; Guarnieri & Pederzoli, 2002; Hirschl, 2004).

By contrast, politicization of justice occurs when the courts become increas-ingly embroiled in politics, but their output is dependent on the preferences of incumbent politicians. During a period of intense political competition, a larger set of cases decided by the courts affects the incumbents' probability of retaining power. As a consequence, the incumbents identify a larger set of cases as salient and important for their reelection chances. This heightened attention to the output of the courts, in turn, leads to the politicization of a larger set of cases.

Political competition thus creates a strategic incentive for weak incumbents not only to try really hard to win each case they are involved in but also to attempt to prevent the opposition from winning cases that it has a stake in. By using the courts as attack dogs, incumbents can hope to weaken their com-petitors or signal strength and thus hurt the opposition's ability to recruit sup-porters. In other words, weak incumbents will choose to interfere in cases that would seem trivial to strong incumbents. For example, weak incumbents may meddle in business disputes involving companies that support the opposition and pressure the judges to deliver rulings that hurt the opposition's financiers. Or, a dispute associated with municipal elections may suddenly become a high-stakes affair for a weak incumbent who is afraid of ceding any ground to the opposition.

The greater the number of cases that become politicized, the greater the number of judges who become subject to pressure. And the more judges are affected, the greater the collective action problem that they face if they wish to resist. In other words, despite the weakness of the incumbents, the "strategic defection" mechanism, identified by Helmke (2002), is less likely to work at the district court level. Rather, a strategic pressure mechanism results in a higher probability that judges will yield to incumbents' demands and deliver biased rulings, thus lowering the overall level of independent judicial output.[3]

## REGIME AGE AND INDEPENDENT COURTS

Time is clearly an important variable in the model I am proposing here. How long can a new regime be called "emerging"? Can regimes hover between consolidated democracy and consolidated authoritarianism forever (or at least for a long time)? There is a vast and still growing body of literature on regime change that suggests that, indeed, many postauthoritarian regimes appear to be stuck in transit to the democracy that they purportedly set out to build (see, e.g., Schmitter, 1994; Carothers, 2002). Or they backslide so significantly in terms of civil and political rights that it no longer makes sense to call them democracies, but they cannot quite consolidate an authoritarian regime either. These regimes have been called competitive authoritarian regimes (Levitsky & Way, 2010).

If we accept the existence of a democracy-autocracy spectrum, rather than a scale or a dichotomy, then we should probably accept that there will not be a sharp border between an unconsolidated democracy and a consolidated one or between a competitive authoritarian regime and a consolidated authoritarian regime. Most agree, however, that the differences between these regime types are meaningful, even if they are difficult to categorize with great accuracy. There are a number of projects that seek to systematize these differences and categorize regimes accordingly – Freedom House, the World Bank's Database of Political Institutions and Governance Indicators, and Polity are the major ones that are widely used in the literature.

---

[3] Of course, weak incumbents in emerging democracies would prefer that many disputes did not reach the courts at all, but would rather that they be decided by government agencies, which should be easier to lean on and control than the courts, ceteris paribus. For example, it may be easier to control elections if all disputes were decided only by the election commissions and if the courts did not have jurisdiction over these disputes at all. However, taking away jurisdiction from the courts requires even more resources than pressuring the courts in individual cases. To go back to the distinction between independence at the level of the case and independence at the level of the rule, taking away the latter entails a stable parliamentary majority (and, often, a two-thirds or larger majority as the political and civil rights are usually constitutionally enshrined). Thus, weak incumbents that are barely holding on to power would find it hard to change the rules as to exclude the courts altogether.

To determine whether a regime has slid back into consolidated authoritarianism, regime classifiers look at whether political and civil rights have been eroded to the point that we cannot argue that elections are meaningfully contested. If political incumbents consolidate power to the extent that they can abolish elections for important offices altogether, it is an easy call – the country has reverted to consolidated authoritarianism. The border between an emerging democracy and a consolidated democracy seems more challenging to pinpoint. How can we tell that democracy has become the "only game in town"? I have argued that emerging democracies are characterized mainly by a mixed democratic-authoritarian institutional environment and a high level of uncertainty about the sustainability of the regime in its current form. Thus, countries inch closer to democratic consolidation as leftover authoritarian informal institutions and practices start dissipating with time. For example, informal channels of voter coercion give way to greater respect for electoral laws; or civil society becomes stronger and its groups start aggregating interests and communicating them to elected officials. I expect that the "unbounded" uncertainty of the transition stage slowly decreases the longer the main rules and institutions that structure the democratic regime persist without major changes. If, however, change is the name of the game, rather than continuity, I argue that the "emerging democracy" stage would be longer and that consolidation would be delayed. Uncertainty would remain high and time horizons short if major rules change often (e.g., the Constitution is frequently amended) or important institutions come and go (e.g., electoral system switches between PR and majoritarian models) or central players enter and exit politics frequently (e.g., electoral volatility is extremely high with new parties winning majority and then disappearing after one term).

Determining when a regime no longer qualifies as an "emerging democracy" matters to our discussion because the strategic pressure theory applies only under these circumstances. If a regime exits the "emerging democracy" category, then the strategic pressure theory stops being applicable. If the regime morphs into a consolidated democracy, then we can expect that the traditional political competition theories of judicial independence would start to apply – intense political competition would motivate politicians to refrain from leaning on the courts, whereas strong incumbents would occasionally impose their preferences on judicial output. If the regime backslides into full-blown authoritarianism, then we should look to theories of judicial behavior in authoritarian regimes to explain the relationship between political incumbents and judges (see, e.g., Moustafa, 2007; Ginsburg & Moustafa, 2008).

CONCLUSION

This chapter argued that traditional political competition theories of judicial independence have important boundary conditions. First, they are better at explaining the variation in judicial independence in consolidated democracies than in other competitive regimes. In the former set of regimes, political competition increases the benefits that incumbents can reap from independent courts and boosts the costs of pressuring the judiciary. As a result, political competition promotes judicial independence, *in consolidated democracies*. Second, they are better at explaining judicial independence at the level of the high courts, than at the level of the lower courts, which in civil law countries do not adjudicate constitutional disputes.

I argued that in emerging democracies incumbents receive a higher payoff from dependent courts and incur lower costs if they pressure the judiciary. That is why dependent courts are the norm, rather than the exception in emerging democracies. The chapter presented a *strategic pressure theory*, which posits that political competition hinders the establishment of independent courts in such regimes because it creates a stronger incentive for incumbent politicians to interfere in judicial decision making. This inverse probabilistic relationship between political competition and judicial independence results from the fact that incumbents who face a realistic chance of losing power can reap higher benefits from dependent courts. Such weak incumbents also try to impose their preferences on a larger set of cases, which further reduces the level of judicial independence. Strong incumbents, by contrast, have the luxury of being more relaxed about judicial output, which might give some leeway to the judiciary to decide cases free of extrajudicial pressures. As a result, a higher level of judicial independence may result from the strong incumbents' indifference.

# 3

# What Can a Focused Comparison of Russia and Ukraine Tell Us about the Origins of Independent Courts?

To test the *strategic pressure theory* against traditional political competition theories of judicial independence, one needs to measure the volume of independent judicial output in emerging democracies and check whether intense political competition is associated with higher or lower levels of judicial independence. If the highly competitive regimes have courts that are relatively more independent from politicians, then the conventional wisdom is right. If, however, the highly competitive regimes have courts that are more subservient rather than less to the demands of incumbent politicians, the *strategic pressure theory*, rather than the traditional theories, explains the interaction between the judiciary and politicians in emerging democracies.

The choice of measurement method and case selection are both crucial to devising a good research design to test the predictions of the two theories against each other. This chapter starts with a discussion of the limitations and biases of existing measures of judicial independence. The chapter then proposes a new quantitative measure of judicial independence based on multi-stage win-rate analysis of judicial output and describes the data sets on which I apply this measure. The chapter goes on to justify the selection of Russia and Ukraine as the two cases for the application of the new quantitative measure by demonstrating that the two countries share a similar historical, legal, institutional, and economic trajectory but differ significantly on the two crucial explanatory variables, identified in the literature on judicial independence – the degree of structural insulation and the intensity of political competition. Then it explains the choice of two legal issue areas in which to examine judicial independence from politicians – electoral registration disputes and defamation cases against media outlets. The chapter concludes with a brief summary of the predictions of the different theories of judicial independence for Russia and Ukraine.

## EXISTING MEASURES OF JUDICIAL INDEPENDENCE

Operationalizing decisional judicial independence[1] is notoriously difficult, especially if we want to go beyond the reputational index (Larkins, 1996). Some scholars have measured judicial independence by cataloguing threats to the institutional structure of the judiciary as a whole or the careers of individual judges. Gerald Rosenberg assumes that periods of congressional hostility toward the Supreme Court are periods of low judicial independence (Rosenberg, 1992). Scholars have also considered instances of judges getting purged, disciplined, or threatened by the regime as an objective measure of judicial independence (Chavez, 2004; Finkel, 2004). The length of tenure of high court judges is also used to capture the level of judicial independence (Bergara, Henisz & Spiller, 1997; Hayo & Voigt, 2003).

However, defining periods of attacks on the court as low judicial independence and periods without such attacks as high judicial independence may also be misleading. For one, such a measure conceals the difference between a truly independent judiciary and one that is so irrelevant due to its limited jurisdiction that the government does not need to punish rebellious judges. In fact, purges, court packing, and threats might be a symptom of a judiciary's peaking behavioral independence, whereas the absence of such attacks could reflect clear submission. Without looking at actual outcomes of trials, we cannot reliably interpret the true meaning of attacks on judicial independence. In addition, promotion can be just as effective as dismissal in establishing a dependent relationship between the judiciary and another branch of government.

Measures based on a comparison of the promotion rates of loyal and disloyal judges offer an effective improvement upon these static career indicators. Salzberger and Fenn apply this measure to gauge the level of behavioral independence in the U.K., and Ramseyer and Rasmusen apply it to career data from Japan (Ramseyer & Rasmusen, 1997, 2001a, 2001b; Salzberger & Fenn, 1999). Ramseyer and Rasmusen trace the career paths of young judges who have the audacity to rule against the government in cases that are highly salient to politicians and find that these judges never achieve the career success of fellow judges with similar level of promise coming out of university. They interpret this career bifurcation as evidence that the typical Japanese judge would be deferent to the political power holders in order to safeguard

---

[1] As opposed to institutional judicial independence, which, as I argued in Chapter 2, is actually an independent variable that might or might not affect the volume of independent judicial output, rather than a conceptualization of the judicial independence idea envisioned in the rule-of-law doctrine.

his or her career, which in effect violates the equality of the litigants before the law. In other words, politicians have a better chance of consistently maximizing their preferences than other litigants. This seems to be a reliable, albeit indirect measure of behavioral judicial independence from politicians.

Unfortunately, the longitudinal career measure is hard to apply beyond the industrialized democracies. In many countries, it is simply too hard to find reliable longitudinal data on career trajectories. More importantly, however, in most countries outside of North America and Western Europe regime changes, political instability, and/or civil war have punctured development to a significant extent. Hence, fewer people spend their whole life in one career in one institution. In the postcommunist states, specifically, the 1990s were a period of substantial personnel turnover in the judiciary so the career paths of communist-era judges could hardly be used as an indicator. Not enough time has passed to evaluate the career trajectories of younger judges.

The optimal measure of decisional judicial independence would be a direct measure based on individual case outcomes. Measures of this type usually record the overall percentage of cases the government wins in court (Gonzalez Casanova, 1970; Schwarz, 1973, 1977). The more sophisticated versions of this operationalization control for the salience of the cases to incumbents (Molinelli, Palanza &Sin, 1999; Helmke, 2002; Iaryczower, Spiller & Tommasi, 2002).

The existing versions of this indicator do not reflect the substantive difference between a government that puts pressure on the courts in order to secure favorable outcomes and a government that does a good job of complying with its own laws. Also, in order to turn the win-rate of the government into an effective tool for capturing cross-national variation in judicial independence, we would need to develop a measure for the volume of frivolous claims against the government and control for it. A judiciary that is subservient to the government should be less likely to receive frivolous claims against the government than a judiciary independent from the incumbents. The incidence of frivolous claims should be extremely hard to measure, however, as it probably cannot be gleaned from court documents and plaintiffs would not admit in a survey to filing a frivolous claim.

A more serious complication of existing win-rate measures, however, is the selection bias associated with analyzing only the last stage of a multi-stage process that narrows down the pool of participants. Priest and Klein (1984) show that the selection bias stems from the fact that litigation represents only a tiny fraction of the universe of disputes in any given issue area. More importantly, litigated cases are not a random sample of all disputes. In fact, Priest and Klein posit that the parties to a conflict carefully weigh the probability of success and follow cases through to trial only when they think the outcome of the trial is uncertain. In all other cases, the parties are likely to settle in order to avoid the costs of a trial. As a result of this strategic behavior the win-rates will always hover around 50 percent, regardless of whether a judge is biased or impartial. The win-rate will differ significantly from 50 percent only when the relative stakes to the parties also differ significantly. The Priest-Klein model predicts that the party for whom the stakes are higher will tend to win more often.

Other theoretical accounts and empirical tests have extended the Priest-Klein framework. Spitzer and Cohen (2000) have shown that the U.S. government has a significantly higher win-rate at the Supreme Court than other litigants. Spitzer and Cohen have hypothesized that this advantage stems not from the politicians ability to impose their preferences on the courts, but from the fact that the Solicitor General files only petitions he or she estimates to have a very high chance of winning. Thus, if we looked only on the win-rate without considering the strategic calculation that goes on before a case is even filed, we would reach misleading conclusions about the level of judicial independence.

## MULTISTAGE WIN-RATE ANALYSIS AS A METHOD OF MEASURING JUDICIAL INDEPENDENCE

Despite its drawbacks, we should continue to search for a reliable measure of behavioral judicial independence based on analysis of individual case outcomes. Such a measure would not only directly capture the concept of judicial independence but also allow disaggregation according to the source of potential dependence. I argue that judicial independence can be measured reliably and systematically through a direct measure based on trial outcomes. Researchers can construct the proposed multistage win-rate measure in four steps: (1) choose a legal issue area that is salient to the principal of interest; (2) compare the win-rate in court of the principal to the win-rate of other litigants; (3) correct selection bias by incorporating multiple stages of the litigation process; and (4) supplement with interviews or survey data on judges' attitudes to assess the potential influence of judges' personal ideology on trial outcomes. The drawback of this measure is that it is very contextual and labor-intensive, which makes it harder to create a large-*n* database that would allow us to test hypotheses on the whole world sample. Thus, for large-*n* tests, we currently need to rely on the reputational indices. However, the empirical chapters of this book will demonstrate that the measure is feasible, fine-tuned, and robust and thus can be used very effectively in focused small-*n* comparisons between similar countries.

The first step is to choose the legal issue according to the type of judicial independence to be assessed. If the goal were to determine whether the judiciary is independent from the other branches of government, analyzing individual case outcomes in areas such as family law, for example, would be misleading. Rather it would be more suitable to examine the record in politically salient issue areas such as freedom of political speech, election law (such as registration of candidates, redistricting, and campaign finance), or large-scale privatization (or nationalization) of state assets. If we were interested in gauging the degree of judicial independence from public pressure, we would choose an issue area that attracts significant public attention, such as high-profile criminal cases, or consumer protection. To assess the degree of independence from individual litigants, we could look at routine contract enforcement cases. If individual litigants had significant power over judicial decision making, then victory would go to the richest litigants, who can offer the biggest bribe to the presiding judge. Of course, the salience of some issue areas may vary across countries – for example, abortion rights cases are probably politically salient in few countries apart from the U.S., and family law (such as divorce and child custody cases) might have significant political salience in Islamic countries.

The second step is to compare the win-rate in court of the potential principal to the win-rate of other groups of litigants. The goal is to determine whether different groups of litigants have a different probability of winning in court and look for differences, which could not be attributed to the content of the relevant laws. For example, when the objective is to assess the degree of independence from the other branches of government, we could check whether the partisan affiliation of the litigant is a good predictor of success in court. If litigants who are politically linked to the incumbents have a higher probability of a trial victory than litigants affiliated with the opposition, then judicial independence from politicians seems to be low.

If we stopped at this step, this measure would be vulnerable to potential selection bias. Imagine that the judicial process is truly stacked against opposition-affiliated litigants and the players are well aware of the existence of bias and its direction. If only the cases with unpredictable outcomes end in trial, then the win-rates for government-affiliated and opposition-affiliated litigants could be roughly equal even in the presence of judicial dependence. Cognizant of the size and direction of the bias, opposition-affiliated litigants would go to court only if they have cases strong enough to overcome the bias, whereas government-affiliated litigants would go to court with much weaker cases, but still achieve the same rate of success. Conversely, government-affiliated litigants may actually be much more risk averse than opposition-affiliated litigants because for them the costs of a loss in court may outweigh the benefits of a win. If this were the case, government-affiliated litigants would go to court only with stronger cases, and consequently an equal win-rate would suggest that the courts favor the opposition.

A third step aimed at correcting selection bias is thus crucial to the construction of an unbiased measure of judicial independence based on trial outcomes. One way to correct for selection bias is to incorporate the decision to go to court into the equation. To do that we need information on the whole universe of potential litigants. Such information is available, for example, in disputes associated with privatization procedures, electoral registration, or dismissal of civil servants. Only companies that have participated in privatization procedures, declared candidates, and fired civil servants could possibly participate in one of these disputes. By incorporating the selection stage into the equation, we can see whether, for example, judicial dependence is so pervasive that opposition-affiliated litigants simply self-select out of participating in a court case. Once we have a clearer idea of the dynamics of the decision to go to court in the first place, we can conduct unbiased analysis of the actual trial outcome.

Collecting information about all potential litigants is not always possible or feasible, however. For example, it is hard to identify all potential medical malpractice litigants and see who decided to sue and who decided to let it go because there is no reliable way of defining the whole pool of victims of medical malpractice. One would have to consider the whole universe of patients. Determining who the victims are is the prerogative of the court, rather than an a priori established fact.

One strategy for getting around the selection bias in issue areas where we cannot identify the whole universe of potential litigants is to focus on areas of judicial decision making where the judge has considerable flexibility of action, but the litigants cannot self-select in or out of the group. In civil cases that involve compensatory damages, the size of the award could be an indicator of judicial bias toward one group of litigants. In criminal cases the length of the sentence (where sentencing is flexible and the prerogative of the judge) could reveal information about judicial biases.

Finally, in-depth interviews with judges are an indispensable supplement to the quantitative measures because we want to know what role judges' ideology might play in the decision-making process. In certain legal issue areas, judges may be biased in favor of politicians not as a result of low judicial independence but as a result of norms of deference. For example, judges may simply believe that elected officials deserve higher compensation awards for defamation than other, "ordinary" plaintiffs because they deserve more respect for the difficult job that they do.

## MEASURING JUDICIAL INDEPENDENCE FROM POLITICIANS IN RUSSIA AND UKRAINE

To determine the levels of judicial independence from politicians in Russia and Ukraine through multistage win-rate analysis, I first chose two legal issue areas that are potentially salient to politicians because they can significantly alter politicians' chances of assuming or retaining office: electoral registration disputes and defamation lawsuits against media outlets. Electoral registration disputes affect who gets to run for elected office. An electoral registration dispute can arise when a candidate is removed from the ballot for campaign law violations before election day. The candidate can either appeal his or her canceled registration in court or simply drop out of the race without a fight. In addition, both registered candidates and voters can file complaints in court seeking the cancellation of a candidate's registration again on grounds that he or she has violated electoral laws. Defamation lawsuits against media outlets affect how far the media can go in examining the incumbents' record. They arise when media coverage offends the subject of the story and he or she goes to court to prove that the facts are both false and damaging to the subject's reputation and dignity.

Second, I collected data on over 1,000 cases decided by the Russian and the Ukrainian courts between 1998 and 2003. The datasets that I constructed include 118 Russian and 134 Ukrainian electoral registration disputes, and 695 Russian and 105 Ukrainian defamation lawsuits. I not only recorded the trial outcome but also tracked down and coded information about the political affiliation, socioeconomic status, and administrative and legal resources of the litigants involved in each of these cases.

Third, I collected additional data in order to correct the selection bias, associated with looking only at trial outcomes. For the electoral registration disputes analysis, I collected data on *all* individuals who wanted to run for parliament in a single-mandate district. The dataset included 1,974 candidates from 141 of Russia's 225 single-mandate districts and 1,957 candidates from 134 of Ukraine's 225 single-mandate districts. I tracked down and coded the political affiliation, socioeconomic status, and administrative and legal resources of each one of the 3,931 candidates. Then I traced who got involved in an electoral registration dispute and decided to go to court over it. The analysis presented in Chapter 4 checks whether the candidates' political affiliation can predict either the candidate's appeal-rate or their win-rate in court. If government-affiliated candidates have higher win-rates than neutral or opposition-affiliated candidates, that is an indication of low judicial independence and less rule of law, as the requirement for equality under the law would be violated.

In order to correct the selection bias associated with looking only at trial outcomes in defamation lawsuits, I collected data on the size of the compensation award given to each victorious plaintiff. In defamation cases, we cannot collect information on all potential plaintiffs because there is no way to systematically identify the whole universe of people offended by media reports about them. But consider how misleading it may be to look only at trial outcomes. Maybe incumbent politicians would go to court only when they have air-tight proof that they have been slandered, because having a court certify the published information as truthful would be even more detrimental than simply having the information in the public domain. Oppositionists, on the other hand, might be much more opportunistic in bringing cases to court because they could much more easily spin a loss in court as a sign of political persecution, which might enhance, rather than undermine their political clout. This calculation may be especially common in countries where the courts are widely perceived as dependent on incumbent politicians.

This scenario would produce a higher win-rate for government-affiliated plaintiffs, but not because of any judicial dependence, but because of systematic differences in case merit between the two groups of litigants. To avoid the selection bias, therefore, I checked whether the plaintiff's political affiliation can help us predict the size of the compensation award. Differences in case merit could explain the probability of winning in court, but they should not affect the size of the award. Chapter 5 presents this analysis in detail.

The fourth step, aimed at supplementing and checking the results of the quantitative analysis, was to conduct interviews with a variety of actors involved in both types of cases. During five research trips to Russia and Ukraine, I did over 100 semistructured interviews. I spoke with judges, court administration officials, and Ministry of Justice civil servants about their interpretation of the laws on the books and the dynamics of adjudicating electoral registration and defamation disputes. I also met with lawyers who represented candidates in electoral registration cases and lawyers who represented litigants in defamation lawsuits. Finally, I interviewed some of the actual litigants, as well as potential litigants (i.e., candidates who decided not to go to court to appeal a cancelled registration) and journalists who were warned by offended parties that they would take them to court unless they print a retraction.

The role of the interviews in the process of measuring judicial independence was to get a sense of whether any bias in favor of a particular group of litigants that showed up in the quantitative analysis could be attributed to judges' ideology, rather than dependence from incumbent politicians. A strong norm of deference to elected officials and widespread "reactionary" attitudes among judges (e.g., dislike of democratic competition or a free press) can both produce biased judicial output in favor of incumbent politicians. However, it seems that a judiciary that produces such output is simply conservative, rather than dependent.

## WHY RUSSIA AND UKRAINE?

But why are Russia and Ukraine good cases for a test of the theories of judicial independence? The case selection follows the most similar systems design. Ukraine and Russia share a common history since the ninth century. They also share a very similar initial post-Soviet institution building and economic trajectory. Both states pursued judicial reforms, which resulted in an institutional setup that insulated the judiciary from the other branches of government. Russia and Ukraine, however, vary on the main independent variables identified in theories of judicial independence – structural insulation of the judiciary and political competition. Russia has taken the structural insulation project further than Ukraine. Ukrainian politics became increasingly competitive during the 1990s and beyond, while Russian politics became less competitive. This section first goes on to describe the similarities and differences between the two states in more detail.[2] Then, it summarizes the theoretical predictions about the relative level of judicial independence in the two countries.

### *Similarities between Russia and Ukraine*

Both Russia and Ukraine trace their history back to the same early East Slavic state – the Kyivan Rus. During its Golden Age in the tenth through eleventh centuries, the Kyivan rulers adopted Orthodox Christianity. While several Western Ukrainian provinces belonged to Poland, Lithuania, and the Austro-Hungarian Empire, most of the territory of contemporary Ukraine was part of the Russian Empire following the 1654 Treaty of Pereiaslav. In 1940, the Western regions were annexed by the Soviet Union and in 1954 Nikita

---

[2]  There are also, of course, some significant differences between Russia and Ukraine. An obvious difference is that Russia is much larger in terms of territory and population than Ukraine. Russia also has nuclear weapons and massive energy resources, whereas Ukraine has neither. Russia has also assumed the role of the main successor state to the Soviet Union in terms of its superpower position in the international community. Finally, while both states are multiethnic, post-Soviet Ukraine has had a tougher time arriving at a definition of what constitutes a Ukrainian nation than post-Soviet Russia. In Shevel's terms, while Russian elites came up with a consensus definition of the nation, Ukrainian elites, divided along regional lines, had to settle for a compromise definition (Shevel, 2003). Significant as they are, all of these differences are not expected to influence the level of judicial independence and therefore should not bias the analysis.

Khrushchev "gave" Crimea, which belonged to the Russian Soviet Federal Socialist Republic, to the Ukrainian Soviet Socialist Republic. Thus, the two countries share all the twists and turns of a common legal history – from the creation of the first written legal code, the *Russkaya Pravda* during the Kyivan Rus period, through the cycle of Europeanization-inspired judicial reforms and Slavophile counterreforms of the Tsarist period, the early Soviet legal nihilism and finally to the late Soviet rule *by* law (Kistiakovskii 1916; Berman 1963; Wortman 1976; Walicki 1979; Barry, 1992; Beirne, 1992; Hendley 1996, etc.).

Not surprisingly given the common historical, cultural, and economic legacy, Ukraine and Russia embarked on parallel post-Soviet trajectories and established remarkably similar post-authoritarian institutions. Russia adopted its current Constitution through popular referendum in December 1993 after a bloody confrontation between President Yeltsin and the communist-dominated parliament. Ukraine's Constitution was adopted in 1996 after prolonged negotiations between President Kuchma and a highly fragmented parliament. Both constitutions establish a semipresidential form of government and a formally independent judiciary.

The term semipresidential is somewhat misleading because Russia and Ukraine have the two strongest presidencies in Eastern Europe and scholars tend to call both systems superpresidential, rather than semipresidential (Holmes, 1993–1994; Easter, 1997; Fish, 1997; Huskey, 1999; Ishiyama & Kennedy, 2001; McFaul, 2001; D'Anieri, 2003). In both countries, the president not only appoints the prime minister, but can also remove the government without parliament's consent. Both presidents also enjoy secure tenure since parliament cannot call preterm presidential elections and impeaching the president is extremely hard (Clark & Wittrock, 2005, p. 183). Both the Russian and the Ukrainian president can call preterm parliamentary elections, except during the last six months of his or her term in office (Constitution of Ukraine, 1996; Clark & Wittrock, 2005, p. 183). Finally, Russian and Ukrainian presidents have also taken full and roughly equal advantage of the broad decree powers to initiate policies, direct the implementation of laws, and make appointments (Protsyk, 2004).

During the 1990s and early 2000s, Russia and Ukraine also used the same electoral system to form their 450-member lower house of parliament. 225 members of parliament were elected in single-mandate districts (SMDs) using a majoritarian voting; the other 225 seats were filled by party lists, using proportional representation (PR) system. In addition, the balance sheet of formal powers of the legislature is almost identical, as the Fish-Kroening Parliamentary Powers Index shows (Fish, 2006).

In addition, Russia and Ukraine's paths from a command to a market economy went through virtually the same stages. The main thrust of economic reforms consisted of price liberalization and macroeconomic stabilization, followed by privatization. Price liberalization in the early 1990s led to hyper-inflation of over 1,000 percent in both countries. Russia managed to bring inflation under control by 1995 and Ukraine – by 1996. The reforms led to a significant decline in GDP – between 1990 and 1996 both economies were contracting by double digits every year – to a deterioration in living standards, to slowing industrial production, and to the infamous "wage arrears." The last term is a euphemism for thousands of employees not getting paid at all for months, even years, or getting paid in kind. Both Russia and Ukraine got their economies back on track toward economic growth in the late 1990s, and both economies were booming in the early 2000s.

The identical economic reform trajectories allow us to test a couple of judicial independence theories. First, the "blame deflection" theory seems to predict that incumbents in both countries would have the same incentive to delegate unpopular economic reforms to an independent judiciary in order to avoid taking responsibility for the painful effects. The stunning contraction that both economies experienced during the 1990s also allows us to test Haggard and Kaufman's hypothesis that politicians who operate during a period of economic hardship would be less willing to tolerate independent courts (Haggard & Kaufman, 1995). This theory also predicts equal levels of judicial independence in Russia and Ukraine.

In both countries, the 1990s were also the decade of "crony capitalism." State property was privatized through nontransparent insider deals, which resulted in the creation of a group of powerful oligarchs. Boris Berezovski, Vladimir Gusinski, and Mikhail Khodorkovski in Russia and Pavlo Lazarenko, Viktor Medvedchuk, and Rinat Akhmetov in Ukraine (among quite a few others) amassed personal fortunes and built powerful financial-industrial groups largely through asset-stripping and monopoly government contracts. According to one estimate, in 2003 ten groups owned 60.2 percent of the Russian stock market and made 39 percent of all sales in Russia (Guriev & Rachinsky, 2005, p. 133). The oligarchs also held key government positions, which gave them enormous influence over the policy-making process. To list just a few examples – Vladimir Potanin was deputy prime minister in Russia; Berezovki was the deputy head of the National Security Council; Lazarenko was prime minister; Medvedchuk was head of the presidential administration. They all formed parties and built media empires, both of which gave them additional political clout.

A scholarly debate on the role of the oligarchs in Russian and Ukrainian political and economic development is heating up. Some scholars view the rise of the oligarchs as detrimental to the countries' prosperity due to asset-stripping, capital flight, tax evasion, and rent-seeking (e.g., Stiglitz,

1999; Black & Tarassova, 2002; Hoffman 2003). The oligarchs have also purportedly stunted democratic consolidation by increasing inequality and significantly undermining popular trust in the post-Soviet political regime and approval of democratic procedures (e.g., Hoff & Stiglitz, 2002; Braguinsky & Myerson, 2003). Others argue that oligarchs may actually have contributed to the economic recovery in both countries by restructuring their businesses and investing more in them than smaller companies (e.g., Boone & Radionov, 2002; Aslund, 2004; Guriev & Rachinski, 2005; Gorodnicheko & Grygorenko, 2006). In addition, for more than ten years now, Anders Aslund has been predicting the establishment of independent courts through the prodding of oligarchs keen on safeguarding their property rights. He interprets the Orange Revolution, which in his words pitted "millionaires against billionaires," as a confirmation of his prediction (Aslund, 1995, 2004).

Regardless of whether we believe the positive or the negative view of oligarchs, the parallel rise of oligarchic crony capitalism in Russia and Ukraine suggests that the level of judicial independence in the two countries should be quite similar. If the positive view of oligarchic capitalism is the better representation of reality, and if we believe the "policy stability" story of the rise of independent courts, both Russia and Ukraine should be on the path to establishing judicial independence. Oligarchs keen on protecting their property rights and creating an auspicious business climate for their businesses to thrive will demand that politicians provide independent courts. If, on the other hand, we adopt the negative view of oligarchic capitalism, we should expect to observe equally low independent judicial output in Russia and Ukraine as a result of limited public backlash in response to pressure on the judiciary. Oligarchic media ownership should decrease transparency and prevent detecting of attacks on judicial independence. Moreover, the low level of public trust in institutions attributed to crony capitalism will also rub off on the judiciary. Indeed, studies have shown that both the Russian and the Ukrainian electorate deeply distrust the judiciary (Rose, 2001).

*Structural Insulation of the Judiciary in Russia and Ukraine*

Most importantly for the purposes of this study, Russia and Ukraine are both civil law countries. They share the civil law view of judges as more, rather than less mechanistic implementers of the laws on the books, not as interpreters of the law and creators of new jurisprudence. Their legal systems frown upon the common law concept of precedent (i.e., decisions by any court are binding to future adjudication of similar cases and become part of the law). And they maintain a very strict distinction between constitutional interpretation and application of ordinary legislation. Only the Constitutional Court can interpret the Constitution and can decide disputes that have a constitutional dimension. The ordinary courts (including the highest one, the Supreme Court) cannot decide constitutional cases.[3]

Russia and Ukraine both significantly reformed the judiciaries they inherited from the Soviet period and by the late 1990s their judiciaries had more formal guarantees against interference by politicians than many old consolidated democracies do. Both constitutions, as well as additional legislation, proclaim a commitment to the principle of judicial independence (Constitution of Ukraine, Art. 126; Constitution of the Russian Federation, Art. 120 and 124; Law of the Russian Federation on the Judicial System, Art. 5). In addition, both constitutions and specific statutes on the status of the judiciary established security of tenure, provided objective appointment criteria, and granted control over judicial careers to organizations staffed mostly by judges, rather than to politicians.

During the late 1990s through early 2000s, which are the focus of the present analysis, both countries had Judicial Qualification Commissions, which controlled the selection process for new judges. In Ukraine, two-thirds of Qualification Commission members were judges, elected by their colleagues from the local court to serve for a five-year term, and the rest are jurists selected by the regional legislative body (Law of Ukraine on the Qualifying Commissions, Qualifying Certification, and Responsibility of Judges of the Courts of Ukraine, Art. 2–3). The important point is that judges, elected by their peers dominated the institution, which is a clear sign of structural insulation of the judiciary from the other branches of government.

In Russia up until the Kozak reforms of late 2001, all Qualification Commission members were judges, elected to their positions by their peers (Solomon, 2002, p. 120). In 2002, Russia adopted a system more similar to the Ukrainian one, where a third of the members had to be "representatives of the public," elected to these positions by the legislature. In addition, the Russian president gained the power to appoint one representative to each Qualification Commission. Still, judges continued to dominate Qualification Commissions

<hr />

[3]   There is a big legal literature on the Soviet legal system as a civil law system, which has spawned both the Russian and the Ukrainian contemporary legal systems. Some classic texts on the subject include: Harold Berman, *Justice in the USSR: An Interpretation of Soviet Law*, (Cambridge, MA: Harvard University Press, 1963); Peter Maggs, John N. Hazard and William E. Butler, *The Soviet Legal System*, 3rd ed. (Dobbs Ferry, NY: Oceana Publications, 1977). On the contemporary Russian legal system, see William Burnham, Peter Maggs, and Gennady Danilenko, *Law and the Legal System of the Russian Federation*, 4th ed. (Huntington, NY: Juris Publishing, 2009). On the contemporary Ukrainian legal system, see Alexander Biryukov and Inna Shyrokova, *Law and the Legal System of Ukraine* (Huntington, NY: Juris Publishing, 2005).

in numerical terms. In fact, the very impetus for the Kozak reforms came from the widespread view that the judiciary had unchallenged corporate control over personnel decisions (i.e., it was structurally impervious to input from the other branches of government) (Solomon, 2002; Trochev, 2006).

The appointment process for new judges was also quite similar in both countries. Candidates with the requisite combination of education and experience would take an exam administered by the Qualification Commission of any local court with a vacancy. The Qualification Commission would then forward its recommendations to the High Council of Justice (in the Ukrainian case) or to the High Qualification Commission (in the Russian case), which in turn made recommendations to the president (Constitution of Ukraine, Art. 128; Constitution of the Russian Federation, Art. 128). After a three-year probationary period in Russia and after five years in Ukraine, judges would receive life tenure if they were confirmed by the legislature (Constitution of the Russian Federation, Art. 119 and 121; Constitution of Ukraine, Art. 128)[4].

In addition, the Qualification Commissions and/or court chairs, rather than the executive, had formal powers over the promotion and disciplinary process in both countries. Promotions to a higher rank, to an administrative position within a court, or to a higher court were all subject to objective criteria such as age and years of legal and judicial experience (Law of the Russian Federation on the Judicial System, Art. 6(1), Art. 7; ABA/CEELI, 2002b, p. 21). The position of court chair has always been very powerful in both systems where a judge could make promotion recommendations. Judges enjoyed statutory immunity from prosecution for official actions (Law of the Russian Federation on the Status of Judges, Art. 16; Law of Ukraine on the Status of Judges, Art. 13), but they could be disciplined, demoted, or removed from office through a process that only a qualification commission could initiate at the recommendation of the court chair (Law of Ukraine on the Status of Judges, Art. 35.1; Law of the Russian Federation On the Status of Judges, Art. 16).

In sum, in both countries, judicial careers were firmly under the corporate control of the judicial bureaucracy, which is a sign of the structural insulation of the judiciary from the other branches of government (Trochev, 2006; ABA/ CEELI, 2002b). Contrast the Russian and Ukrainian judicial career organization to the highly politicized appointment procedures for U.S. courts, where both branches of government and/or the public have more input in appointing

---

4   There have been substantial changes in the formal institutions since 2009–2010 in both countries (see Solomon, 2010). Ukraine has abolished regional-level qualification commissions and has centralized the process of selecting new judges. Russia has added another layer to the disciplinary hierarchy with the creation of a special body above the Supreme Court.

judges than the judiciary, as well as the widespread practice of having judges fight to remain in office in competitive or uncompetitive elections (Ramseyer, 1994; Russell & Malleson, 2006). Or to the Canadian practice of granting the prime minister unchecked power to appoint Supreme Court justices and the continuing practice in some provinces to allow the provincial attorney general (i.e., a member of the executive) to appoint all judges without any input by either the judiciary or the legislature (Russell & Malleson, 2006). Even in the context of continental civil law systems (like Russia's and Ukraine's), the Russian and Ukrainian judiciary displayed significant structural insulation from the other branches. In Germany, as in Canada, judges sitting in the ordinary courts in half of the federal regions (*Lander*) are appointed by the regional justice minister, without any input from outside of the executive branch. In the other half, where there is a selection committee that nominates judges (an institution roughly equivalent to the Qualification Commissions in Russia and Ukraine), the committee is not dominated by members of the judiciary, as in Russia and Ukraine, but displays a power balance between representatives of the legislature, the executive, the bar, and the bench. At the federal level, appointments to Germany's five Supreme Courts take place without any input from the judiciary – the committee advising the executive on appointments and promotions includes only representatives of the executive and the legislative branches (Guarnieri & Pederzoli, 2002, pp. 51–52).

While both Russia and Ukraine insulated judiciaries during the period under study, Russia went further than Ukraine in instituting formal safeguards against extrajudicial interference in judicial affairs. In Russia, the legislature played no role in appointing judges to the lower courts, whereas in Ukraine, the Rada had the final say. In Russia, local Qualification Commissions heard allegations of misconduct against judges and decided whether the misconduct was serious enough to warrant dismissal. The judges who chose not to appeal a dismissal decision were thus fired directly by their local Qualification Commission (i.e., by their peers and superiors within the judiciary). Qualification commission rulings could be appealed to the High Qualification Commission, and the actions of the latter were subject to review by the Supreme Court (Law of the Russian Federation on the Status of Judges, Art. 16). In other words, in Russia, the final arbiter in dismissal procedures was a judicial actor.

By contrast, in Ukraine extrajudicial actors played an important role in dismissal proceedings. As in Russia, in Ukraine judicial misconduct investigations were initiated and conducted at the local Qualification Commissions. However, upon deciding that there were sufficient grounds for dismissal, the Qualification Commissions forwarded the recommendation to the High Council of Justice, which then conducted its own hearings (Law of Ukraine on the High Council of Justice, Art. 32). The council has functioned basically as an extrajudicial actor, because only four of its twenty members are judges. The rest are nominees of the president and the Rada, representatives of the Procuracy and the Congress of Advocates, and renowned jurists. The minister of Justice is also an ex officio member (Constitution of Ukraine, Art. 131). If the High Council of Justice decided that the investigated judge should indeed be dismissed, it forwarded its recommendation to the branch that has appointed the judge in the first place – the president, in the case of untenured judges, or the Rada, in the case of tenured judges (Law of Ukraine on the Status of Judges, Art. 14.2).

Russia went further in insulating its judiciary than Ukraine in budgetary matters as well. The chairmen of the three high courts (Constitutional Court, Supreme Court, and Supreme Arbitrazh Court), as well as the director of the Court Department and the Council of Judges all participated in the drafting of the judiciary's budget by the cabinet (Law of the Russian Federation on the Judicial System, Art. 33.3). In the event of disagreement over the projected allocation, the government had to attach a note with the judiciary's figures to the draft budget that goes to the legislature for a vote (Law of the Russian Federation on the Judicial System, Art. 33.3). Moreover, the judiciary's representatives could participate in the deliberations on the federal budget, which preceded its adoption by the Duma (Law of the Russian Federation on the Judicial System, Art. 33.4). Finally, the law provided a guarantee that the size of the judiciary's budget cannot be reduced without broad consent by the judiciary in the form of decisions of the All-Russia Congress of Judges or the Council of Judges (Law of the Russian Federation On the Judicial System, Art. 33.5).

If the government happened to drag its feet on transferring money to the judiciary, courts could access the government's accounts and draw funds without additional authorization (Solomon & Foglesong, 2000, pp. 16–18). Once the judiciary's budget was appropriated, the judiciary assumed full control over its disbursement. The task of managing the judiciary's budget belonged to the Court Department of the Supreme Court, and its regional offices had the responsibility to manage it. The Court Departments dealt with all court administration issues, from building repairs to judicial salaries, as well as with the collection and systematization of court statistics. Notably, the director of the Court Department was appointed and dismissed by the chairman of the Supreme Court with the consent of the Council of Judges (Law of the Russian Federation on the Judicial System, Art. 31.2; Law of the Russian Federation on the Court Department at the Supreme Court, Art. 8.1).

The Ukrainian judiciary, on the other hand, was dependent on the executive in budgetary matters. Until 2002, local departments of the Ministry of Justice (MOJ) in each region received proposals for funding by the local courts and consolidated it into a single request. This practice made each individual court vulnerable to pressure from the MOJ because courts did not have line item budgets (ABA/CEELI, 2002b, p. 17). In August 2002, Kuchma established a new institution to take over the management of the courts from the MOJ. The State Court Administration of Ukraine (SCA) inherited the MOJ's regional offices, as well as the court management portion of the MOJ's competence. This decision of the Kuchma administration, however, was hardly a step toward greater insulation of the judiciary from the executive, despite the decrease in MOJ's power. Since the SCA head was appointed and dismissed by the President at the proposal of the Prime Minister (Cabinet of Ministers of Ukraine), the new institution was just as beholden to the president and similarly positioned within the executive as the MOJ.

### Political Competition in Russia and Ukraine

Despite all their similar historical, institutional, and economic legacy and postcommunist trajectory, Russia and Ukraine have ended up with dramatically different regimes twenty years after the collapse of the Soviet Union. Today Ukraine is classified as a fully free regime, just as the most successful postcommunist democratizers in East Central Europe and the Baltics, whereas Russia has reverted to authoritarianism, just like the Central Asian former Soviet (FSU) countries (Freedom House, 2010). During the late 1990s through mid-2000s period, which is the focus of this book, both Russia and Ukraine were emerging democracies that hovered in the "partially free" category of countries (in Freedom House's terms), but they did differ starkly in terms of the intensity of political competition. Well before the massive Putin reelection victory in March 2004 and the Orange Revolution that followed the November 2004 Ukrainian presidential election, Russia and Ukraine had been on a divergent path. Even though both regimes were quite competitive during the early and mid 1990s, Russia became less and less competitive after 1999, whereas Ukraine became more and more competitive. This contrast holds whether we define political competition as electoral uncertainty or as the ideological distance between the major political actors and however we choose to operationalize these variables.

    One widely used method of capturing electoral uncertainty is to calculate the degree of electoral volatility of each electoral cycle. An electoral volatility score is calculated by summing all the percentages gained or lost by each party from one election to the next and dividing by two (Pedersen, 1983, pp. 29–66). As Tables 3.1 and 3.2 show, electoral volatility for the 1998–2002 election cycle

TABLE 3.1. *Electoral volatility in Russia, 1999–2003*

| Party name | 1999 % vote | 2003 % vote | Difference |
|---|---|---|---|
| Unity (Edinstvo) | 23.3 | 38.0 | 1.4 |
| Fatherland-All Russia (OVR) | 13.3 | | |
| Communist Party of the Russian Federation (KPRF) | 24.3 | 12.8 | 11.5 |
| Zhirinovskii Bloc (Blok Zhirinovskogo) | 6.0 | 11.7 | 5.7 |
| Yabloko (Yabloko) | 5.9 | 4.4 | 1.5 |
| Union of Right Forces (SPS) | 8.5 | 4.0 | 4.5 |
| Rodina (Rodina) | 0 | 9.2 | 9.2 |
| Sum of the absolute change in percentage of votes gathered by each party | | | 33.8 |
| **Electoral volatility score** | | | **16.9** |

in Ukraine is almost twice the size of the score that Russia receives for the 1999–2003 cycle.

Since both Russia and Ukraine are presidential republics, it probably makes more sense to estimate the electoral uncertainty faced by the president, rather than parliament. In Russia, the incumbent president has never lost a presidential bid. By contrast, each post-Soviet Ukrainian president has lost an election. In 1994, Leonid Kravchuk failed to win a second term; in 2004, Leonid Kuchma was unsuccessful in securing the election of his chosen successor, Viktor Yanukovych; and in 2010, Orange Revolution hero Viktor Yushchenko came an embarrassing third in his bid for reelection.

Moreover, whereas all Ukrainian presidential elections have been close and have included a runoff second round, all Russian presidential races after 1996 have been entirely predictable. The difference between the winner and the runner up has been between 7 and 18 percent in Ukraine. In Russia, Boris Yeltsin secured his reelection in 1996 after a close second round in which he defeated Communist Party leader Gennadii Zyuganov by 13.5 percent. Both in 2000 and in 2004, however, Vladimir Putin won the election in the first round. In 2004, he trounced his nearest competitor, Nikolay Kharitonov, by a staggering 57.5 percent! In 2008, Dmitrii Medvedev, Putin's anointed successor, defeated Gennadii Zyuganov by a 53.3 percent margin. By contrast, the 2010 Ukrainian presidential election, which again pitted Viktor Yushchenko against Viktor Yanukovych, produced another very close result, although this time Viktor Yanukovych

TABLE 3.2.  *Electoral volatility in Ukraine, 1998–2002*

| Party name | 1998 % vote | 2002 % vote | Difference |
|---|---|---|---|
| Communist Party of Ukraine (KPU) | 24.7 | 20.0 | 4.7 |
| Rukh/ Our Ukraine (NU) | 9.4 | 23.6 | 14.2 |
| Socialist Party of Ukraine (SPU) * | 8.6 | 6.9 | 1.7 |
| Greens (ZPU) | 5.3 | 1.3 | 4.0 |
| National Democratic Party of Ukraine (Pustovoitenko)/ For a United Ukraine (Za Edu) | 5.0 | 11.8 | 6.8 |
| Hromada | 4.7 | 0 | 4.7 |
| Progressive Socialist Party/ Nataliya Vitrenko Bloc | 4.0 | 3.2 | 0.8 |
| Social-Democratic Party of Ukraine-united (SDPU-o) | 4.0 | 6.3 | 2.3 |
| Yuliya Tymoshenko Bloc | 0 | 7.2 | 7.2 |
| Women for the Future (Zhinki za maibutne) | 0 | 2.1 | 2.1 |
| Winter Crop Generation (Komanda Ozimoho Pokolinya) | 0 | 2.0 | 2.0 |
| Yabluko | 0 | 1.2 | 1.2 |
| Unity (Ednist) | 0 | 1.1 | 1.1 |
| Sum of the absolute change in percentage of votes gathered by each party | | | 52.8 |
| **Electoral volatility score** | | | **26.4** |

defeated former "Orange" leader and acting prime minister, Yuliya Tymoshenko. Figure 3.1 shows the stark contrast between the two trends by plotting the difference (in percent) between the two top vote-getters in the first round of each country's three post-Soviet presidential elections. The first round better reflects the closeness of an election, because it includes multiple candidates and it is often uncertain which two among them would make it to the runoff.

If we conceptualize political competition in terms of the ideological distance between the major political actors, Russia again scores lower than Ukraine. One way to measure ideological polarization is to consider the ideological diversity of the parties represented in parliament, as well as the level of parliamentary fragmentation. Another route is to evaluate the ideological distance between the legislature and the president.

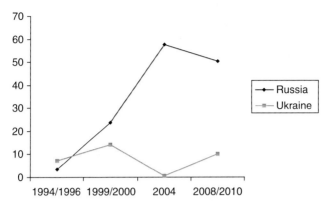

FIGURE 3.1. Difference in the vote garnered by the top two candidates in the first rounds of all Russian and Ukrainian presidential elections (in percent).

At first glance, Russia and Ukraine have very similar party systems. Whether as a result of superpresidentialism, or the mixed-member electoral system, or for other reasons, both states have failed to develop stable party systems with programmatic parties (Ishiyama & Kennedy, 2001; Clark & Wittrock, 2005). Instead, both regimes feature an unreformed, revisionist Communist Party, a fragmented liberal-democratic movement, some unsavory nationalists, and a revolving door of centrist "parties of power."[5] After a brief banishment from political life between 1991 and 1993, the communists in both countries came back with a vengeance as the largest faction in parliament. Then during the last parliamentary election cycle (2002–2003), the popular appeal of the communists waned significantly, perhaps due to generational change in the electorate, and both parties became much weaker. The Russian and Ukrainian centrists are also strikingly similar – light on ideology, but heavy on connections to oligarchic clans and clientelistic ties to the executive (Wilson & Birch, 1999; Colton, 2000; Protsyk & Wilson, 2003). Finally, both the Duma and the Rada included a large set of assorted independent members of parliament (MPs), who did not find it useful to run under any party label.

Notably, however, even though Ukrainian elites continue to regroup, Russian parties have been converging ideologically since Putin's rise to power.

---

[5] Ukraine may finally be on the road towards party system consolidation with the survival of the Party of Regions and Yulia Tymoshenko's Bloc as viable parties for more than one election cycle and the imminent disappearance of the unreformed Communists of Petro Symonenko. But it is too early to tell. As of August, 2010, I am not aware of any studies claiming a significant leap in party system institutionalization in Ukraine. On the contrary, scholars still treat the Russian and Ukrainian party systems as largely similar (Booth & Robbins, 2010).

The unification of Unity and Fatherland-All Russia (OVR) into United Russia (ER) early in the Third Duma is only the most obvious manifestation of this trend. Ideological boundaries between the parties have become increasingly blurred as all of them rushed to rally around the strong president. The Liberal Democratic Party of Russia (LDPR) has kept only a perfunctory and theatrical semblance of their original virulent nationalism. The Communist Party of the Russian Federation (KPRF) and the Agrarians pay only lip service to communist ideology but have repositioned themselves as a similarly patriotic, left alternative to United Russia. The SPS vies to be the right alternative and Yabloko – a more democratic alternative. It is hard, however, to call any one of these parties a veritable opposition to the ruling majority because, as Table 3.3 indicates, all of them vote with United Russia most of the time. Table 3.3 shows in what percentage of the votes the majority of the MPs of one faction casts the same vote as another faction's majority. The dataset analyzed includes 3,387 votes taken during the Third Duma term.

A good proxy for the ideological distance between the president and the legislature is the frequency with which the president uses his veto powers to strike down bills passed by parliament. The more bills vetoed by the president, the greater the ideological polarization between the two branches of government. The level of success of parliament in overriding the vetoes also reflects the level of political competition, because it indicates whether parliament is an effective check on presidential power or not. The greater number of overridden vetoes, the more intense the competition between the two branches of government.

Presidential veto statistics show that the confrontation between the two branches of government has been stronger in Ukraine than in Russia, even before the notoriously contentious relationship between Yushchenko and the Rada during the latter part of his term. During the term of the Third Duma (1999–2003), Putin vetoed 41 of the 771 laws adopted by parliament, which comes out to a veto rate of roughly 5 percent. Both Kuchma and Yushchenko used the presidential veto powers twice as often, striking down 108 (10 percent) of the 1,114 laws that the Rada passed between 2002 and 2006. Moreover, the Rada was much more successful in overriding presidential vetoes than the Duma – 23 (21 percent) of Kuchma's and Yushchenko's vetoes did not stand, while only 3 (7 percent) of Putin's vetoes failed to achieve their goal. Finally, as Table 3.4 suggests, the Russian president managed to establish effective control over the Duma early in his first term and thus has not had to use his veto power much since. By contrast, both Kuchma and Yushchenko have faced significant opposition from parliament – both of them used their veto power more often than Putin, but less effectively, as fewer of their vetoes stuck.

TABLE 3.3. *Overlapping votes among factions in the 3rd Duma (in percent)*

| | Edinstvo | KPRF | LDPR | OVR | SPS | Yabloko | Agrarian | Narodnyi Deputat | Regiony Rossii |
|---|---|---|---|---|---|---|---|---|---|
| Edinstvo | * | 55,2 | 62,3 | 81,9 | 61,5 | 59,9 | 54,3 | 78,8 | 76,1 |
| KPRF | 55,2 | * | 45,1 | 60,9 | 49,6 | 56,4 | 91,0 | 62,0 | 62,2 |
| LDPR | 62,3 | 45,1 | * | 68,8 | 60,9 | 53,7 | 45,4 | 67,9 | 66,0 |
| OVR | 81,9 | 60,9 | 68,8 | * | 70,0 | 66,5 | 60,3 | 86,8 | 85,6 |
| SPS | 61,5 | 49,6 | 60,9 | 70,0 | * | 65,3 | 49,4 | 66,5 | 66,7 |
| Yabloko | 59,9 | 56,4 | 53,7 | 66,5 | 65,3 | * | 55,5 | 65,5 | 65,1 |
| Agrarian | 54,3 | 91,0 | 45,4 | 60,3 | 49,4 | 55,5 | * | 61,7 | 61,8 |
| NarDep | 78,8 | 62,0 | 67,9 | 86,8 | 66,5 | 65,5 | 61,7 | * | 85,4 |
| RegRoss | 76,1 | 62,2 | 66,0 | 85,6 | 66,7 | 65,1 | 61,8 | 85,4 | * |

Source: Yu. K. Malov, *Informatsionno-analiticheskii Byulleten' 2000–2003 gg. Gosudarstvennaya Duma Tret'ego Sozyva (itogovyi)* (Informatsionno-analiticheskoe upravlenie, Gosudarstvennaya Duma) http://wbase.duma.gov.ru:8080/law?d&nd=981601043&mark=c

TABLE 3.4. *Presidential veto dynamics in Russia and Ukraine*

| Year in legislative term | Russia (2000–2003) | | | Ukraine (2002–2006) | | |
|---|---|---|---|---|---|---|
| | Total # of laws passed | # vetoes (% of all laws) | # vetoes overriden (% of all vetoes) | Total # of laws passed | # vetoes (% of all laws) | # vetoes overriden (% of all vetoes) |
| 1st | 145 | 9 (6%) | 0 (0%) | 191 | 19 (10%) | 4 (21%) |
| 2nd | 207 | 23 (11%) | 3 (13%) | 333 | 10 (3%) | 1 (10%) |
| 3rd | 210 | 5 (2%) | 0 (0%) | 279 | 20 (7%) | 11 (55%) |
| 4th | 116 | 4 (3%) | 0 (0%) | 311 | 59 (19%) | 7 (12%) |
| **Total** | **771** | **41 (5%)** | **3 (7%)** | **1114** | **108 (10%)** | **23 (21%)** |

*Source:* Information compiled by the author from statistical data available on the official Web sites of the Duma and the Rada. For Russia, the data are available in the *Informatsionno-analiticheskie Byulleteni o Deyatel'nosti Gosudarstvennoi Dumy*: http://wbase.duma.gov.ru:8080/law?d&nd=981600047. For Ukraine, the data are available in the *Zakonodavstvo Ukrainy* section: http://zakon.rada.gov.ua/cgi-bin/laws/main.cgi and the *Plenarni Zasidannya* section: http://www.rada.gov.ua/plenar.htm

Finally, political competition can be conceptualized in terms of the constraints on contestation, rather than the manifestations of it. The more constraints there are, the lower the level of political competition. Way (2005) uses this approach and discusses four constraints on fair contestation in the post-Soviet regimes: government manipulation of elections, incumbent monopolization of the media, opposition weakness, and de facto power of executive over parliament. Way argues that both Russia and Ukraine became less competitive in the 1999–2004 period, compared to the 1990–1999 period. However, he also argues that Ukraine has been more competitive than Russia throughout the whole post-Soviet period (Way, 2005, p. 242).

## THEORETICAL PREDICTIONS ABOUT JUDICIAL INDEPENDENCE IN RUSSIA AND UKRAINE

A focused comparison between Russia and Ukraine allows us to test the predictions of all theories of judicial independence that include political competition and the institutional structure of the judiciary (i.e., structural insulation) as independent variables. Applying existing theories, plus the theory that I propose, yields three distinct predictions about the existence of independent courts in Russia and Ukraine. Table 3.5 summarizes the predictions of the different theories.

TABLE 3.5. *Theoretical predictions about the level of judicial independence in Russia and Ukraine*

| Theory | Prediction about absolute level of JI | Prediction about relative level of JI |
| --- | --- | --- |
| Structural insulation theory | High | Higher in Russia Lower in Ukraine |
| Traditional political competition theories: • Political insurance mechanism • Strategic defection mechanism | Variation | High in Ukraine Low in Russia |
| Strategic pressure theory | Low | Higher in Russia Lower in Ukraine |

The structural insulation theory predicts that both Russia and Ukraine should have fairly high levels of judicial independence, as both have adopted formal institutions with few formal channels through which extrajudicial actors can influence or pressure the judiciary. Since Russia has gone further than Ukraine in establishing an institutional fortress around the judiciary, Russia should display higher levels of judicial independence. The traditional political competition theories (whatever the mechanism) make a very different prediction. They predict a stark contrast between Russia and Ukraine – subservient courts in Russia, where political competition is low and the incumbents are electorally secure, and independent courts in Ukraine where political competition is high and the incumbents are electorally insecure. Finally, my strategic pressure theory predicts that both Russia and Ukraine would have low judicial independence because during the late 1990s through early 2000s both were emerging democracies, where politically subservient courts should be both more useful for incumbents *and* easier to achieve. However, judicial independence would be somewhat higher in Russia than in Ukraine because Russia's electorally secure incumbents do not need to subordinate the courts in as many cases as Ukraine's insecure incumbents.

# 4

## The Role of Ukrainian and Russian Courts in the Provision of Free and Fair Elections: Judicial Independence from Politicians during the 2002 Rada and the 2003 Duma Campaign

Russian and Ukrainian courts played an important role in shaping the final roster of candidates who contested a single-mandate district seat in the 2002 and 2003 parliamentary elections. At least 134 candidates in Ukraine and 118 candidates in Russia went to court to either defend their registration or challenge an opponent's registration. Moreover, most of these candidates were not also-rans, but viable contenders for seats. In fact, 18 percent of the single-mandate-district winners in both Russia and Ukraine were involved in electoral registration court cases[1].

In comparative terms, these numbers are massive. Electoral registration disputes are exceedingly rare in consolidated democracies. Apart from Alan Keyes's lawsuit, which challenges Barack Obama's eligibility to be the U.S. president on the basis of purported evidence that Obama was born in Kenya, rather than the United States, one would be hard-pressed to find a U.S. politician who has had to defend his right to stand in an election in court. Any type of election-related litigation appears to be much rarer in consolidated democracies than in emerging democracies, such as Russia and Ukraine. U.S. courts at all instances received 341 election-related lawsuits in total during 2004, which was a presidential election year (Hasen, 2005). The total number of electoral disputes in France for 2002 was 143 (Wright, 2003). Czech courts adjudicated 12 cases in 2002 and a record 70 cases in 2006 (Williams, 2007). By contrast, Russian courts heard 1,739 electoral cases in 1999 (Sudebnyi Departament pri Vekhovnom Sude RF, 2000). Ukrainian courts heard 200 electoral cases in 1994, 1,753 cases in 1998, and 5,896 in 2002 (). In 2004, the year of the Orange Revolution, Ukrainian courts received 134,000 election-related petitions! (Verkhovnii Sud Ukraini, 2004)

---

[1] Calculations are by the author on the basis of information from Ukraine's Central Election Commission and multiple Russian sources (newspaper coverage, interviews with candidates, court Web sites, regional election commission Web sites, etc).

Given their substantial involvement in the electoral process, one can hardly overstate the importance of finding out whether the courts were impartial adjudicators in electoral disputes. This question is a central component of the debate about the fairness of the election process and outcome. If the courts were independent in reaching their decisions, then those who tried to get ahead in the horse-race by violating electoral laws and procedures rightfully suffered the consequences and had their registration canceled. Even if the courts did not go after all transgressors, the punishments that they did mete out would create an incentive for other candidates in future campaigns to abide by the law. The end result would be a cleaner campaign and a long-term trend toward fair elections. However, if the courts acted as instruments in the incumbents' attempt to hold on to power, then the elections were deeply flawed and unfair. Moreover, the long-term consequences of such judicial behavior include the gradual hollowing out of elections of their meaning and legitimacy and the undermining of the rule of law project.

The 2002–3 elections are a useful tool for comparing the level of judicial independence from politicians in the two countries because they are, at the same time, similar to each other and typical, rather than idiosyncratic. First, each country had previously held at least one parliamentary election under the same electoral system (225 SMD seats and 225 seats filled through PR lists), which means that all actors involved in the electoral process were already accustomed to the formal electoral rules. Moreover, in both countries, candidates and the "political technologists" they employed used the same campaign techniques: oligarchic media-orchestrated "black PR," technical and clone candidates, deregistration, and administrative resources. Finally, although the Ukrainian election was clearly more competitive than the Russian election (which is the main independent variable under investigation), both elections were fairly uneventful, that is, none involved idiosyncratic factors, such as the mass-scale protests of the Ukrainian Orange Revolution (which briefly empowered the Ukrainian Supreme Court) or the violent executive–legislative confrontation that preceded the 1993 Russian parliamentary election (which also threatened the integrity of the Russian judiciary). Therefore, we can be confident that conclusions about the level of judicial independence that stem from the comparison of these particular two elections are likely to reflect the effects of political competition rather than ad hoc circumstances.

In this chapter, I argue that both countries' courts failed to meaningfully constrain the incumbent regime. Both the 2002 Rada and the 2003 Duma electoral campaigns showcased widespread use of administrative resources by the incumbent Kuchma and Putin regimes. "Administrative resources" is a term that refers to the benefits that come with holding administrative or elected office. When used by the office/position holder during the campaign, those benefits give him or her an unfair advantage over the other participants in the race. For example, university rectors used large auditoriums to hold rallies or allegedly threatened to evict students from dormitories if the rector's preferred candidate did not garner the most votes in the dormitories polling station; military personnel coerced subordinates into campaigning or voting for a particular candidate; and enterprise directors provided employees with bonuses or paid leave in exchange for participation in campaign events (for discussions of administrative resources, see, e.g., Fish, 2005 on Russia; Kuzio, 2003 on Ukraine). If the courts were independent from the incumbents, we should expect to observe a lower win-rate in court for progovernment candidates and a higher win-rate for all other candidates. Neither the Ukrainian nor the Russian data show this result, which means that in both countries progovernment candidates bolstered their reelection chances through violations of the electoral laws with impunity. This result is in line with the prediction of the strategic pressure theory that judicial independence will be low in both countries. In addition, and again in line with the strategic pressure theory's predictions, Ukrainian judicial output in electoral registration disputes displays larger systematic bias toward progovernment candidates than the output of Russian courts. Since the size of the progovernment bias reflects the level of judicial dependence from incumbent politicians, I conclude that Ukrainian courts were more dependent on politicians than Russian courts were.

I arrive at this conclusion through statistical analysis of the candidates' litigation experience. First, I compare the Russian and Ukrainian legislative framework on the issue and explain what electoral registration disputes are. The next section of the chapter describes the data that I collected. The third section discusses my hypothesis about the relationship between candidates' political affiliation and judicial independence and the control variables needed to assess it. The fourth section describes the measures of the independent variables, a candidate's political affiliation, his or her viability at the outset of the campaign, and district competitiveness. The last section presents the statistical analysis of the data and summarizes the predicted probabilities of victory in an electoral registration case for various groups of Russian and Ukrainian plaintiffs.

## WHAT ARE ELECTORAL REGISTRATION DISPUTES?

In any democracy, citizens who wish to run for elected office need to take formal steps in order to appear on the ballot on election day. In Canada, for example, each prospective candidate files a Nomination Paper, as required by Art. 66 of the Canada Elections Act. The form contains the prospective candidate's personal information, declarations on his or her eligibility to run for office, as well as the names, addresses, and signatures of 50–100 constituents in the district where the candidate intends to run. The Nomination Paper is accompanied by a $1,000 deposit, which is returned to the prospective candidate should Elections Canada, the straightforwardly named administrative agency that oversees elections in Canada, reject the application for nomination or should the candidate die between registration and election day (Elections Canada, 2011).

This administrative process of becoming an officially recognized candidate is usually called electoral registration. Electoral registration disputes are court cases that arise in the course of the electoral registration process. Russian and Ukrainian courts adjudicated three types of electoral registration disputes during the parliamentary election campaigns of 2002–3. The first type involved candidates who submitted documents declaring their intention to run in a single-mandate district, but were denied registration by a District Election Commission (DEC). Many of these individuals filed court appeals asking the court to direct the DEC to register them. The second type of dispute involved candidates who initially became registered by the DEC, but who were later deregistered (i.e., their registration was revoked or canceled) by a DEC. Some of these individuals went to court seeking to overturn the DEC decision and get back on the ballot. The final category of plaintiffs were candidates, ordinary citizens, and election commission officials who appealed to the court to take down a candidate's registration (or to deregister a candidate) for alleged election law violations.

In all case types, the plaintiffs relied on electoral law legislation that gave them the right to challenge decisions of the election commissions in a court of law. In Russia, the relevant pieces of legislation were the Federal Law on the Election of Deputies of the State Duma of the Federal Assembly of the Russian Federation, the Federal Law on Basic Guarantees of Electoral Rights and the Rights of Citizens of the Russian Federation to Participate in a Referendum, as well as the Civil Procedural Code of the Russian Federation, which governs the mechanism through which citizens file court grievances against the action (or inaction) of state actors. The Ukrainian legislation that regulates the same issues was the Law on the Election of People's Deputies of Ukraine and the Civil Procedural Code of Ukraine. Both Ukrainian and Russian electoral law stipulated that any DEC decision or action could be reviewed by a district court. Both laws also provided plaintiffs with the option of challenging any perceived failure to act on the part of DEC in court (Law on the Election of

People's Deputies of Ukraine, Art. 29; Law on the Election of Deputies of the State Duma of the Federal Assembly of the Russian Federation, Art. 94 and Art. 95). For example, if a candidate filed with the DEC a complaint that one of his opponents had been violating election law provisions, but the DEC simply ignored the complaint or decided that it was unfounded, the unsuccessful complainant could take his or her case to court.

The Russian and Ukrainian election laws that were in force in 2002–3 were similar to each other and largely consistent with their counterpart legislation in consolidated democracies. According to the Office for Democratic Institutions and Human Rights (ODIHR) subunit of the Organization for Security and Cooperation in Europe (OSCE), the leading international organization that monitors democratic elections around the world, both Russian and Ukrainian electoral legislation in the early 2000s met democratic standards. Specifically, OSCE/ODIHR believes that the Ukrainian electoral law "provides an adequate framework for the conduct of democratic elections" (OSCE/ODIHR, 2002, p. 6). The OSCE's assessment of the Russian laws is virtually identical – "[the] legal framework is generally consistent with OSCE commitments and other international standards relating to democratic elections" (OSCE/ODIHR, 2004, p. 4).

The OSCE/ODIHR's positive and similar assessment of Russian and Ukrainian electoral legislation suggests that neither Russian, nor Ukrainian legislation overtly favored progovernment candidates or hurt opposition-affiliated candidates. This is an important point for our analysis of judicial behavior, because the content of the laws on the books can be highly consequential to the types of decisions that courts deliver in the disputes that may arise in the process of electoral registration. Imagine, for example, that one law were drafted in such a way that oppositionists would have to jump through hoops to secure registration, whereas registration for progovernment candidates was facilitated. Or that one law gave progovernment candidates carte blanche to use administrative resources, while the other law stipulated that such practice would lead to the immediate deregistration of the candidate. In such scenarios, differences that we observe between the two countries in the win-rates of different types of plaintiffs are likely to stem as much from the bias built into the law as from any bias at the court. Thus it is important to examine the electoral legislative framework in both countries.

So, first, how did citizens register to run in an SMD in Russia and Ukraine in the early 2000s? The steps and necessary documentation stipulated in the two electoral laws are very similar. Table 4.1 lists the documents that comprise the electoral registration package in each country and illustrates the significant overlap between the two laws.

TABLE 4.1. *Required registration documents for SMD candidates*

| Russia | Ukraine |
| --- | --- |
| Notice of self-nomination (Art. 38, par. 6 and 9) or documentation confirming date and procedure of party/electoral bloc nomination (Art. 41). | Self-nomination application (Art. 38, par. 2) or documentation confirming date and procedure of party/electoral bloc nomination (Art. 42, par. 1) |
| Candidate's biographical information (Art. 38, par 7):<br>• full name<br>• date of birth<br>• home address<br>• education<br>• party membership<br>• place of work or service<br>• occupation, if currently unemployed<br>• identity card details<br>• citizenship, including disclosure of current or past foreign citizenship<br>• criminal record | Candidate's biographical information (Art. 42, par. 5):<br>• full name<br>• date and place of birth<br>• home address<br>• education<br>• party membership<br>• place of work/service; position held<br>• occupation, if currently unemployed<br>• family members' names<br>• citizenship<br>• duration of residence in Ukraine<br>• criminal record |
| Declaration that, if elected, the candidate will cease any activities incompatible with position as State Duma deputy (Art 38, par 7) | Declaration that, if elected, the candidate will cease any activities incompatible with position as Rada deputy (Art 42, par 4) |
| Income and property documentation (Art 38, par. 7) | Income and property documentation, both for candidate and for family members (Art. 42, par. 7; Art. 44) |
| Documentation certifying that the nominating party/electoral bloc (if applicable) has been registered by the Central Election Commission (Art. 41) | Documentation certifying that nominating party/electoral bloc are officially recognized by Ministry of Justice (Art. 42, par. 2, par 3) |
| Constituent signatures; either 1% of SMD registered voters or 1000 signatures, whatever is the bigger number (Art. 41 and Art 42) OR an electoral deposit of 900,000 rubles (~$30,000) (Art. 66, Art. 68, par. 4) | Electoral deposit in the amount of 60 untaxed minimum citizens' incomes (12,000 hryvny or ~$2,500) (Art. 43, par. 2) |
| | Candidate's photo (Art. 42, par. 9)<br>Candidate's election program (Art. 42, par. 6) |

The comparison reveals two interesting differences in the registration process in Russia and Ukraine, but those differences do not suggest that the electoral laws in any country gave an implicit advantage to progovernment candidates over opposition candidates. Russian SMD candidates could choose whether to register by collecting signatures or by submitting an electoral deposit. Ukrainian legislators implemented OSCE/ODIHR's advice to remove the signature collection option (OSCE/ODIHR, 2001, p. 7), and candidates had only the second option. Second, Russian candidates were required to disclose only their personal income and property information, whereas Ukrainian candidates had to provide the same information about family members as well. The signature collection option may appear to be democracy enhancing because it allows candidates with limited finances to achieve registration through door-to-door signature collection drives by committed volunteers. Thus, signature collection may contribute to increased levels of political participation and to the establishment and maturing of grass roots political organizations – both democracy-enhancing (or -entrenching) developments. The drawback of the signature collection route to registration is that the authenticity of the collected signatures (usually collected by volunteers and without witnesses) is harder to ascertain than the authenticity of the official documents that make up the rest of the registration application package. Thus, the signature option may tempt political opponents to try to sideline each other by challenging the authenticity of the signatures. In OSCE/ODIHR's words, the signature system created "very many practical problems of regulating and verifying in a fair manner the collection of signatures in support of a candidate or party" (OSCE/ODIHR, 2001, p. 7). The OSCE/ODIHR concern was well-founded, as indeed, invalid signatures was a leading motivation that Russian DECs cited in denial of registration decisions, and it also figured prominently in the electoral registration disputes that made it to court (Lubarev, 2006). It is important to stress again that there is no reason to believe that the signature collection option in the Russian law favored progovernment candidates over opposition candidates in the registration process – both types of candidates faced the possibility of having to defend the authenticity of the signatures that their campaign had collected. Hence, we could maybe expect Russian courts to receive more complaints than Ukrainian courts, but we have no reason to expect that they would favor progovernment candidates in those disputes, simply as a result of the content of the electoral law.

After receiving the entire list of documents along with the signatures and/or electoral deposit, the district election commission decided whether to officially register the candidate. Both the Russian and the Ukrainian election laws ensured that progovernment and opposition parties got DEC representation

(OSCE/ODIHR, 2002, p. 6; OSCE/ODIHR, 2004, p. 4). This guarantee suggests that DECs in both countries behaved similarly during the registration process. For example, we have no reason to believe that Russian DECs were more likely than Ukrainian DECs (or vice versa) to deny registration to opposition candidates on shaky grounds, which would in turn result in oppositionists in one country going to court with consistently stronger cases, than oppositionists in the other country.

Achieving registration did not mean that a candidate was guaranteed a spot on the ballot on election day. Candidates in both countries could have their registration canceled for electoral law violations committed in the course of the campaign. The grounds for cancellation identified in Russia's Federal Law on Basic Guarantees of Electoral Rights and the Rights of Citizens of the Russian Federation to Participate in a Referendum and in Ukraine's Law on the Election of People's Deputies of Ukraine were virtually identical.

First, candidates could lose their registration upon the discovery of vital inconsistencies in the information that they submitted as part of their electoral registration application (Art. 76 of the Russian law; Art. 49, par 8 of the Ukrainian law). The implication of these provisions was that the veracity of all components of a candidate's biography and his/her property and income statements could be challenged by opponents who sought to take the candidate out of the election race. In both countries, these provisions became the grounds for numerous lawsuits, some containing rather comical allegations. For example, in St. Petersburg's SMD#207, a similar lawsuit led to the deregistration of the main district's front-runner, incumbent municipal council deputy, Alexander Morozov. His opponent, Irina Rodnina, filed a complaint alleging that Morozov lied about holding higher degrees from two universities, when, in fact, he held only one. The court sided with Rodnina and deregistered Morozov, citing the discovery of "vital inconsistencies" in his registration application. Curiously, even after successfully taking her main opponent out of the race, Irina Rodnina failed to secure the Duma seat – on election day, the largest share of votes in SMD#207 went in the "against all" category (Novaya Gazeta, December 1, 2003; www.cikrf.ru). In Ukraine, the State Tax Authorities discovered inconsistencies in the income declarations of over 600 candidates (both SMD and party list) (*Kyiv Post*, March 14, 2002). Dozens of SMD candidates were deregistered as a result and had to fight to get back on the ballot.

Second, both the Russian and the Ukrainian law contained explicit and detailed formal measures designed to minimize the use of administrative resources and the outright bribery of candidates. Elected incumbents and administrative leaders in both countries could not recruit campaign volunteers from among their subordinates or employees; could not use the premises of state institutions and/or the organizations they managed to hold rallies, unless they provided the exact same premises under the same conditions to their political competitors; could not use their office phones, faxes, and other office resources in their campaign; could not use free transportation or preferential rates available to them to campaign; could not use their the access to state media granted to their office to spread their message to voters or to organize the collection of signatures (in the Russian case) (Art. 40 of the Russian law; Art. 49, par. 10 of the Ukrainian law). In addition, candidates could not provide voters with "money, goods, services, securities, credits, lottery tickets or other things or material values for free or at discount prices" (Art. 56 of the Russian law; Art. 49, par. 9 of the Ukrainian law). The formal provisions thus allowed courts to curb the use of administrative resources and buying of votes by government-affiliated candidates. Finally, both the Russian and the Ukrainian law stipulated that candidates whose campaign spending exceeded the legally provided maximum would also lose their registration (Art. 76 of the Russian law; Art. 49, par. 12).

There was also no shortage of lawsuits filed using these provisions. In Russia, for example, incumbent, oppositionist Duma deputy Viktor Cherepkov was taken to court by a rival (Evgenii Kolupaev) in his Primorskii Krai SMD#52. Kolupaev argued that Cherepkov was abusing his entitlement to free transportation for the purposes of his campaign (Kommersant, no. 220, 2/12/2003). Despite being an outspoken opposition figure, Cherepkov defended himself successfully in court and remained on the ballot. In Ukraine, Evgenii Sukhin, a businessman rumored to have spent over a million dollars on his campaign in provincial Vinnitsya's SMD#18, had to defend himself against allegations of voter bribery. Sukhin reportedly paid for a new roof for a village church, provided new equipment to a state orthodontal office, serving a rural district, and, at a campaign rally with female voters, gave out terry towels to all attending. Despite his "generosity" on the campaign trail, he lost out to the pro-government candidate (Parkhomchuk, 2002).

Unfortunately, as the statistical analysis described later in this chapter shows, neither the Russian nor the Ukrainian courts took advantage of the opportunity given to them by the law on the books. Despite ample evidence collected by journalists and documented by plaintiffs that progovernment candidates regularly used administrative resources in their campaign, progovernment candidates, on average, did not lose their electoral registration cases more frequently than other candidates.

In sum, both my analysis and the OSCE/ODIHR reports suggest that Russian and Ukrainian laws were adequate, on paper, in providing electoral rights from the standpoint of democratic standards (OSCE/ODIHR, 2002, p. 6; 2004, p. 4). It is the similarity in the election laws that allows me to draw reliable conclusions about the independence of the courts in the two countries on the basis of a systematic comparison of their decisions, which follows.

## THE DATASETS

To answer the question of whether the Ukrainian and Russian courts applied election law provisions impartially in electoral registration disputes, I started with data sets that included all candidates who vied for a seat in one of the 225 SMDs – 3,084 people in Ukraine and 3,018 in Russia. Information on all candidates, rather than only those who participated in court proceedings, is essential to the process of evaluating court bias. In order to understand whether electoral registration lawsuits were politicized, we need to know who were those not involved in court cases in the first place.

In both Russia and Ukraine, the Central Election Commission (CEC) provides information on the political affiliation, previous election experience, age, gender, and occupation of each candidate. The CEC also lists the final vote tally in each SMD. In Ukraine, the CEC compiled a set of court decisions delivered by district courts during the campaign (Tsentral'na Viborcha Komisiya, 2002). Unfortunately, the CEC electoral registration dispute collection does not provide court decisions from 10 of Ukraine's 25 regions, which all together contain 90 of the 225 SMDs. Fortunately, the incomplete information should not skew the results of the analysis in any significant way because the excluded districts come from all parts of the country – the industrial, propresidential East, the nationalist West, and the rural, communist- and socialist-leaning South. After this exclusion, my dataset includes information on all 1,953 candidates who set out to run in 135 SMDs and participated in 134 electoral registration disputes[2].

In Russia, the CEC does not provide systematic information on electoral registration disputes. What it does provide is a media coverage section, which is an extensive compilation of articles from the national and regional media that deal with campaign issues. The section provides information on quite a few court cases, but its collection could be biased as it may cover only the cases involving more famous candidates. To avoid this potential pitfall, I contacted the election commissions in each of the 89 subjects of the Russian

---

[2] Fifteen of Ukraine's twenty-five provinces are included in the sample. These regions are Krym AR, Vinnytsia, Volyn, Chernihiv, Zakarpattia, Zaporizhzhia, Kyiv, Kirovohrad, Lviv, Mykolaiv, Odessa, Poltava, Ternopil', Kharkiv, Cherkasy, Kyiv, and Sevastopol.

Federation and asked for information on electoral disputes adjudicated in their region during the 2003 campaign. I also contacted all regions' highest courts and searched the decisions database of the Supreme Court of the Russian Federation. Finally, I scoured reports by election monitoring nongovernment organization NGO *Assotsiatsiya "Golos"*. These information-gathering techniques yielded information on 118 cases decided in 141 of the country's 225 SMDs, where a total of 1,974 candidates ran for a seat. As in the Ukrainian dataset, the excluded regions represent the entire political spectrum – from reformist regions, through moderate and Red Belt communist regions, to authoritarian ethnic republics.[3]

Finally, I collected information on the viability of each of the candidates who were initially registered in the SMDs, whose electoral dynamics I analyze. During the roughly two months between registration and election day, both the regional and national press covered the SMD races and identified the main contenders for most seats. Many local newspapers ran series of articles on their region's SMDs and pointed out who were viable (*prokhodnye*) candidates in each district. In addition, think tanks and pollsters conducted weekly public opinion polls in many districts and sifted the candidates who had a shot at a victory from the also-rans. Using a diverse set of sources, I identified 283 candidates in Russia (14 percent of the sample) and 255 candidates in Ukraine (13 percent of the sample) as viable contenders with a realistic chance of winning their district seats.

At the end of the data-gathering process, I ended up with detailed information about 1974 Duma candidates and 1953 Rada candidates – their political affiliation, their viability at the start of the campaign, and their experience with going to court over an electoral registration dispute. Table 4.2 lists the main cumulative figures that describe the two samples. The data are highly comparable as each country's sample includes roughly the same number of SMDs and the same number of candidates. Moreover, the rates at which candidates go to court are roughly the same. This similarity suggests that Russian and Ukrainian candidates have roughly the same proclivity toward using the courts to resolve electoral disputes, rather than extrajudicial methods and venues. It also suggests that the courts in both countries are roughly equally used

---

[3]  Forty-five of the eighty-nine subjects of the Russian Federation are included in the sample. These regions are Buryatiya, Karelia, Komi, Marii-El, Tatarstan, Chuvashiya, Krasnoyarsk, Astrakhan, Bryansk, Volgograd, Novosibirsk, Chelyabinsk, Primorskii Krai, Stavropol, Khabarovsk, Amur, Arkhangelsk, Ivanovo, Irkutsk, Kamchatka, Kurgan, Kursk, Moskovskaya oblast, Nizhnii Novgorod, Novgorod, Omsk, Orenburg, Perm, Pskov, Rostov, Ryazan, Samara, Saratov, Sverdlovsk, Smolensk, Tver, Tomsk, Tula, Tyumen, Ulyanovsk, Yaroslavl, Moscow, St. Petersburg, Nenetsk, and Khanty-Mansy.

TABLE 4.2. *Descriptive statistics of the electoral registration datasets*

|  | Russia | Ukraine |
|---|---|---|
| **Number of candidates who** | | |
| • Ran in all 225 SMDs | 3018 | 3084 |
| • Ran in the SMDs in the sample | 1974 | 1953 |
| • Participated in a registration dispute | 118 | 134 |
| • Participated in a registration dispute and then won the SMD seat | 26 | 24 |
| • Were viable from the start of the campaign | 282 | 255 |
| **Information about the SMDs** | | |
| • SMDs in the sample | 141 | 135 |
| • Number of competitive districts | 52 | 72 |
| • Average number of candidates per SMD | 14 | 14 |
| **Information about the court cases** | | |
| • Total number of cases in the sample | 118 | 134 |
| • Number of losses | 66 | 61 |
| • Number of victories | 52 | 73 |
| • Win-rate at trial for all candidates | 44% | 54% |

as an important arena for the implementation of "electoral technologies." The general win-rate is also similar at around 50 percent in both countries. The one major difference is that there were more competitive districts[4] in Ukraine than in Russia, which is additional evidence that political competition, exemplified by electoral uncertainty, was higher in Ukraine than in Russia in the early 2000s.

## WHAT CAN A PLAINTIFF'S POLITICAL AFFILIATION TELL US ABOUT JUDICIAL INDEPENDENCE?

I hypothesize that when judicial independence from politicians is low, the political affiliation of litigants is a significant predictor of success in court. In the case of electoral registration disputes, if judicial independence from politicians is low, progovernment candidates will win more often than anybody else, ceteris paribus, and opposition candidates will win less often than anybody else, again ceteris paribus. The size of the difference between the chances of victory of progovernment and opposition candidates is thus a direct measure

---

[4] I defined a competitive district as a district where the difference between the winner and the runner-up was under 10 percent (plus all districts where a viable candidate did not participate in the race due to deregistration). I elaborate on the reasons for this oprationalization in the section that describes how I measured all independent variables.

of the level of judicial independence from politicians – the larger the difference, the lower the level of judicial independence. To examine the relationship between candidates' political affiliation and their chances of success in
court, I control for two other factors that may affect judicial decision making:
a candidate's viability and the competitiveness of the district.[5]

*Candidate viability.* Viable candidates are both more likely to participate
in a court case and more likely to eventually win in court. By viable candidates, I mean those who were widely believed to be among the top contenders for a given SMD seat at the outset of the campaign, before any registration
disputes could arise. Candidates who have a realistic chance of winning the
seat from the outset of the campaign should definitely be more likely than
the average candidate to fight a decision by the DEC to cancel their registration. In addition, viable candidates probably also become the target of
court challenges by their opponents more often than candidates who stand
no chance of gathering a significant percentage of the vote. For starters, it
seems wasteful to try to take down the registration of someone who does not
threaten your chances of winning the seat. Moreover, even if the challenge
of a powerful opponent's registration fails in court, the plaintiff can probably
claim that the defendant escaped punishment either due to a technicality or
thanks to corrupting or pressuring the judge into delivering an unfair ruling.
Given the low esteem in which the public holds both judges and politicians,
many voters would probably be inclined to believe the alleged misdeeds even
if the charges do not stick. Therefore, lawsuits and counterlawsuits could be
an effective "black PR" strategy for viable candidates. In other words, viable

[5]   In addition, the degree of legal expertise that a candidate has at his or her disposal might
also affect the likelihood of going to court and winning, not just for front-runners, but for all
candidates regardless of their rating going into the campaign. For one, a candidate with a legal
background or strong representation is likely to be quicker to detect any election law violations committed by his or her competitors. Naturally, such a candidate should also be more
likely to bring a lawsuit to court, as well as appeal a DEC decision to deregister him or her.
And, it almost goes without saying that legal expertise should increase a candidate's chances
of winning in court, all other factors being equal. I collected data on the personal legal expertise of the candidates (whether the candidate herself was a jurist), but the variable was not
significant in any of the models and had the opposite sign. The decision to omit it from the
analysis, however, stems from the fact that I could not find data on the strength of candidates'
legal representation, which should be the more relevant operationalization. Even if I could
track down such information, I expect it to be highly correlated both with a candidate's administrative resources (i.e., political affiliation with the incumbent regime) and with his or her
viability. Since these variables are included in the model, the only omitted variable bias that
this analysis may suffer from might be a slight overestimation of the influence of viability and
administrative resources on the court. The overestimation, however, should affect both states
to a similar extent, so it should not affect conclusions about the relative level of judicial independence in Russia and Ukraine.

candidates should be more likely to become involved in electoral registration lawsuits.

Electable candidates probably also have a higher probability of winning in court than also-rans. The first reason why this advantage may exist is that even the most impartial judges would probably be reluctant to deregister a candidate who appears headed for an election victory because such an act seems countermajoritarian and somewhat undemocratic. Of course, it is crucial to find out whether only propresidential candidates enjoyed this advantage or whether it extended to opposition nominees. Another reason why viable candidates might have a better batting average in court is that they probably, on average, devote more resources to the legal fight. Since their stakes in the ultimate outcome are higher, it seems reasonable to assume that they would try harder to influence the race (Priest & Klein, 1984).

*District Competitiveness.* Finally, I hypothesize that the probability of being involved in a court case in the first place is affected not only by the candidate's characteristics but also by environmental factors. Specifically, it seems that competitive districts should yield more court cases than districts where the campaign is but a chronicle of an election victory foretold. Both meritorious and frivolous lawsuits should be more numerous in competitive districts. "True" cases should abound because candidates are more likely to push the limits of acceptable campaigning when they are facing stiff competition. For example, all leaders in the polls with access to administrative resources would mobilize them if their opponents were breathing down their necks. Frivolous lawsuits would also occur more frequently, since, as I previously mentioned, they can be an effective campaign strategy.

## MEASURING THE INDEPENDENT VARIABLES

*Political Affiliation.* To measure the main variable of interest, I created two dummy variables – a pro-government variable, where I assigned a 1 (one) to all candidates who had the incumbent regime's backing and an opposition variable, where I assigned a 1 (one) to all candidates who openly challenged the incumbent regime. How to measure a candidate's position vis-à-vis the incumbent regime was somewhat easier in the Russian than in the Ukrainian context.

In 2003, the Kremlin openly supported one party, United Russia, so all its candidates in the SMDs were unambiguously propresidential. United Russia ran 100 candidates in the 141 SMDs in the sample. In most of the districts where United Russia did not put forward a candidate, the federal center nevertheless threw its weight behind one of the candidates. I classified 55 candidates as unofficially supported by the Kremlin.

I was conservative in identifying such candidates because of a tendency by the regional press to exaggerate certain candidates' ties to the center. Since Putin's stamp of approval carried enormous political value due to his popularity, independent candidates and nominees of parties other than United Russia had a strong incentive to portray themselves as being close to the president. I expected that the regional press that often publishes prepaid articles and passes them off as reporting or editorializing would reflect this bias. Therefore, to classify independent candidates as Kremlin protégés, I used only objective criteria such as an official endorsement by the *United Russia* leadership or by the governor, if the latter was a member of United Russia. For example, Vyacheslav Shport in Khabarovsk and, the Nizhnii Novgorod governor's wife, Gulii Khodyreva, fit the bill (Tselobanova, 2003; Sokolov, 2003). Finally, some candidates, such as former Minister of Justice, incumbent Duma deputy and head of the Duma's Committee on Law-making, Pavel Krasheninnikov ran both in an SMD and on United Russia's federal list (Grankin.ru, 2004). Thus, even though in the Magnitogorsk SMD he was officially an SPS nominee, I classified him as a candidate supported by the federal center.

I also classified as propresidential some "technical candidates" for United Russia (UR) and any existing "clones" of UR nominees' main rivals in each district. The main goal of "technical candidates" in entering the race was either to campaign in favor of the United Russia nominee and pull out of the race in favor of the principal a few days before election day or to take away votes from a viable competitor. Such candidates were, for example, Igor' Artemenkov in Moscow's SMD #200, who withdrew from the race in favor of eventual winner, Vladimir Vasil'ev, and Anatolii Shiryaev in Volgograd's SMD #72, whose task was take away votes from the communist, Aleksandr Kulikov, in order to bolster the chances of victory for *United Russia* nominee, Aleksandr Ageev (Artemenkov, 2004; Kuts, 2006). Corroboration that a candidate named "Sergei Vladimirovich *Kprf*" (Ryazan SMD #149) had a single-minded mission to undermine the KPRF nominee in the district seems unnecessary. "Clones," or candidates who share the same name as a viable candidate, also register with the sole purpose of confusing voters and thus lowering the viable candidates' final tally.

Deciding who the opposition was in Russia in 2003 also required making some analytical choices. Ostensibly and rhetorically United Russia faced opposition from all sides. From the left – in KPRF and Rodina; from the democratic right – in SPS and Yabloko; and from the far right – in LDPR. In reality, however, Rodina and the LDPR were hardly a veritable opposition to the incumbents.[6] The voting record of the LDPR in the Third Duma shows that their leader's inflammatory pronouncements were empty bravado and the party was more useful than harmful to the Putin administration because it provided an outlet for disgruntled voters, yet behaved loyally and predictably in parliament (Levada, 2004, p. 49). Rodina also postured as opposition, but the extensive media coverage that it received led many observers to believe that the Kremlin saw Rodina as a useful and acceptable version of the KPRF. There were indeed reports that the Kremlin (and more specifically, deputy head of the Presidential Administration, Vladislav Surkov) created Rodina, which was to play the role of a "technical party" for United Russia.[7]

The Kremlin's attitude toward Yabloko and SPS was ambivalent. On the one hand, many believe that the main trigger of Khodorkovski's arrest and prosecution was his decision to fund Yabloko and the SPS, which suggests that the Kremlin perceived the democratic parties as dangerous competitors, which could undermine its goal to garner a constitutional majority for United Russia (Mereu, 2003). In addition, Rodina's anti-SPS tirades also might have been indirect digs by the Kremlin. But, on the other hand, Putin appeared with SPS leader Chubais a few days before the election, which could be interpreted as a token gesture of support by the Kremlin. Khodorkovski himself actually ventured a radically different take on the Presidential Administration's relationship with the right opposition. He argued that for the first time since 1991, the Kremlin simply refrained from actively supporting the SPS and Yabloko and both floundered in the polls as a result of their inherent unpopularity with the electorate (Khodorkovskii, 2004).

Following the different interpretations, I constructed four political affiliation dummy variables – two to capture opposition status vis-à-vis the regime and two to reflect propresidential bloc affiliation. The first opposition variable, *KremOpp1*, codes only KPRF nominees and independents openly aligned with the communists. The second one, *KremOpp2*, also includes SPS and Yabloko nominees, as well as the independents these parties campaigned for. The first propresidential variable, *KremBacked1*, codes only United Russia nominees and independents overtly supported by the Kremlin. The second variable,

---

[6] McFaul and Petrov (2004) actually argue that LDPR and Rodina were basically part of an informal pro-Kremlin coalition with United Russia.

[7] There are probably dozens of articles alleging that the Kremlin created Rodina. For a succinct formulation of the idea, see an interview with Ol'ga Sagareva, Dmitrii Rogozin's press secretary who later wrote a tell-all book about Rodina and an article on the popular *Comporomat. ru* Web site (Sagareva, 2004; Ishchenko, 2004).

*KremBacked2*, includes also LDPR and Rodina nominees, as well as protégés of these two parties.

Classifying Ukrainian candidates according to where they stood along the main propresidential/antipresidential cleavage also required in-depth investigation of local politics and the background of smaller parties. The first complication arose from the fact that a lot of candidates registered as independents, but in effect belonged firmly to one of the two camps. An initial cut at the problem was to look at the party affiliation that each candidate was required to report in his or her registration application. It seems evident that a self-nominated candidate who is a member of SDPU(o) or one of the constituent members of the Za Edu bloc (Kinakh's Trudova Ukraina or Yanukovych's Partiya Regioniv, for example) would not be a "true" independent.

Another obvious step in the proper identification of the political leanings of each candidate was to code all "clones" as political opponents of the viable candidate in their district, whatever his or her political affiliation. Since clones register only to take away votes from viable contenders, they cannot possibly be independent players. The final easy step was to code the major party and bloc representatives along the progovernment/opposition cleavage. The propresidential forces included Za Edu and all its constituent parties, SDPU(o), Zhinki za Maibutne, Democratic Party-Democratic Union, and the Green Party. The opposition camp consisted of Yushchenko's Nasha Ukraina, Simonenko's Communist Party of Ukraine, Moroz's Socialist Party of Ukraine, and the Yuliya Tymoshenko Bloc.

The incumbents' desire to split every portion of the opposition vote was also fairly transparent. To this end, several party "clones" sprung up shortly before the campaign started. Narodnyi Rukh Ukrainy Bloc (which included the ironically named National Rukh of Ukraine For Unity) aimed to steal nationalist votes from Nasha Ukraina, which contained the "real" Rukh, but it was not particularly successful at the national level. Hence, the irony in the "for unity" part in the name of a party that seeks to break up rather than unite the vote. It garnered only 0.16 percent of the vote or around 40,000 votes. Komanda Ozimoho Pokolinnya (KOP) had the task of attracting young liberal voters who would otherwise probably support Nasha Ukraina. This ploy worked better as KOP got over half a million votes (2.02 percent). The Communist Party of Ukraine (renewed) was also somewhat successful in splitting the communist vote and received 1.39 percent of the vote. The 362,712 votes that went to KPU(o) constituted percent of the communist vote. Finally, the Natalia Vitrenko Bloc was designed to mop up the votes of people frustrated by the loss of the Soviet social safety net but, for some reason, reluctant to support the communists. The bloc's leader was also a rather effective attack dog who constantly spewed conspiracy theories about Yushchenko's ties with the United States and even the Nazis. Vitrenko's cozy relationship with the incumbents was evident from her wide media exposure. Given her extremist antimarket rhetoric, one would think that the oligarchs close to the president would dislike her as much as they feared Communist leader Simonenko. Yet Vitrenko was all over national TV, while Simonenko was almost completely shut out (Wilson, 2002).

Some parties that ran quite a few candidates in the SMDs were much harder to place on the main political cleavage of 2002. The most problematic cases are Mikhail Brodskii's Yabluko and Kyiv mayor Omelchenko's Ednist. At first glance, Yabluko appears to be the government's attempt to attract the votes of liberal and democratic-minded citizens by creating a party that echoes Russian Yabloko's established oppositionist stance. Yabluko's leader, Mikhail Brodskii, made his sizable fortune in a joint venture with the leader of SDPU(o), Viktor Medvedchuk, the grey cardinal of the Kuchma regime. Finally, Yabluko almost outspent Nasha Ukraina on TV advertising, so it is no surprise that most observers consider Yabluko to be a Za Edu satellite (Wilson, 2002).

If Yabluko was indeed doing the regime's bidding, however, it is hard to explain why Mikhail Brodskii initiated a legal battle with the Za Edu right from the start of the election campaign. In late February, at the outset of fierce campaigning, Brodskii filed a complaint at the CEC arguing that the First National TV Channel, UT-1, was illegally campaigning for Za Edu. The plaintiff also alleged that the Za Edu might be providing free transportation to the Ukrainian Paralympics team in violation of Art. 29, par. 4 of the election law. Based on these charges, Brodskii demanded nothing short of the temporary closing of UT-1 and the deregistration of Za Edu's top party-list candidates: Litvin, Kinakh, Seminozhenko, Tihipko, Sharov, Derkach and Pustovoitenko. To no one's surprise, the CEC did not go for the bold move of disqualifying the leaders of the main propresidential force. In fact, the CEC did not even consider the merits of the complaint, but refused to hear it on a procedural technicality. Brodskii, however, took his appeal to the Supreme Court, which on February 20, 2002, passed the hot potato back to the CEC – it ordered the commission to rule on the merits of Brodskii's complaint (Tsentral'na Viborcha Komisiya, 2002, pp. 78–9). On February 25, the CEC dismissed the complaint as unfounded and the issue was soon back at the Supreme Court. Finally, on March 11, the Supreme Court closed the case by denying Brodskii's appeal and upholding the CEC decision (Tsentral'na Viborcha Komisiya, 2002, pp. 70–2).

The story did not end there. Only four days after the second Supreme Court decision, the CEC found significant discrepancies in the income declarations filed by both Brodskii and Yabluko's #2 figure, Viktor Chaika, and deregistered both candidates. With the top two candidates on the party list disqualified, the party as a whole faced exclusion from the ballot. Brodskii and Chaika immediately appealed the CEC decisions to the Supreme Court, and by March 21 their registrations were reinstated (Tsentral'na Viborcha Komisiya, 2002, pp. 33–6). Since Brodskii, Chaika, and Yabluko ultimately did participate in the election, a conspiracy-minded observer could interpret the whole affair as the government's attempt to create a Trojan horse in the opposition camp. The court cases, the conspiracy theory would go, were just instruments in the chiseling of Yabluko's image as legitimate opposition, but once Yabluko entered parliament, they would cooperate fully with its sponsors from the pro-presidential camp.

This theory seems rather far-fetched because it seems somewhat risky to attract public attention to Za Edu's abuse of administrative resources at such a high level as the Supreme Court and the CEC. Moreover, after successfully defending its leaders' registration, Yabluko came out with a scathing declaration, which urged voters to support "all opposition forces". Yabluko's leadership went on to call the establishment "not a government, but a criminal regime [...] which has to be replaced at every level – from lower ranks to the very top" (Unian, 2002). Yabluko did not make it into parliament, but remained in opposition throughout the rest of Kuchma's presidency and supported Yushchenko's presidential candidacy in 2004, so it seems that they did move into the opposition camp for real. It seems that the party was simply the personal vehicle of an opportunistic oligarch, Mikhail Brodskii, whose ego tempted him to confront the establishment and gradually left him no choice but to support the opposition. Based on this contextual analysis, I concluded that Yabluko's candidates in the SMDs were probably the closest things to "true" independents because they were neither clearly aligned with the opposition, nor actively helped by the establishment.

Ednist is another difficult nut to crack. Oleksandr Omelchenko was certainly cozy with the president himself; however, like Brodskii his personal ambition made him a fickle ally. Unlike Brodskii, he had access to his own administrative resources, which gave him confidence in the success of his candidates on election day. It seems that Omelchenko expected that the Ednist faction in the new Rada could find itself in the position of being the tie-breaker between the propresidential and antipresidential camp. Consequently, during the campaign, Omelchenko wanted to keep his options open as much as possible. The "nonaggression pact" that Ednist and Nasha Ukraina purportedly signed at the start of the campaign seems to support such an interpretation of Omelchenko's position (Storozhenko, 2001).

In addition, Ednist was overtly hostile to SDPU(o), Za Edu's major ally in the propresidential camp. The Ednist faction in the outgoing Rada had initiated a petition demanding Viktor Medvedchuk's resignation, so there was no love lost between Omelchenko and the SDPU(o) leader. However, the president himself seemed somewhat supportive of the Kyiv mayor, Omelchenko. When Brodskii charged that Omelchenko was illegally holding both the office of mayor and the office of head of the Kyiv state administration, Kuchma seemed to take Omelchenko's side by calling for an "expert opinion" on the issue before any steps were taken (Chernaya, 2001).

In conclusion, like Yabluko, the Ednist candidates seemed to be in a neutral position vis-à-vis the main political cleavage of the 2002 elections. Even though they benefited from the administrative resources available to their leader in Kyiv and Kyiv oblast, in regions controlled by Omelchenko's foes (e.g., Donetsk), they suffered intimidation at the hands of state authorities. So I coded Ednist candidates as neutral in all regions, except for Kyiv and Kyiv oblast where judges were likely to perceive an Ednist candidate as a representative of the party of power.

Table 4.3 provides comparative descriptive statistics on the political affiliation of the candidates in the Ukrainian and Russian samples. The data show that in both countries the groups of opposition-affiliated and government-affiliated candidates are roughly equal. However, in Russia, the proportion of neutral candidates was much higher than in Ukraine, perhaps as a reflection of the lower level of political competition in Russia.

*District Competitiveness.* It might seem reasonable to assume that the difference between the number of votes that the winner receives and the number of votes that go to the runner-up captures the competitiveness of the campaign. Given this operationalization of the concept, both countries display a wide variation in district competitiveness. In Russia, the closest majoritarian race took place in SMD #163 in Sverdlovsk Oblast, where incumbent Duma deputy Georgii Leont'ev beat provincial oligarch Aleksandr Ryavkin by only five votes! By contrast, in Saratov's SMD#156, the deputy leader of United Russia's Duma fraction, Vyacheslav Volodin, overtook his KPRF opponent, Ol'ga Alimova, by more than 250,000 votes, winning 82 percent of the vote to her 9 percent. In the closest Ukrainian race in Odessa's SMD #135, propresidential candidate Ihor Reznik defeated independent Serhii Bovbalan by 0.25 percent or 260 votes. At the other end of the spectrum, in Ternopil's district #168, Nasha Ukraina's nominee Mihailo Polyanchich beat his closest competitor, independent Oleg Povadyuk, by 69 percent or 92,290 votes.

TABLE 4.3. *Descriptive statistics of candidates' political affiliation*

| Type of candidate | Russia | Ukraine |
|---|---|---|
| Opposition affiliation | KPRF and its protégés only: 158 (8%) KPRF, SPS, and Yabloko: 300 (15%) | Nasha Ukraina, Yuliya Tymoshenko Bloc (BYuT), Communist Party of Ukraine (KPU), Socialist Party of Ukraine (SPU): 500 (26%) |
| Progovernment affiliation | UR and its protégés only: 159 (8%) UR, LDPR, and Rodina: 314 (16%) | Za Edu, SDPU (o), Zhinki za Maibutne, Democratic Party-Democratic Union, Green Party, Nataliya Vitrenko Bloc, Narodnyi Rukh Ukrainy Bloc, Komanda Ozimoho Pokolinnya, KPU (o): 545 (28%) |
| Neutral affiliation | Higher estimate: 1,657 (84%) Lower estimate: 1,360 (69%) | Independents, Yabluko, Ednist (except in Kyiv and Kyiv oblast): 908 (46%) |
| **Total** | **1,974 (100%)** | **1,953 (100%)** |

Instead of using the continuous variable, however, I created a DistComp dummy variable, where I assigned 1s to all SMDs where the difference between the winner and the runner-up was less than 10 percent. After applying this coding scheme, I ended up with seventy-two competitive districts in the Ukrainian sample (53 percent of the total) and fifty-two competitive districts in the Russian sample (37 percent of the total). This result is in line with all the other pieces of evidence that the Ukrainian election was more competitive than the Russian election. The rationale for using a dummy variable, which required me to choose a cut-off point, which is inherently somewhat arbitrary, is that beyond a certain threshold an increasing difference between the two top vote-getters stops reflecting competitiveness. Whether the winner beats his closest rival by 25 or 45 percentage points does not really seem to matter much – in both cases the race seems rather uncompetitive.

An important caveat of measuring district competitiveness through election results is that if a major competitor is deregistered by the courts and cannot participate in the election, an extremely competitive district may appear uncompetitive if we only look at the election outcome. To avoid this problem, I classified the five Ukrainian and seven Russian SMDs, where a viable candidate was deregistered, as competitive, regardless of the size of the difference between the winner and the runner-up. In Ukraine, these SMDs were #6, 71, 99, 147, and 148; in Russia, they were SMDs #9, 47, 96, 97, 120, 159, and 179. There were, of course, SMDs where nonviable candidates were deregistered. However, since these candidates were not expected to affect the overall result of the race, I assumed that their deregistration also had no effect on the district's competitiveness.

*Candidate Viability.* Capturing candidate viability in a variable is even more challenging and definitely more labor-intensive than gauging district competitiveness. The most obvious operationalization based on looking at the election results and estimating with the benefit of hindsight that anyone within a reasonable shot of the winning percentage must have had a chance at victory when the campaign started could be quite misleading. For one, this method would leave out perfectly viable candidates who did not participate in the election at all as a result of a canceled registration. In Ukraine's SMD #99 in Kirovohrad oblast, a court deregistered Batkivshchyna candidate Valerii Kalchenko on the very eve of the election. Kalchenko was running both for the parliamentary seat and for mayor of Kirovohrad, and it appears that he was the front-runner in both races. Not only did the local press identify him as clearly viable (*prokhodnoi* in Russian), but after the elections thousands of people protested his deregistration (Gorobets, 2002; Gotsuenko, 2002). In Russia, a similar fate befell former vice-president and ex-Kursk governor, Aleksandr Rutskoi, who failed to secure registration in Kursk, where he had sky-high name recognition and a very realistic chance of winning. In Nizhnii Novgorod, Krasnoyarsk, and Kurgan, shady businessmen Andrei Kliment'ev, Anatolii Bykov, and Pavel Fedulev were deregistered by court decision. Their high name recognition and virtually bottomless campaign coffers made them viable contenders for the SMD seat. Moreover, Kliment'ev had already proven his electability by winning the 1998 NizhniiNovgorod mayoral race.

Another problem with this approach to estimating viability is that election results reflect the success or failure of administrative resources and administrative resources are usually mobilized precisely to benefit or hurt viable candidates. For example, if we looked at the distribution of the vote in SMD #70 in Western Ukraine's Zakarpattia oblast, we might conclude that the viable candidates in the district were only two: Serhii Ratushniak, an independent who scored a 35.47 percent victory, and the Nasha Ukraina nominee Ihor Kril' who received 20.14 percent of the vote. With 9.2 percent of the vote,

SDPU(o) nominee Nestor Shufrich would not appear to be among the viable candidates. However, only several months later, Shufrich, whose political base is in his native Zakarpattia, managed to win repeat elections in a district with an opposition-leaning electorate (SMD #201 in Cherkasy). Amazingly enough, despite being an outsider in the Cherkasy election, Shufrich easily defeated both the winner of the regular election, Nasha Ukraina nominee Mykolai Bulatetskii, and Natalia Vitrenko (the leader of the Natalia Vitrenko Bloc), which almost received national representation (Lubenskii, 2002). This development suggests that Shufrich was a viable candidate in his home Zakarpattia district as well, but his election strategies failed to yield the desired results.

A more reliable way of estimating candidate viability is to scour the regional and national press for assessments by people familiar with the politics of each SMD, and this is what I did. Based on a media search for each of the 1,974 Russian candidates and each of the 1,953 Ukrainian candidates, I created a dummy variable where 1 was assigned to viable (or to use the Russian language term *prokhodnye*), candidates and 0 to candidates who, *at the outset of the campaign*, stood no realistic chance of winning the seat. Whereas some publications surely exaggerate the chances of success of the candidates they support, if the exaggeration is of staggering proportions, then the candidate probably has significant resources. In a way, such exaggerations indicate that the candidate is in this race for real and acts *as if* he or she were a viable contender for the seat, which for the purposes of this analysis is as important as actual viability.

I supplemented the results of the press reports with data from public opinion polls conducted by regional research institutes and NGOs during the campaign. For example, the Institute for Regional Issues (Institut Regional'nykh Problem) in Odessa conducted weekly polls on a sizable sample of 2,064 respondents and calculated the approval rating of all candidates in the Odessa oblast SMDs. The institute's reports identify the viable candidates in each SMD (Institut Regional'nykh Problem, 2002). For the Russian sample, I used the assessments contained in the Russian Regional Report[8] and reports by Group 7/89.[9]

---

[8]   A biweekly publication jointly produced by the Center for Security Studies at the Swiss Federal Institute of Technology (ETH) Zurich, http://www.isn.ethz.ch (May 8, 2006) and the Transnational Crime and Corruption Center (TraCCC) at American University, Washington, DC, http://www.American.edu/traccc (May 8, 2006).

[9]   *Gruppa 7/89 Assotsiatsiya Regional'nykh Sotsiologicheskikh Tsentrov*, is an organization of seventeen regional polling agencies that conduct public opinion research, http://www.789.ru/portal/index.php (May 8, 2006).

## ADMINISTRATIVE RESOURCES AND CASE MERIT: WHY 2002–2003 PROGOVERNMENT CANDIDATES SHOULD HAVE BEEN LOSING IN COURT

Finally, before proceeding with the model that estimates the importance of political affiliation to a candidate's victory in an electoral registration dispute, I consider case merit as a potential source of omitted variable bias. Case merit refers to the strength of a plaintiff's case. Ideally, the rule-of-law doctrine envisions a legal system in which case merit, determined impartially and faithfully by the judiciary on the basis of the laws on the books, should be the one and only predictor of victory in court. Courts, which are independent and impartial, will grant victory to plaintiffs who bring strong cases. Plaintiffs who file frivolous or weak cases, on the other hand, will lose more often than other litigants. It is essential to know whether the political affiliation of the candidates is highly correlated with case merit or not. If candidates of one political stripe have systematically stronger cases, then we should, in fact, expect an impartial and independent court to side with them more often than with other candidates.

Unfortunately, it is all but impossible to capture case merit in an observable variable. If we could, judges and courts would be superfluous. It is also extremely hard to capture judges' true perceptions of case merit, not least because judges themselves may find it impossible to distinguish between faithful interpretation of case merit according to the legal text and their personal prejudices on the subject or preconceptions about the litigants. Case merit is basically unobservable in individual cases, but it is important to know whether as a variable it might be correlated with our main variable of interest, candidate political affiliation, in order to avoid potential omitted variable bias. In other words, if we happen to find out that progovernment plaintiffs win more often than other plaintiffs, we want to know whether that is because they have stronger cases on average or it is because judicial independence from incumbents is low and judges have to deliver favorable rulings.

Fortunately, there is significant empirical evidence on the relationship between candidate political affiliation and case merit in the context of the 2002 Rada and 2003 Duma elections. We can assume that both in Russia and in Ukraine progovernmental candidates did not have stronger cases than other plaintiffs. If anything, as the main beneficiaries of the practice of using administrative resources (which is an electoral law violation in both countries), progovernment candidates should have weaker cases both as plaintiffs and as defendants. Finally, given electoral technologies that allowed the incumbents to stack the DECs with loyal representatives, we can also assume that most

DECs would be reluctant to deregister a progovernment candidate. When they did, they were probably responding to particularly egregious electoral law violations. This dynamic should also lead to progovernment candidates having weaker cases than everybody else.

Domestic and foreign election monitors in both countries cited ample evidence to support these assumptions. The administrative resources and mechanisms employed in both campaigns to boost propresidential candidates and hurt oppositionists were very similar. Both the Committee of Voters of Ukraine (CVU), the country's largest NGO devoted to monitoring campaigning, and the OSCE/ODIHR observers reported high levels of administrative resource use (Committee of Voters of Ukraine, 2002; OSCE/ODIHR, 2002, p. 12). In Kharkiv oblast, for example, CVU representatives noted that the oblast administration bused people to attend a public "Youth Forum for a United Ukraine," distributed leaflets and encouraged everyone to support the For United Ukraine (Za Edu) bloc. In Chernihiv, professors and students from local universities were required to take part in a state-organized rally for Za Edu. And in Kyiv, local businesses that refused to purchase Ednist (Mayor Omelchenko's party) election materials received warnings from city officials to expect rent increases and frequent tax and fire inspections after the election (Committee of Voters of Ukraine, 2002). OSCE observers reported that in Lviv, the head of the local branch of Za Edu distributed free coal and used state vehicles during working hours. In Kharkiv, citizens received free electrical appliances along with notes soliciting votes for Za Edu (OSCE/ODIHR, 2002, p. 13).

In Russia, the main beneficiary of administrative resources was, of course, United Russia. OSCE observers noted that regional governments often supplied all the equipment and most services to the local United Russia campaign headquarters. Opposition candidates, on the other hand, often did not receive permits from the regional authorities to hold rallies and could not find public organizations willing to provide them space to hold meetings. The OSCE also received numerous complaints about police detaining oppositionists' campaign workers and impounding opposition campaign materials (OSCE/ODIHR, 2004, p. 5).

Some will argue that the OSCE was biased against the incumbents in both elections and as a result painted a skewed picture of the situation. Maybe these were no-holds-barred campaigns, in which all competitors used every dirty campaign trick in the book. If the opposition lagged behind the presidential supporters in administrative resources, it compensated in illegal campaign financing by friendly oligarchs and maybe even the United States. This theory was the leitmotif of propresidential election technologists and Commonwealth of Independent States (CIS) and Russian observers in Ukraine. The official publication of the Russian government, Rossiiskaya Gazeta, hinted that the US$5 million earmarked by the USAID for programs aimed at ensuring the transparency of the elections, was in fact spent on behalf of Nasha Ukraina's campaign, which of course would be a violation of election law (Bogdanov, 2002). Even if this were an accurate description of both parliamentary campaigns, no one has attempted to argue that oppositionists were the main perpetrators of campaign rules violations, so we can safely dismiss the possibility that the propresidential candidates who went to court had stronger cases, all else being equal.

In short, although case merit is unobservable and omitted from the model, it is unlikely that its omission would lead us to find a progovernment bias in court decision making where none exists. On the contrary, if Russian and Ukrainian courts were adjudicating electoral registration cases independently and impartially, we should observe a lower win-rate than average for progovernment plaintiffs.

## SARTORI SELECTION MODEL OF COURT APPEAL-RATE AND WIN-RATE

To test the proposed hypotheses and determine what candidate and district characteristics can best predict which way the court would go in a dispute over electoral registration, I estimated a Sartori selection model with candidate court experience as the dependent variable. The Sartori estimator is a selection-effects model, which is appropriate to use in cases when the dependent variables in the selection equation and the outcome equation might have correlated error terms. In the case of electoral registration disputes, the decision to pursue a court appeal and the trial outcome are probably both affected by similar unobservable variables, such as case merit. The Sartori estimator assumes that the correlation between the error terms is 1. While such an assumption is probably wrong, the estimator is very robust to that assumption being wrong, whereas the Heckman model (which is a more venerable selection model) is less robust. Moreover, unlike the Heckman, the Sartori estimator allows us to use the same independent variables in both equations. Since the decision to go to court is probably affected by the exact same factors as the ultimate court decision, and the two decisions are close together in time, the Sartori estimator is more appropriate than a Heckman estimator (Sartori, 2003).

The two binary dependent variables of the selection and the outcome equation (decision to go to court and trial outcome) are coded in one trichotomous variable. If a candidate did not participate in any court proceedings during the campaign, he or she received a 0 for court experience. All candidates who went to court to demand the cancellation of an opponent's registration, to appeal their own deregistration, or to defend their registration from an opponent's challenge but did not win in court received a 1. Finally, all candidates who scored a victory in court received a 2. The independent variables include the main variables of interest, progovernment and opposition affiliation, as well as the control variables: candidate viability and district competitiveness. The two models' coefficients are summarized in Table 4.4[10].

The Sartori models first suggest that judicial independence was low in both Russia and Ukraine during 2002–3. This would actually be a rather uncontroversial statement if we relied only on cross-country rule of law indices. The World Governance Indicators (WGI) puts both Russia in 2003 and Ukraine in 2002 in the bottom 25 percent in the world in terms of rule of law (Kaufmann, Kraay, and Mastruzzi, 2010). My data lend a more fine-tuned and direct confirmation of this empirical claim as they show that in neither country did progovernment candidates have *a lower* win-rate than other candidates. This finding indicates that the courts did *not* effectively constrain the incumbent regime and did not check the abuses of power associated with the widespread use of administrative resources. Progovernment candidates bolstered their reelection chances by violating the electoral laws with impunity. Had the courts been independent from the incumbents, we would have observed a lower win-rate for progovernment candidates and a higher win-rate for all other candidates. In other words, the statistical analysis of electoral registration disputes that made it to court during the campaign for the 2002 Rada and the 2003 Duma elections is in line with the charges of oppositionists and Western and local observers that these were not fair elections.

Next, the models confirm the hypothesis that viable candidates participated and won court cases more often than nonviable candidates. This relationship is strong in both countries, and we can be very confident that it exists as it is highly significant. The tendency of viable candidates both to go to court

[10]  I estimated four models for each country with different specifications of the progovernment and opposition variables. The results for the most part were the same. One interesting finding from the Russian models is that LDPR candidates seemed to have a significantly lower probability of winning in court, so including LDPR either in the progovernment or in the opposition-camp led to that camp posting a disadvantage in court. Given reports that LDPR has for years been "leasing" its party label to unabashed criminals seeking to get immunity from prosecution which comes with a parliamentary seat, it should not be too surprising that LDPR nominees often faced insurmountable registration hurdles. In interviews, judges often expressed concern about the "infestation" of parliament by criminal elements, so LDPR's disadvantage probably has little to do with the interests of the center and more to do with judges' personal preferences to keep criminals out of contention. In the model reported in this chapter, the LDPR is neither opposition, nor progovernment.

TABLE 4.4. *Results of Sartori models for Russia and Ukraine*

| Candidate and district characteristics | Coefficient (standard error) | |
|---|---|---|
| | Russia | Ukraine |
| Selection stage: Decision to go to court | | |
| Viability | .90*** | .78*** |
| | (.12) | (.11) |
| Progovernment affiliation | .24 | .08 |
| | (.15) | (.11) |
| Opposition affiliation | .26* | .15 |
| | (.16) | (.11) |
| District competitiveness | .30** | .06 |
| | (.10) | (.09) |
| Constant | −2.01 | −1.75 |
| | (.08) | (.09) |
| Outcome stage: Court decision | | |
| Viability | 1.34*** | .96*** |
| | (.16) | (.12) |
| Progovernment affiliation | .20 | .30** |
| | (.17) | (.14) |
| Opposition affiliation | .12 | .12 |
| | (.19) | (.15) |
| District competitiveness | .13 | .00 |
| | (.13) | (.11) |
| Constant | −2.57 | −2.17 |
| | (.13) | (.12) |
| Number of observations | 1974 | 1953 |
| Log likelihood | −455 | −538 |
| Wald $X^2$ | 116.88 | 64.56 |

*Note:* *$p < .1$ one-tailed test; ** $p < .05$ one-tailed test; *** $p < .01$ one-tailed test

more often and to win more often could reflect these candidates' higher level of commitment to the race. But the result also lends systematic support to much-discussed anecdotal claims that registration disputes were a prominent weapon in the black PR arsenal and that therefore viable candidates were both the main perpetrators and the main victims of such cases. Theoretically, the results confirm the contention of the strategic pressure model that in emerging democracies, like Russia and Ukraine during the late 1990s and early 2000s, justice is more politicized. The comparative data shows that in both countries, the courts are very useful to politicians as tools of political competition and hence viable politicians use them more often than everybody else.

The rest of the results indicate substantial differences between how courts decided registration disputes in Russia and in Ukraine. In Russia, candidates running in competitive districts were significantly more likely to become involved in a court case. The optimistic interpretation of this result suggests that candidates were trying in earnest to play by the rules, but those who tried to get the upper hand in a very close race, predictably crossed the line into forbidden campaign tactics more often, which resulted in the significantly larger number of disputes in competitive districts. The cynical, and arguably more plausible, interpretation is that the use of "election technologies" was more prevalent in the highly competitive districts where viable candidates dug up dirt on each other and tried to use it to derail competitors' quest for the seat.

The Ukrainian data, however, hint at a worse situation than the cynical Russian scenario. The district competitiveness coefficient is not only insignificant but also very small. This result suggests that district competitiveness likely had no effect whatsoever on the likelihood that candidates would go to court over registration disputes. In other words, during the 2002 Rada campaign, candidates sued each other regardless of whether the race was competitive or not. There are two ways to account for this outcome. One possibility is that electoral law violations took place regardless of whether the race was close. This means that candidates had complete disregard for election law provisions and violated them even when a victory seemed secure. Another possibility is that lawsuits are not highly correlated with actual electoral law violations, but are just a method for harassing the competition. In all likelihood, both possibilities describe the 2002 Rada campaign. The point is that the Ukrainian courts were deeply embroiled in politics because they were useful tools for competing politicians.

Another difference is that in Russia, opposition candidates were significantly more likely to go to court, whereas in Ukraine political affiliation had no bearing on the decision to go to court. We should not overestimate this difference, though, because the Russian result barely meets a low significance threshold and because both coefficients are positive and of similar size. In other words, in both countries, opposition candidates were probably slightly more prone to filing lawsuits, it is just that in Russia we can make this claim with somewhat more confidence. This result may be interpreted as confirmation of anecdotal observations that opposition candidates had more registration problems than progovernment candidates and thus were more likely to end up involved in a registration dispute.

The most important result, however, is that in Russia the political affiliation of the plaintiff has a smaller effect on a candidate's probability of victory in an electoral registration trial. The coefficients indicate that any advantage that Russian progovernment candidates may enjoy in court is about two-thirds the size of the Ukrainian progovernment candidates' advantage. Moreover, the Russian coefficient is not statistically significant, which suggests that we are not certain that such an advantage even exists. In Ukraine, on the other hand, progovernment candidates enjoyed a significant advantage when their registration disputes end up in court. This contrast suggests that judicial independence from politicians is lower in Ukraine than in Russia, as Ukrainian judicial output consistently reflects the preference for the incumbent regime.

It is important to emphasize that the model indicates that political affiliation matters in Ukraine even after we control for candidate viability. In other words, propresidential candidates win not simply because a larger percentage of them have a realistic chance of winning and the courts are reluctant to foil the will of the electorate by deregistering a front-runner. Rather, Ukrainian propresidential candidates win more often simply thanks to their affiliation with the establishment.

## EFFECT MAGNITUDE AS A MEASURE OF JUDICIAL INDEPENDENCE

The Sartori estimator not only suggests that political affiliation is a significant predictor of success in court but also allows us to predict exactly *how much* more likely a propresidential candidate is to win in court in comparison to other candidates. The difference in the predicted probability of court victory represents the extent to which politicians can impose their preferences on the courts. In other words, the greater the difference between the predicted win-rates of progovernment and opposition candidates, the lower the level of judicial independence from incumbent politicians.

I use the Sartori model coefficients to calculate and compare the predicted probabilities of court victory for four groups of plaintiffs, depending on their political affiliation and viability. District competitiveness is held constant at its modal value (0 in Russia; 1 in Ukraine). Figure 4.1 compares the probability of court victory for nonviable opposition-affiliated and government-affiliated candidates in Russia and Ukraine.

The contrast between Russia and Ukraine is quite stark. In Russia, nonviable candidates have roughly the same probability of winning a registration dispute in court. If progovernment candidates have any advantage at all over opposition-affiliated candidates, it appears to be about 5 percent. In Ukraine, on the other hand, progovernment candidates enjoy a big advantage over opposition-affiliated candidates – almost 25 percent. Candidates close to the

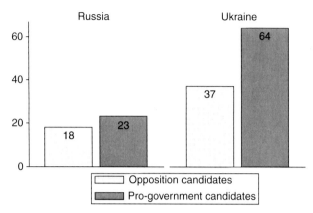

FIGURE 4.1. Predicted probabilities of success in court according to the political affiliation of non-viable candidates: Comparison between Russia and Ukraine.

Kuchma regime were twice as likely to win a court case, as they were to lose, even if they were opportunists who did not have a realistic chance of being elected through a fair process.

I also calculated the 95 percent confidence intervals for each predicted probability in order to show the amount of uncertainty associated with each estimate. In Russia, the difference between the predicted win-rates of Russian candidates is not statistically significant – progovernment candidates have a 12 to 40 percent probability of victory, and opposition candidates have an 8 to 34 percent probability of victory. By contrast, the results suggest that Ukrainian candidates of different political stripes have statistically different chances of winning a registration lawsuit because the confidence intervals associated with the two estimates barely overlap. The confidence interval for progovernment candidates is 46 to 83 percent, and for opposition candidates it is 23 to 54 percent.

The difference between Russia and Ukraine is also significant when we compare the predicted probabilities of success of viable candidates. As Figure 4.2 shows, in Russia progovernment candidates appear to have about a 12 percentage point advantage over opposition-affiliated candidates. The confidence intervals of the two predictions overlap significantly – progovernment candidates have a 46 to 100 percent probability of victory, and opposition candidates have a 34 to 96 percent probability of victory. Ukrainian government protégés' advantage is more than twice as big, at 27 points. In fact, viable candidates who were close to the Kuchma administration had a tight lock on the courts. They were almost assured to win any electoral registration dispute that they were involved in, their predicted probability of winning being at 89 percent.

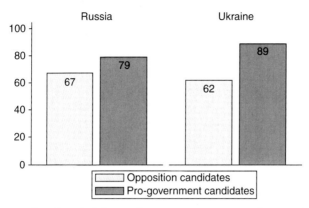

Figure 4.2. Predicted probabilities of success in court according to the political affiliation of viable candidates: Comparison between Russia and Ukraine.

The confidence intervals also do not overlap as in the Russian model, which points to a statistically significant difference between the two predicted probabilities. Pro-government candidates have a 74 to 100 percent probability of victory, while opposition candidates have a 43 to 89 percent probability of winning in court.

## IMPLICATIONS OF THE ELECTORAL DISPUTE ANALYSIS FOR JUDICIAL INDEPENDENCE THEORIES

The direct measure of judicial independence, which Chapter 3 proposed and this chapter applies, allows a fine-tuned comparison of the level of judicial independence in two very similar countries. The results indicate that, contrary to impressionistic accounts and presumptions, the Russian courts had slightly more independent output from politicians' preferences, than Ukrainian courts, even if we cannot really talk about independent courts in either country.

More importantly, however, this methodological innovation facilitates a test of the predictions of existing theories of judicial independence. The traditional political competition theories predict just the opposite results. They expect that as weak incumbents, Kuchma and his political circle, would refrain from pressuring the courts and, in fact, would bolster judicial independence. The political insurance theory expects the Kuchma regime to promote independent courts as a guarantee against future persecution by the next incumbent. The strategic defection theory expects that by 2002, Ukrainian judges should have been abandoning the sinking ship of the Kuchma regime. The policy stability hypothesis posits that the Kuchma administration would try to buttress independent courts in order to make sure that after the loss of power (which by 2002 should have seemed a plausible turn of events) would not mean a complete loss of policy control. Rather Kuchmists would retain some policy control by being able to rely on independent courts. On the other hand, Putin's electorally secure regime supposedly had none of these incentives to allow independent courts. Russian judges also purportedly had no incentive to stray from supporting the strong Putin regime through favorable rulings for pro-Kremlin candidates involved in registration disputes.

None of these predictions are borne out by the electoral registration data. On the contrary, the data show that Ukrainian courts produced more decisions in favor of the incumbent regime than Russian courts did. This finding bolsters the prediction of the *strategic pressure* theory that the more competitive regime would display a lower level of judicial independence.

The quantitative analysis of electoral registration trial outcomes does not in itself illustrate the mechanism of the strategic pressure theory, though. In other words, the fact that Ukrainian courts have delivered more progovernment rulings than Russian courts is not in itself proof that the Kuchma regime has pressured judges into reaching the decisions that they did. Evidence that this is the reason behind the notable progovernment bias in electoral registration cases is provided in Chapter 7. In addition, the finding that, despite a nontrivial difference, judicial independence from politicians was low in both Russia and Ukraine challenges the predictions of the institutional theories of judicial independence. According to these theories, the structural insulation of the Russian and Ukrainian judiciaries should have facilitated the emergence of independent courts, as formal institutional safeguards should have made it difficult for incumbent politicians to impose their preferences on the courts. Instead, the electoral registration data show that both the Russian and the Ukrainian courts failed to hold incumbent politicians accountable for electoral law violations. Despite incumbents' ubiquitous use of administrative resources, neither Russian nor Ukrainian government politicians had a *lower* than average win-rate in court, when oppositionist candidates decided to fight back and attempted to seek redress through the courts. "Good", purportedly rule-of-law-fostering institutions have not produced a "good" enough outcome in either Russia or Ukraine.

Because structural insulation of the judiciary is higher in Russia than in Ukraine (as shown in Chapter 3), however, it is still possible to attribute the slightly less dependent Russian judicial output to institutional constraints, rather than to strategic incentives (as the strategic pressure theory does). In other words, maybe Russian courts were slightly less dependent on politicians because the institutional setup of the judiciary made interference in judicial decision making slightly more complicated for Russian politicians? Maybe the "good," insulated judicial institutions have begun to foster rule-of-law-abiding behavior among Russian politicians? Maybe it just takes time for these gains to be solidified, so that we can observe the entrenchment of independent courts in the postcommunist context? Maybe in time Russia's judicial insulation will produce a high judicial independence ranking not just relative to Ukraine but in absolute terms as well? Chapter 6 addresses this alternative explanation of the empirical results presented in this chapter. It argues that the formal insulation of the Russian (and the Ukrainian) judiciary can and is routinely circumvented by enduring informal practices, which make it easy for any motivated Russian (or Ukrainian) political incumbent to intervene in judicial affairs and impose his or her preferences on individual case outcomes.

Before I get to the mechanism testing, however, the following chapter (Chapter 5) expands the analysis of judicial independence to another politically salient issue area, namely defamation lawsuits against media outlets. The goal is not only to check how independent Russian and Ukrainian courts are when it comes to guaranteeing another central civic right, namely the right to free speech. The goal is also to perform a robustness check on the comparative results presented in this chapter. If the contrast between Russian and Ukrainian courts holds beyond the electoral registration cases, then we can be more confident that these results are not some random artifact of the electoral laws. If Russian courts are more independent than their Ukrainian counterparts in two distinct types of politically important cases, we can be more certain that there is indeed an underlying difference in judicial independence between the two countries.

# 5

# The Role of Ukrainian and Russian Courts in the Provision of Press Freedom: Judicial Independence in Defamation Lawsuits, 1998–2003

February 2002 was a bad month for Russia's oppositionist newspaper *Novaya Gazeta*. First, a Moscow court ruled that an article about the lavish lifestyle of a provincial court chair contained false information and ordered the newspaper to pay the slandered judge US$1 million (Abdullaev, 2002a). Within a week, *Novaya Gazeta*'s luck went from bad to worse. A bank the paper had linked to a money-laundering scandal won its defamation lawsuit, and the paper was slapped with a US$500,000 punitive damage fine. Since *Novaya Gazeta*'s annual turnover barely approached the total sum of the awarded damages, domestic and foreign observers started writing the paper's obituary. The dominant interpretation of the events centered on a Kremlin-backed campaign to muzzle the independent media (Abdullaev, 2002a). Yabloko's deputy chair, Sergei Mitrokhin, was probably speaking for most Russian liberals when he lamented that the defamation suits against *Novaya Gazeta* represented the "direct use of the judicial authorities for political goals, rather than in compliance with the law" (Yabloko Press Release, 2003). Eventually, though, *Novaya Gazeta* survived because both victorious plaintiffs decided not to collect their awards ("Novaya Gazeta Could Get a Reduced Fine," 2002).

Ukrainian opposition newspaper *Vseukrainskie Vedomosti* was not so fortunate. In December 1997, it wrote about rumors that Dynamo football club owner Grigorii Surkis had talked about the possibility of selling Dynamo's star player, Andriy Shevchenko, to an Italian club. Surkis claimed the rumors were slanderous and demanded US$1.75 million in compensation for the moral damages he sustained as a result of the article. In January 1998, a Chernivtsy court ruled in favor of the plaintiff. A month later the court froze the newspaper's assets to ensure payment. In March, right before the parliamentary elections, *Vseukrainskie Vedomosti* officially closed down because they could not pay their bills (Fond Zashchity Glasnosti, 1998). In 1999, Shevchenko was indeed sold to Milan for US$26 million (ESPN SoccerNet,

2009). The newspaper had not lied after all. Few believed, though, that the dispute had ever been over Shevchenko. Rather it seemed to be all about politics. As one of the leaders of the Social Democratic Party of Ukraine (united) (SDPU(o)), Surkis was a main figure in the propresidential Kuchmist camp. *Vseukrainskie Vedomosti*, on the other hand, had obvious financial links to Kuchma's arch-rival in 1998 – *Hromada* leader, Pavlo Lazarenko (European Institute for the Media, 1998).

These high-profile cases are just the tip of the iceberg. Between 1999 and 2003, the Russian courts of general jurisdiction heard between 4,235 and 5,499 defamation cases per year.[1] In 1999, Ukrainian courts reportedly heard 2,258 defamation cases against media outlets (Razumkov Centre, 2001, p. 33). In comparative context, these figures are huge. In 2003, Australians initiated 150 defamation lawsuits, Americans filed 110 suits, and the British, known for their supposed litigiousness when it comes to defamation, filed a total of 206 cases. If we calculate the per capita incidence of defamation lawsuits, the contrast is even more striking. In the United States, there is one lawsuit per 2.3 million people. In Delaware, the defamation law capital of the United States, there were 166,000 people. England is indeed more litigious than the United States, as its data show that there is one lawsuit per 121,000 people. Australians also turn out to be quite litigious, as there is one lawsuit per 131,000 people (Caslon Analytics, 2005). By contrast, in Russia, in 2003, there was one defamation lawsuit per 26,000 people. In Ukraine in 1999, there was one defamation lawsuit per 22,000 people. In other words, Russians and Ukrainians were about five times more likely to file a defamation suit than Australians and the English, and about ten times more likely than Americans.

While litigation rates are vastly different, win-rates in defamation trials are similar in Russia and Ukraine and in the United States. In Russia, the courts ruled in favor of the plaintiff in about 65 percent of cases (Sudebnyi Departament data, 2004)[2]. In Ukraine, the plaintiff won approximately 70 percent of the time (Razumkov Centre, 2001, p. 33). In the United States during the 1990s, lawsuits against media outlets specifically were successful about 63% percent of the time (Logan, 2001, p. 513).

The high defamation litigation rates in Russia and Ukraine add detail to the picture of a highly litigious society that is already emerging in other research on Russian courts. Hendley (1997; 1999; 2001; 2004) has shown that Russians

---

[1] Data provided to the author by the Court Department of the Supreme Court of the Russian Federation on April 5, 2004.
[2] Data provided to the author by the Court Department of the Supreme Court of the Russian Federation on April 5, 2004.

use the courts extensively to collect debts and settle business disputes. Cashu and Orenstein (2001) have described the 200,000 case strong litigation campaign that Russian pensioners pursued against a government-mandated inflation-indexing coefficient. Solomon (2004) has shown that Russians have used administrative litigation extensively to press many grievances against state institutions. In short, defamation (and electoral registration) litigation rates are part of a broader phenomenon – post-Soviet citizens' eagerness to use the courts to resolve disputes.

The high volume of defamation cases has serious implications for media development and freedom of the press and whether the impact is positive or negative hinges squarely on the independence of the courts. Independent and impartial judicial output in defamation cases probably discourages journalists from becoming information hit men out to kill anybody's reputation for the right sum of money. If the courts are likely to punish the willful dissemination of false and damaging information about people, journalists are going to think twice before doing it. The earnest and impartial enforcement of defamation legislation by the courts should boost the quality of investigative journalism. Journalists wary of running afoul of defamation legislation rules would use a high reliability threshold before they put anything in print. Eventually, the information that the media disseminates will be more reliable.

By contrast, judicial output that systematically reflects the preferences of politicians or other powerful and rich plaintiffs significantly curtails freedom of speech. Under the guise of fighting for their good name, politicians could effectively use the courts to punish media outlets, which report damaging (but true) information about them. The more cases politicians win, the more afraid journalists will be. Eventually, investigative reporting will suffocate under the blanket of defamation litigation. If the courts participate in this politicization of the judicial process, they would effectively become state censors.

Thus, it is essential to find out whether the Russian and Ukrainian courts were independent from politicians and other plaintiffs in adjudicating defamation disputes. The analysis presented in this chapter estimates whether a plaintiffs' political affiliation and administrative resources have a significant effect (both statistically and substantively speaking) on their chances of victory, as well as on the size of the moral compensation award that usually accompanies a successful defamation claim. When politically powerful plaintiffs win much more often and receive larger compensation awards than other plaintiffs, that is an indication that the courts are biased, rather than impartial adjudicators.

The comparison between Russian and Ukrainian judicial output in defamation cases provides a second test of the predictions of the political competition theories of judicial independence. To remind the reader, the strategic pressure theory proposed in this book predicts that Ukrainian courts are going to be more politicized than Russian courts, because Ukraine's electorally insecure incumbents would be much more interested in securing favorable outcomes in each case than Russia's stronger incumbents. The traditional political competition theories make the opposite prediction – Ukraine's higher level of political competition should serve as an incentive for the incumbents to provide independent courts.

## THE STATUTORY FRAMEWORK FOR DEFAMATION LAWSUITS

The defamation cases analyzed in this chapter are civil suits brought by individuals and organizations under civil code provisions rather than criminal offenses pursued by the prosecution office under the criminal code. The Civil Code of the Russian Federation and the Civil Code of Ukraine both stipulate that citizens can use the courts to seek redress for the public denigration of his or her "honor, dignity and business reputation."[3] In both countries, the person disseminating the allegedly slanderous piece of information has to prove its veracity to the court's satisfaction. If the court establishes that the defendant has not met the burden of proof, the judge can order the defendant to publish an official retraction and/or compensate the plaintiff for the moral damage that he or she has incurred. The civil codes define "moral damage" as "physical or emotional suffering" that results from the violation of a citizen's personal nonmaterial rights, such as the right to protect his or her honor, dignity, and business reputation from denigration and defamation (Grazhdanskii Kodeks Rossiiskoi Federatsii, 1996; Grazhdanskii Kodeks Ukrainy, 1992).

Since the size of the compensation award can be exorbitant and reach several million dollars, it is important to explain how moral damage is quantified. Article 152 of the Civil Code of the Russian Federation stipulates that the plaintiff can propose an estimate of the moral damage in his or her complaint. However, as article 151 stipulates, the court is the ultimate arbiter on the matter and determines, first, whether the plaintiff is entitled to any monetary compensation, and, second, whether the plaintiff should receive the full

---

[3] The Russian phrase is *chest', dostoinstvo i delovaya reputatsiya*. Coverage of defamation cases in the Russian-language sources refers to a defamation lawsuit as *isk o zashchite chesti, dostoinstva i delovoi reputatsii*. For more on defamation law in Russia, see Peter Krug, "Civil Defamation Law and the Press in Russia: Private and Public Interests, the 1995 Civil Code, and the Constitution (Part One), *Cardozo Arts and Entertainment Law Journal*, 13 (1995), pp. 847–79 and Peter Krug, "Civil Defamation Law and the Press in Russia: Private and Public Interests, the 1995 Civil Code, and the Constitution (Part Two), *Cardozo Arts and Entertainment Law Journal*, 14 (1996), pp. 297–342.

compensation that he or she has indicated in the complaint or some fraction of it. To arrive at a precise figure, the court takes into account a variety of factors such as (1) the degree to which the defendant is responsible for the inflicted damages; (2) the intensity of the physical and emotional suffering endured by the plaintiff; (3) the characteristics and circumstances of the plaintiff. In addition, article 1101 provides that the size of the award has to be "reasonable and just" (Grazhdanskii Kodeks Rossiiskoi Federatsii, 1996).

Resolution No. 4 of the Plenum of the Supreme Court of Ukraine from March 31, 1995, which interprets Article 4401 of the Civil Code of Ukraine and is entitled "About Court Practice in Cases Involving the Adjudication of Moral (non-material) Damages," stipulates a virtually identical mechanism to the Russian one. The court determines the size of the award by considering the defendant's culpability, the type and seriousness of the injury, the degree to which his or her reputation and prestige have been damaged, and the efforts that would be needed to the restore them. This list of factors is not exhaustive and court practice has shown that judges also consider how widely the slanderous information has been disseminated (Civil Chamber of the Supreme Court of Ukraine).

This chapter focuses on a subgroup of the whole universe of defamation cases, namely lawsuits in which the defendant is a print or broadcast media outlet. In those cases, the Russian Law on the Mass Media applies in conjunction with the civil code. Article 51 of the media law stipulates that journalists are prohibited from disseminating false and discrediting information about a physical or a juridical person (Law of the Russian Federation on Mass Media, 1991). In addition, the Plenum of the Supreme Court of the Russian Federation has issued a binding resolution, which defines discrediting information as "information that does not correspond to reality, denigrates a citizen's honor and dignity, contains statements which accuse a citizen or an organization of violating the law or moral principles (such as dishonest act, improper behavior at work, at home, and other information discrediting business or public activity, reputation, etc.)" (Council of Europe/Directorate General of Human Rights/Media Division, 2003).

Ukrainian practice also envisions a victory for the plaintiff if the court finds simply that the disseminated information is false. While the law provided for a distinction between inadvertent and deliberate defamation, in reality judges did not consider this factor, because "malicious intent" was not clearly defined anywhere (Shevchenko, 2003). Moreover, even the new amended Law on Guarantees for Freedom of Speech, adopted in the spring of 2003, does not say who needs to prove the presence of malicious intent. The laws on the books and Supreme Court rulings and resolutions on the matter also fail to determine whether the media outlet or the author of the article found to be defamatory carry the bulk of the responsibility for the false information's dissemination (Civil Chamber of the Supreme Court of Ukraine).

In other words, all the legislation discussed so far gives enormous leeway to the judge to determine the outcome and impact of each case. Since there are no objective guidelines the court could use in determining either the appropriateness or the size of the moral damage award, the judge can easily act upon his or her own biases and predispositions. Alternatively or in conjunction, the judge could hand down a ruling that is more in line with a powerful actor's agenda, than with any abstract notion of justice or reasonableness. Because of this built-in legal flexibility, defamation cases are a particularly useful tool for examining judicial behavior.

## THE DATASETS

Each one of the 695 defamation cases that make up the Russian dataset analyzed in this chapter is described in considerable detail in the Glasnost Defense Foundation Monitor, which tracks media-related disputes and journalist rights violations in Russia and the other CIS states.[4] The Glasnost Defense Foundation (GDF) is a Moscow-based human rights watchdog with ten regional centers, which serve as hubs for collecting and sorting information about media disputes. The foundation also provides legal advice and representation to media outlets who cannot afford to retain a lawyer to defend them in a defamation suit. Table 5.1 summarizes how the data break down by federation unit.

GDF researchers did not follow scientific random sampling techniques but rather recorded the entire yield from three information-gathering channels: (1) references to defamation cases in the regional press; (2) direct accounts of trials provided to a GDF center by trial participants (usually the defendant); and (3) accounts of trials provided by lawyers involved in defamation disputes. While not all federal units are equally represented in the dataset, the data contain information from a politically and geographically diverse group of regions. As Table 5.1 shows, all major geographic areas of Russia are represented. More importantly, however, the represented regions cover the entire political spectrum – from reformist regions, through moderate and Red Belt communist regions, to authoritarian ethnic republics. The last group is the only regional type that seems underrepresented in the sample. It is possible

[4] Sluzhba Monitoringa, Fond Zashchity Glasnosti, information accessed at http://www.gdf.ru/monitor/index.html

TABLE 5.1. *Regions represented in the sample (number of cases; percent of total)*

| Region | Number of cases (% of total) | Region | Number of cases (% of total) |
|---|---|---|---|
| Moscow city | 92 (13%) | Orenburg | 5 (0.7%) |
| Volgograd | 89 (13%) | Belgorod | 4 (0.6%) |
| Primor'e | 45 (6.5%) | Kaluga | 4 (0.6%) |
| Sverdlovsk | 40 (5.8%) | Penza | 4 (0.6%) |
| Rostov | 29 (4.2%) | Bashkortostan | 3 (0.4%) |
| Krasnoyarsk | 23 (3.3%) | Kabardino-Balkaria | 3 (0.4%) |
| Bryansk | 23 (3.3%) | Altai Republic | 3 (0.4%) |
| Kirov | 22 (3.2%) | Arkhangelsk | 3 (0.4%) |
| Voronezh | 20 (2.9%) | Moscow oblast | 3 (0.4%) |
| Tatarstan | 20 (2.9%) | Murmansk | 3 (0.4%) |
| Kursk | 16 (2.3%) | Perm | 3 (0.4%) |
| Nizhnii Novgorod | 14 (2.0%) | Saratov | 3 (0.4%) |
| Chelyabinsk | 14 (2.0%) | Tula | 3 (0.4%) |
| Pskov | 14 (2.0%) | Adygeya | 2 (0.3%) |
| Lipetsk | 13 (1.9%) | Udmurtiya | 2 (0.3%) |
| Vladimir | 11 (1.6%) | Chuvashiya | 2 (0.3%) |
| Khanty-Mansy | 11 (1.6%) | Ivanovo | 2 (0.3%) |
| Mordovia | 10 (1.4%) | Kaliningrad | 2 (0.3%) |
| St. Petersburg | 10 (1.4%) | Orel | 2 (0.3%) |
| Tomsk | 9 (1.3%) | Samara | 2 (0.3%) |
| Kurgan | 8 (1.2%) | Sakhalin | 2 (0.3%) |
| Novgorod | 8 (1.2%) | Smolensk | 2 (0.3%) |
| Novosibirsk | 8 (1.2%) | Tambov | 2 (0.3%) |
| Tyumen' | 8 (1.2%) | Komi-Permyatsk | 2 (0.3%) |
| Kareliya | 7 (1.0%) | Altai krai | 1 (0.1%) |
| Omsk | 7 (1.0%) | Karachaev-Cherkessiya | 1 (0.1%) |
| Ryazan' | 7 (1.0%) | Kalmykiya | 1 (0.1%) |
| Ul'yanovsk | 7 (1.0%) | Komi | 1 (0.1%) |
| Krasnodar | 6 (0.9%) | Vologda | 1 (0.1%) |
| Irkutsk | 6 (0.9%) | Kamchatka | 1 (0.1%) |
| Kemerovo | 6 (0.9%) | Tver' | 1 (0.1%) |
| Tuva | 5 (0.7%) | Chita | 1 (0.1%) |
| Stavropol | 5 (0.7%) | Evreiskii AO | 1 (0.1%) |
| Astrakhan | 5 (0.7%) | Marii El | 1 (0.1%) |

**Regions not represented in the sample:** *Buryatiya, Dagestan, Ingushetiya, Sakha, Khakasiya, Severnaya Osetiya-Alaniya, Khabarovsk, Amur, Kostroma, Leningradskaya oblast, Magadan, Yaroslavl, Aginskii Buryatskii AO, Koryakskii AO, Nenetskii AO, Taimyrskii AO, Ust'-Ordynskii AO, Chukotskii AO, Evenkskii AO, Yamalo-Nenetskii AO*

that since most ethnic republics are under the tight control of the governor, there are hardly any oppositionist media outlets. Consequently, where there would be few controversial articles, there would be fewer offended parties and hence we should expect to observe fewer defamation cases. This logic suggests that any conclusions reached on the basis of this dataset are less applicable to the most authoritarian Russian regions.

The Ukrainian dataset contains 105 cases, which were adjudicated between 1998 and 2003. About one-fifth of the cases ($n = 19$) are described in GDF's CIS Monitor. The rest of the data come from GDF's Ukrainian counterpart – IREX Promedia and lawyers who have represented media outlets in defamation cases. Like GDF, IREX Promedia is an NGO, which monitors press freedom and provides legal advice and representation free of charge to media outlets that cannot afford to hire a lawyer.

Although the Ukrainian sample is significantly smaller than the Russian one, it accurately represents Ukraine's regional diversity. All of Ukraine's administrative regions, with the exception of Vinnitsya, Rivne, and Sumy, are represented in the sample. Moreover, the sample reflects Ukraine's regional East-West division. Thirty-seven cases (36% percent) were adjudicated by courts in Eastern and Southern Ukraine, thirty-five cases (or 34 percent) were adjudicated in Western and Central Ukraine, and the remaining third of the cases ($n = 31$ or 30 percent) were litigated in the capital, Kyiv. The overrepresentation of Kyiv in the sample reflects the fact that most media outlets with nationwide coverage have address registrations in Kyiv and therefore defamation complaints against them fall within the jurisdiction of Kyiv city courts.

Ideally, the sample of cases analyzed would be a scientifically drawn random sample of all defamation cases decided in Russia and Ukraine every year. However, official court statistics track aggregate rather than case-by-case data. Law reviews (*sudebnaya praktika*), which track and analyze judicial output, represent the best source for court statistics. They publish success rates for different courts and some aggregate socioeconomic data about the plaintiffs, but not on a case-by-case basis. Therefore, their data cannot be used to analyze judicial behavior.

Some may raise a concern that the GDF and IREX-Promedia data could be problematic because they were collected by *pravozashchitniki*, or human rights activists, who are almost by definition in opposition to the incumbent regime. As a result the dataset might not represent a random sample of all cases. Rather, it may contain a disproportionately large number of cases, in which an opposition media outlet has to defend itself against lawsuits filed by politically powerful plaintiffs. Moreover, *pravozashchitniki* might tend to record mainly cases in which politically powerful plaintiffs win in order to attract the public's and the international donors' attention to the plight of opposition journalists. In interviews with the author, experts from both GDF and IREX-Promedia stated that they recorded the outcome of every single defamation case, on which they could gather information (Timoshenko, 2002; 2004; Mycio, 2003). More importantly, even if the data collection were biased, it would be biased in the same direction, because GDF and IREX-Promedia have the same mission and potential biases. In other words, although the absolute level of judicial independence may be underestimated due to the partial data, any difference in the relative level of judicial independence in Russia and Ukraine should reflect a real difference, rather than a contextual one. Therefore, GDF and IREX-Promedia appear to be the best available data sources for a comparative analysis of judicial behavior in defamation cases in Russia and Ukraine.

For each case in both samples, I coded the following variables: (1) the administrative unit where the trial took place, (2) the identity of the defendant, (3) the identity of the plaintiff, (4) the month and year the complaint was filed, (5) the plaintiff's estimate of the moral damage inflicted by the slanderous media output, (6) the court where the case was tried, (7) the court's decision, (8) the size of the compensation award as determined by the court, and (9) the month and year the court delivered its ruling.

The GDF/IREX-Promedia case descriptions often provide some context about the political leanings of the litigants, which I used as a starting point for a broader data collection effort. I did an individual Google search on each litigant, which was aimed at collecting as much information about them as possible – their occupation, their ties to any political parties, their relationship (if any) to the regional authorities or to the Kremlin. As in the electoral registration cases, I went mostly through reports from the regional press, but I also used other information sources such as candidate lists for regional and municipal elections, NGO organizers' lists, and employee lists for hospitals and schools. In the end, I had a fairly detailed picture of the professional background and sociopolitical affiliation of each litigant in the database.

I then created several dummy variables. I coded as *central politician* every incumbent Duma/Rada deputy, member of the cabinet, or member of the presidential administration. In the Russian sample, I also created a *regional politician* dummy, which I coded as 1 for all incumbent regional legislature deputies, regional governors, deputy governors, and mayors of the region's capital city. The rationale behind including the mayors in the *regional politician* category, rather than the *municipal politician* category is that in many Russian regions, the mayor of the capital city was a high-profile politician with regionwide name recognition. In many politically competitive regions, the governor and the mayor were bitter rivals (e.g., Primorskii Krai governor Evgeny Nazdratenko and Vladivostok mayor Viktor Cherepkov) (Ross, 2000). The *municipal politician* category includes mayors of smaller cities and city council deputies in Russia and all mayors and city council deputies in Ukraine. One exception – Kyiv mayor, Oleksandr Omelchenko – is classified as a central politician because he was the leader of a viable national party, *Ednist*, and clearly an important player on the national political scene. I also created a *siloviki* dummy, which includes employees of the *militsiya* (i.e., police), tax police, the security services (FSB in Russia, SBU in Ukraine), prosecutors, and judges.

Following the same data collection methodology and coding scheme as in the electoral registration cases (which is described at length in Chapter 4), I also created political affiliation plaintiff groups – opposition-affiliated and government-affiliated plaintiffs. In the Russian case, I additionally distinguished between being a protégée or an oppositionist vis-à-vis the central government (i.e., the Kremlin) or vis-à-vis the regional government (i.e., the incumbent governor in your region).

I included a regional dimension in the Russian data because during the period that the data covers (1998–2003), the degree of electoral competition varied significantly across Russia's eighty-nine constituent regions (Golosov, 1999; McMann and Petrov, 2000; Marsh 2000; Moraski and Reisinger, 2003; Sharafutdinova, 2006, etc.). Some (mainly ethnic republics) had evolved into personal fiefdoms of powerful governors/presidents where the incumbent's electoral position was unassailable. For example, during Murtaza Rakhimov's or Kirsan Ilyumzhinov's tenure, the level of electoral competition in Bashkortostan and Kalmykiya (respectively) was probably closer to that in Uzbekistan, than to that in Moscow. Others were about as competitive as the center – meaningful opposition existed and provided some challenge to the incumbent, but was not strong enough to unseat the incumbent (as mentioned in Chapter 3, the incumbent president has never lost an election in Russia). In at least a fifth of Russian regions, however, electoral competition was vigorous during the 1990s and early 2000s. In nineteen out of Russia's eighty-nine regions, the incumbent lost in *each* gubernatorial election held between 1994 and 2001 (Moraski and Reisinger, 2003, p. 284).

It is important to note that while some dummy variables are mutually exclusive, not all are. For example, a plaintiff cannot be both a regional *and* a central politician by definition. However, politicians at all levels can have either a progovernment or an opposition affiliation, or in some cases can be neutral vis-à-vis the incumbents. Finally, I created an *ordinary citizens* dummy, which is not a residual category that includes all plaintiffs who are not known to have financial or formal administrative resources. Rather, this dummy seeks to capture a group of plaintiffs who are known to be cashed-strapped and vulnerable to administrative resource pressure. Therefore the dummy lumps teachers, doctors, unemployed and pensioners together. Certainly, some individuals who fall in this category may, in fact, have informal ties to politically powerful actors or may simply be proxies for powerful interests, which may introduce some noise in the statistical analysis. In the worst-case scenario, such exceptions would introduce bias and as a result the model might underestimate the difference between the win-rates of powerful and nonpowerful actors in court. Such bias is arguably preferable to bias in the opposite direction, which would lead us to find a difference where none exists in reality. Table 5.2 summarizes how the data break down according to plaintiff group.

As mentioned in the discussion of the applicable legal provisions, the court could deliver one of three rulings at the end of each trial. If the defendant meets the burden of proof and shows that the published information is in fact truthful or if the court decides that the information is false, yet does not denigrate the plaintiff's honor, dignity, or business reputation, the judge rules in favor of the defendant. In the dataset, these trial outcomes are coded as 0, since the focus of the analysis is the success rate of the plaintiff. If the media outlet does not manage to prove the veracity of the published information and the judge agrees that the plaintiff's honor, dignity, and business reputation have been denigrated, the plaintiff's complaint is granted. I coded these outcomes as 1.

Table 5.3 shows the overall plaintiff win-rate for both samples. The breakdown does suggest that the samples reflect the sensitivities of human rights activists (*pravozashchitniki*), as the loss-rate for media outlet is higher than the averages reported in official statistics – 75 percent win-rate in the Russian sample vs. 65 percent reported by the Supreme Court and 82 percent in the Ukrainian sample vs. 70 percent reported by the Supreme Court. Notably, however, the bias seems to be equal in size in both samples, which facilitates a reliable comparison of the level of judicial independence in Russia and Ukraine.

## LOSS, VICTORY, AND "MORAL DAMAGE" AWARDS: MULTISTAGE WIN-RATE ANALYSIS OF JUDICIAL INDEPENDENCE FROM POLITICIANS IN DEFAMATION DISPUTES

The first step in testing the hypothesis that politically powerful actors use the courts to carry out political goals is to examine the win-rate of various types of

TABLE 5.2. *Sociopolitical groups of defamation suit plaintiffs*

| Plaintiff groups | Russian sample | Ukrainian sample |
|---|---|---|
| **Plaintiffs with administrative resources** | | |
| Judges and siloviki (police, tax police, FSB/SBU, prosecution) | 80 cases (12%) | 18 cases (17%) |
| Municipal politician (mayor of smaller city, city council deputy) | 71 cases (10%) | 19 cases (18%) |
| Regional politician (regional legislature deputy, governor, deputy governor, mayor of region's capital) | 181 cases (26%) | — |
| Central politician (Duma/Rada deputy, minister, member of presidential administration) | 57 cases (8%) | 27 cases (26%) |
| **Plaintiff groups according to political affiliation** | | |
| Regional oppositionists | 91 cases (13%) | — |
| Protégées of the regional administration | 117 cases (17%) | — |
| Central government oppositionists | 89 cases (13%) | 18 cases (17%) |
| Protégées of the central government | 26 cases (4%) | 24 cases (23%) |
| Ordinary citizens | 135 cases (19%) | 27 cases (26%) |

TABLE 5.3. *Plaintiff win-rates in Russia and Ukraine*

| Cases in which: | Russia | Ukraine |
|---|---|---|
| Plaintiff loses | 171 cases (25%) | 19 cases (18%) |
| Plaintiff wins | 523 cases (75%) | 84 cases (82%) |

plaintiffs. To estimate the probability of success in court for different groups of plaintiffs, I use a logit estimator with the court decision as the outcome variable and the plaintiff group dummies as the explanatory variables. In addition, dummy variables for each year represented in the sample are used as control variables.[5] Finally, the model includes dummies for Moscow and Kyiv. Not only are the capital cities overrepresented in both samples, but it is

[5] The rationale for using year controls is that even in civil law countries precedent plays some role and there might be trends in court rulings over time.

TABLE 5.4.  *Logit coefficients for success rates in court for different plaintiffs*

| Candidate characteristics | Russia | Ukraine |
|---|---|---|
| Judiciary&Siloviki | 1.49*** | .32 |
| | (.42) | (1.11) |
| OrdinaryCitizen | −.31 | .12 |
| | (.24) | (.99) |
| MunicipalPolitician | .21 | 2.04 |
| | (.33) | (1.67) |
| RegionalPolitician | .38 | — |
| | (.36) | |
| CentralPolitician | .28 | 4.45*** |
| | (.44) | (1.62) |
| RegionalOppositionist | .56 | — |
| | (.42) | |
| RegionalAdminProtege | 1.12** | — |
| | (.45) | |
| CentGovtOppositionist | −.17 | −4.15*** |
| | (.38) | (1.41) |
| CentGovtProtege | .07 | −.40 |
| | (.62) | (1.35) |
| Capital dummy | −.61** | −.94 |
| | (.28) | (.83) |
| 1998dummy | .76 | −1.15 |
| | (1.05) | (1.90) |
| 1999dummy | −.004 | −4.30** |
| | (1.05) | (2.06) |
| 2000dummy | 1.03 | −1.94 |
| | (1.05) | (1.89) |
| 2001dummy | .63 | −2.61 |
| | (1.05) | (1.93) |
| 2002dummy | .84 | −2.18 |
| | (1.05) | (1.85) |
| Constant | .22 | 3.78 |
| | (1.03) | (2.01) |
| N | 687 | 103 |
| Log–likelihood | −347 | −35 |
| $X^2$ | 69.85 | 28.81 |
| Pseudo $R^2$ | .09 | .29 |

*Note:* Numbers in parentheses are the standard errors.
*$p < .1$ ** $p < .05$ *** $p < .01$

possible that judges in the capital behave differently than provincial judges.[6] The results of the following model specifications for the two samples are listed in Table 5.4.

Russian Sample:

$CourtDecision = \beta_0 + \beta_1 Judiciary\&Siloviki + \beta_2 OrdinaryCitizen + \beta_3 Municipal$ $Politician + \beta_4 RegionalPolitician + \beta_5 CentralPolitician + \beta_6 Regional$ $Oppositionist + \beta_7 RegionalAdminProtege + \beta_8 CentGovtOppositionist + \beta_9$ $CentGovtProtege + \beta_{10} CapitalDummy + \beta_{11-14} YearDummies + \varepsilon$

Ukrainian Sample:

$CourtDecision = \beta_0 + \beta_1 Judiciary\&Siloviki + \beta_2 OrdinaryCitizen + \beta_3$ $RegionalPolitician + \beta_4 CentralPolitician + \beta_5 CentGovtOppositionist +$ $\beta_6 CentGovtProtege + \beta_7 CapitalDummy + \beta_{8-11} YearDummies + \varepsilon$

The models present several interesting results. The Russian model shows that there are three statistically significant predictors of plaintiff's success in a defamation trial. First, protégés of the regional administration are more likely than other plaintiffs to win a defamation trial. Second, judges and *siloviki* are also more likely than other plaintiffs to win a defamation trial. Third, plaintiffs bringing defamation trials in Moscow are less likely to succeed than anyone else. The Ukrainian model also identifies three statistically significant predictors of plaintiff's success in a defamation trial. First, central politicians (both incumbent and opposition) have a much higher probability of winning the defamation cases that they bring to court. Second, oppositionist plaintiffs won much less often than anybody else. Third, defamation cases decided in 1999 resulted in victory for the plaintiff less often than cases filed in other years.

Each of these results is important, and I will discuss it later on, but for now let us focus on the main comparison of interest. Did the Russian or the Ukrainian courts appear to cater more to the interests of incumbent politicians? Was the politicization of justice higher in Russia or in Ukraine? The evidence suggests a higher level of politicization in Ukraine than in Russia. Oppositionist plaintiffs in Ukraine had a significantly lower probability of

---

[6] There are many reasons why the dynamics of judicial decision making may be different in the capital and in the provinces. Both the type of defamation cases and the degree of judicial independence may well vary. First, because the press in the capital is probably feistier than the provincial press, it may provoke a greater number of defamation lawsuits. In addition, one hypothesis is that judges in the capital are subject to more direct pressure from the political establishment not only because they are physically closer but also because the cases they hear are more salient. As a result, judges in the capital should be more dependent than provincial judges. An alternative hypothesis is that judicial proceedings in the capital are more visible, so the incumbents may be more cautious in exerting pressure in violation of constitutional guarantees for judicial independence.

winning a defamation case. By contrast, oppositionist (vis-à-vis the Kremlin) plaintiffs in Russia did not appear to be at a disadvantage. Because the magnitude of the observed relationships cannot be easily gleaned from the coefficients, I simulated the predicted probabilities of success or failure in court for various types of plaintiffs and calculated the first difference between the probability of a court victory for various types of plaintiffs and the probability for the average (the modal) plaintiff. This technique allows us to estimate how much exactly opposition status and political clout affect a plaintiff's likelihood of success in court.

Figure 5.1 shows the predicted probabilities of victory for four different types of Russian and Ukrainian plaintiffs according to their political affiliation and political clout. The model predicts that in Russia opposition-affiliated and government-affiliated plaintiffs could expect to have roughly the same winrate in a defamation lawsuit. Kremlin protégés might have roughly a 5 percent advantage in court over Kremlin oppositionists, but the difference is not statistically significant as the two estimates' confidence intervals overlap significantly. By contrast, all Ukrainian opposition-affiliated plaintiffs appeared to have a lower win-rate than government-affiliated plaintiffs. Among central politicians, the difference is statistically significant, but not very big substantively. Opposition MPs have a 93 percent probability of winning, which, of course, is very high. Government ministers, MPs from the pro-Kuchma parliamentary factions, and members of the Presidential Administration, however, cannot lose a defamation case, as their expected win-rate is 99 percent! Among plaintiffs who are not central politicians, political affiliation makes a very dramatic difference. Affiliation with the opposition cuts plaintiffs' probability of winning their defamation suit in half.

These results point to more politicized justice and less independent judicial output in Ukraine than in Russia. First, note that the probabilities for all four types of Russian plaintiffs are pretty similar (in fact they are statistically indistinguishable from each other). In other words, whether you are a Duma member or a federal minister or an average Ivan, you have about a fifty-fifty chance of winning a defamation case against a media outlet. Moreover, whether you are a communist sympathizer or a United Russia Duma MP does not appear to significantly affect your chances of success. In short, defamation cases do not appear to be particularly politicized in Russia – the political affiliation and political clout of the plaintiff do not have a significant effect on the outcome of the case.

By contrast, in Ukraine, the outcomes of defamation cases were thoroughly affected both by the political affiliation and by the administrative resources of the plaintiff. Central politicians, regardless of political affiliation, are roughly

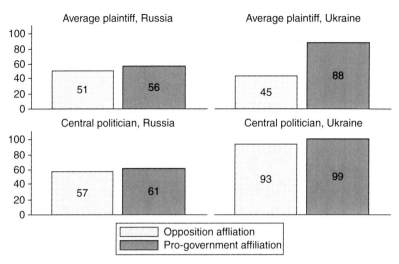

FIGURE 5.1. Predicted win-rates for different types of plaintiffs.

twice as likely as ordinary plaintiffs to win their defamation cases against media outlets. This suggests that both representatives of the Kuchma regimes and major opposition politicians interfered in judicial decision making in order to obtain favorable rulings. Politicians close to the regime, however, were more successful than oppositionists in maximizing their preferences. The 99 percent likelihood of victory in a defamation trial suggests that they almost never lost a case. Both results suggest that defamation trials were highly politicized, and politicians of all stripes in Ukraine used them as a tool in their competition for power.

The win-rate model results suggest that Russian and Ukrainian courts differ significantly when it comes to independence from politicians in defamation lawsuits. However, since the analysis does not include the selection stage of the litigation process, it is vulnerable to selection bias. Without information on the whole universe of potential defamation disputes, we do not know whether Ukrainian politicians win more often because judges are biased in their favor or because they consistently bring stronger cases to court. Collecting information on the whole universe of potential plaintiffs in defamation cases is quite challenging. It is not clear how researchers could identify all people who might have been offended by a newspaper article or a TV exposé, so that we could check who decided to go to court and who did not.

The finding that central politicians of all political stripes in Ukraine enjoy a significant advantage in court over other plaintiffs is consistent with an often-expressed hypothesis that the media outlets themselves are responsible for the explosion of defamation lawsuits. The theory goes something like this. People who hold elected office are exposed to much more intense media scrutiny than ordinary citizens. Given the lack of experience by the post-Soviet media with the responsibilities of free speech and self-regulation, investigative journalism often degenerates into slanderous speculation and innuendo and politicians at all levels and of all political stripes bear the brunt of it. This is the version of the story that gives the benefit of the doubt to the media and attributes their shortcomings to inexperience.

In addition, there is a more cynical view of both the Russian and the Ukrainian press. It posits that *zakazukha* (or "pre-paid" articles) have become standard practice and the main source of income for the major newspapers. The term refers to journalists getting large sums of money either to produce virulent and usually libelous attacks on the ordering party's opponents and mask the article as objective reporting or sincere editorializing or to act as de facto publicists for individual politicians, again using gossip, innuendo, and manipulation, rather than facts to build up a politician's image. (see, e.g., Zassoursky, 2004; Koltsova, 2006; Tsetsura, 2009, etc.) In the fall of 2003, I had the opportunity to sit on a business dinner between a leading Ukrainian journalist and the press secretary of freshly appointed prime minister, Viktor Yanukovych. The conversation illustrated how the line between journalist and publicist was seriously blurred. The journalist and the press secretary were meeting to plan the "coming out" interview of the new prime minister on the journalist's talk show. The journalist started the conversation by sketching out a list of "tasks" for the press secretary. He was to find some footage, in which Yanukovych looks relaxed and which shows him as an ordinary person. The journalist then suggested some scenarios: Yanukovych visiting his grandmother's grave in Belarus, Yanukovych with his *krepkaya sem'ya* (tight-knit family), Yanukovych playing tennis, meeting with Olympic committee chairman, Juan Antonio Samaranch and Soviet Olympic legend Sergei Bubka, meeting with some military officers, maybe, hunting, strolling with Russian Prime Minister Kasyanov like *dva krasavtsa* in Crimea. Then the journalist outlined for the press secretary the topics that he wanted to cover in the conversation: (a) the budget– emphasize how this is a deficit budget, which will stimulate the economy, but talk about stuff only in principle, nothing specific; (b) how his government has lowered taxes to a record low (i.e., very promarket); (c) what Ukraine's entry in the World Trade Organization (WTO) means for specific industries; (d) present himself as a *gosudarstvennoi patriot* (state patriot) and not an *etnicheskii patriot* (ethnic patriot); (e) Ukraine's relationship to Russia, the United States, and Europe – let's talk about diversification in foreign policy like in the economic realm – diversification is good, monopoly is bad. The press secretary took notes and did not say much, except to ask some clarifying questions. The conversation ended with the journalist saying that he would need to meet with the prime minister at least twice before the interview, so that they can prepare well; the journalist's goal is for the premier to have a nice time and be relaxed during the interview in order to achieve maximum impact with the viewers. The journalist and the press secretary agreed on a time for the journalist and the premier to meet and the press secretary left, thanking.

Given the low professional standards of objectivity in both the Russian and the Ukrainian press, the argument goes, politicians were probably more often victims of defamation. As a result, it should not be surprising that they all win more often because they have strong cases more often. Another plausible hypothesis is that public figures cannot afford to be as opportunistic as ordinary citizens in bringing a lawsuit against a media outlet, so they sue only when they are certain that they have an airtight case. A loss in court for an ordinary citizen is not particularly costly. Apart from wasting money on court fees and failing to secure a retraction of the slanderous allegation, the plaintiff does not suffer any additional injury. A politician, however, would clearly prefer to abstain from suing altogether, rather than lose in court. In the absence of a trial, the politician can openly challenge the media's allegations and hope to convince people that malicious political opponents have paid for the nefarious attacks on his or her honor and dignity. However, a loss in court lends additional credence to the published allegations. Certainly, no politician wishes to be officially "certified" a crook (or a lecher, or a dimwit, or whatever the allegation might be) by a court of law.

A final alternative hypothesis that would also produce a higher win-rate for politicians posits that since public figures have higher stakes in the outcome of the trial, they commit more resources to securing a victory. Thus, their lower failure rate could be attributed to their superior legal representation rather than to any court bias in their favor. Unfortunately, we cannot test this alternative hypothesis without survey data on plaintiffs' legal representation.

Defamation lawsuits, however, have an additional litigation stage beyond the decision of the court to side with the plaintiff or with the defendant. The variation in the size of the compensation that judges award to all winning plaintiffs carries information about whether judges are favorably predisposed toward politically powerful plaintiffs or whether the latter simply go to court only when they have a fail-safe case and a good lawyer to argue it. A strong case implies only that the defendant would be clearly hard-pressed to prove the veracity of the published facts. While a strong case would maximize the chance of success in court, it should not have any bearing on the size of the moral damage award.

As mentioned earlier, the size of the compensation award should reflect above all the gravity of the injury to the plaintiff's "honor, dignity and business reputation." The vast majority of the plaintiffs, regardless of whether they are ministers, governors, or village school teachers, go to court over the same allegations of corruption, incompetence, or abuse of office. This similarity suggests that all victorious plaintiffs have suffered comparable injury and should be entitled to comparable compensation packages.

Some may argue that even independent courts would award significantly higher compensation to politicians than to other plaintiffs because politicians' honor, dignity, and reputation are more important to them by virtue of their profession than to other plaintiffs. Interviews both in Ukraine and in Russia, however, suggest that judges are not entirely convinced by such logic. Judge Mykola Zamkovenko, former chair of Kyiv's Pecherskii District Court, succinctly expressed an opinion echoed by many judges I interviewed – politicians are involved in a "dirty" profession, and they are used to being insulted. Therefore, they probably suffer less than anybody else, and, as a result, the law stipulates that they should receive less. A politician should be prepared to take criticism "like a man" (Zamkovenko, 2004). An internal memo of the analytical department of the Supreme Court, which draws general conclusions and offers loose instructions on compensation award determination, makes a related point (Grinenko, 2003). The author of the report urges district court judges not to feel pressured by the exorbitant sums of money that plaintiffs with significant administrative and financial resources usually demand as compensation. Even though he acknowledges that such plaintiffs' reputation is often more important to them, he points out that a mere victory in court and the public promulgation of such victory provides moral compensation for the damages these plaintiffs have suffered (Grinenko, 2003, p. 20).

Another reason why we might expect to find that public officials receive higher compensation awards than ordinary citizens, even if judicial independence is high, is that judges are supposed to consider journalistic intent in determining the award. If journalists deliberately defame anyone, they should be slapped with a heftier fine; if they inadvertently misrepresent the facts or have been misled by a source, the ruling against them should be more lenient. It is likely that public officials are subjected to slanderous and deliberate character assassination more often than ordinary citizens. Ordinary citizens, on the other hand, are more often than not defamed by overzealous journalists or

sloppy investigation reporters. The practice of black-PR and kompromat during election campaigns in both Russia and Ukraine created fertile grounds for
a large crop of defamation lawsuits.

For example, the 1999–2000 parliamentary presidential campaign in Russia
was characterized by a massive media war between the incumbent prime
minister and Yeltsin's chosen successor, Vladimir Putin, and his closest rivals,
former prime minister Evgenii Primakov and Moscow mayor Yurii Luzhkov
(see, e.g., Eremin, 2000; Oates, 2006; Burrett, 2011, etc.). The main weapon
in this war was kompromat. Especially noteworthy was a Sunday show on
ORT, hosted by Sergei Dorenko. ORT was a state-owned channel, but 49 percent of it was privately owned and the biggest private shareholder was Boris
Berezovsky, an oil oligarch then part of Yeltsin's closest inner circle and thus
supportive of Yeltsin's chosen successor, Vladimir Putin. Over the course of
the parliamentary campaign, Dorenko released a number of kompromat stories that aimed to portray both Luzhkov and Primakov as unsuitable presidential candidates. Luzhkov was painted as corrupt and inefficient at governing
Moscow and Primakov was alleged to be in poor health and thus unfit to
govern. Most of the stories presented by Dorenko contained very little fac-
tual proof or backing and were mostly innuendo and gossip. Moreover, the
victims of the mudslinging were effectively denied an opportunity to present
a response to the allegations. Dorenko was reportedly paid millions to present
these stories (White, Oates, and McAllister, 2005, p. 198; Stromback and Kaid,
2008, p. 362). Luzhkov eventually won a defamation lawsuit against Dorenko
for the 1999 parliamentary campaign stories, but it was perhaps too little, too
late.

In the Ukrainian context, all major TV stations (both state-owned and privately held by major oligarchs) engaged routinely in black PR against particular candidates. For an illustrative example, in the run-up to the 2004
presidential election, proregime channel 1+1 had a daily "commentary" show
called "Prote" that followed the evening's most watched newscast. "Prote"'s
hosts, Dmytro Korchinsky and Dmytro Dzhangirov, did nothing else but
editorialize against Yushchenko and his allies every single day. Another daily
show on ICTV (a channel owned by Kuchma's son-in-law, Viktor Pinchuk),
"Details with Dmitrii Kiselev" also methodically undermined the image of
opposition candidate, Viktor Yushchenko (Dyczok, 2005).

In sum, there is good reason to believe that politicians (incumbent or
opposition) have a greater likelihood of being genuine victims of defamation
and hence even independent courts should rule in favor of plaintiffs against
media. Political affiliation, however, should not be correlated with the size of

the compensation if the courts are immune to political influence. It seems that plaintiffs with progovernment leanings and oppositionists are roughly equally likely to be the target of malicious journalists. Incumbents' record can be slammed unfairly by opposition-leaning media. But oppositionists are often attacked by media outlets close to the incumbent regime in an attempt to prevent them from gaining popularity. If we control for the plaintiff's administrative and financial resources, his or her political affiliation should have no effect on the size of the moral damage award.

With these hypotheses in mind, I examine the variation in compensation size in Russia and Ukraine for different plaintiff groups according to their relationship with the incumbent regime. As in all previous comparisons, the same contrast emerges – Ukrainian judicial output seems to be systematically affected by the political affiliation of the plaintiff and Russian judicial output does not. Figure 5.2 shows the median compensation award for opposition-affiliated and government-affiliated plaintiffs in both countries. Russian oppositionists receive basically the same compensation as Kremlin protégés. Plaintiffs close to the Kuchma administration, on the other hand, receive awards that are more than three times bigger than those going to opposition-affiliated plaintiffs. To check whether the last difference is statistically significant, I conducted a comparison of means test using the natural log of the compensation. The rationale for using the natural log of the award, rather than the nominal value is that this reparametrization helps us avoid the problem of huge outliers, such as the million-dollar rulings against Novaya Gazeta, Kyivskie Vedomosti, and Stolichnye Novosti, driving the results. The reparametrization is standard practice when dealing with monetary variables. The test suggests that the difference between the size of the average award in Russia and the average award in Ukraine indeed statistically significant ($t = 1.80$, $p < .10$).

Another difference that jumps out is that Ukrainian awards are much larger on average than Russian awards. This divergence could be an indication that defamation lawsuits in Ukraine are much more politicized than similar cases in Russia. Large compensation awards are an effective tool for influencing editorial policy or outright bankrupting media outlets, and it appears that Ukrainian plaintiffs more often strive precisely for such effects.

## JUDICIAL INDEPENDENCE FROM OTHER PRINCIPALS

The inclusion of other sociopolitical variables besides a plaintiff's relationship with the incumbent regime permits an investigation of other potential principals who may impose their preferences on judicial output. The Russian model

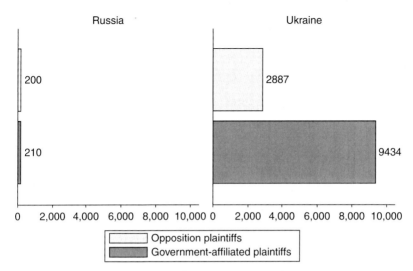

Figure 5.2. Median compensation for oppositionist and pro-government winners of defamation cases (in converted US dollars).

shows that regional politicians, as well as judges and *siloviki* (i.e., prosecutors, police, and, perhaps most importantly, President Putin's former colleagues at the FSB) enjoy a systematic advantage in defamation cases. As Figure 5.3 indicates, judges and *siloviki* have the highest win-rate of any sociopolitical group of plaintiffs in Russia. At 80 percent their expected success-rate in court is 25 percent higher than the success that the modal plaintiff achieves in defamation lawsuits.

Actually, we cannot be sure that there are real statistical differences between the probability of winning between each of the different plaintiff groups. The only group whose predicted win-rate is significantly bigger than the average win-rate are the judges and *siloviki*. To illustrate this point, Figure 5.4 plots the mean predicted probabilities for each plaintiff group and the 95 percent confidence intervals of the estimates.

The large advantage that judges and *siloviki* appear to enjoy in court suggests that judicial unaccountability and judicial dependence on the other "law and order" institutions (*pravookhranitel'nye organy*) were bigger threats to the rule of law in Russia, than interference by federal politicians. The finding seems to back up claims that served as the justification of Putin's judicial reform package of 2001, namely that the Russian judiciary had become "a closed club of judges, closed off from public criticism, public supervision" (Solomon, 2002). The finding also confirms reports that both the Procuracy and the FSB wield significant influence over judicial output. The Procuracy's influence stems

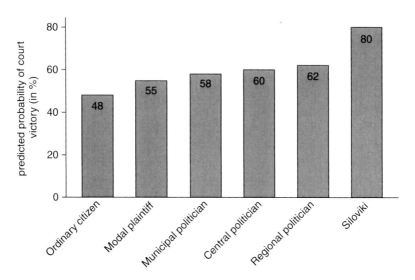

FIGURE 5.3. Predicted win-rates for different sociopolitical groups of Russian plaintiffs.

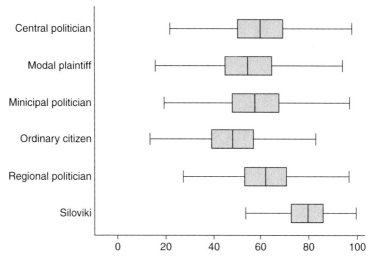

FIGURE 5.4. Predicted win-rates for different sociopolitical groups of Russian plaintiffs (with 95 percent confidence intervals).

from its long-standing mandate of "general supervision" (or *obshchii nadzor*) of legality in the state, which imbues procurators with a sense of superiority over all other jurists. The FSB's influence, besides being a strong historical legacy, is currently perpetuated by the continuing practice of informal FSB vetting of candidates for judicial posts.[7] Finally, Genri Reznik, the head of a leading Moscow law firm with a sizable defamation practice, estimated that the only instances, in which he felt that judges were subject to significant pressure and interference were cases, in which the FSB had a strong and direct interest (Reznik, 2004).

Politicians at different levels of the federal hierarchy also seem to have a slightly higher chance of court victory than the average plaintiff, but none of these differences are either substantively or statistically significant. Regional politicians have the highest win-rate among politicians. This result may not be surprising given that until 2002 regional legislatures controlled the process of granting life tenure to judges and regional executives provided extrabudgetary financing to the cash-strapped courts, which sometimes could not even afford to buy pens and paper with their federal appropriations (Solomon & Foglesong, 2000, pp. 36–42).

The data on plaintiffs' relationship with the regional incumbents allow additional exploration of the link between political competition and judicial independence. Political competition has been much more intense in Russia's regions than in the federal center. Russian governors have had a tough time getting reelected. In the 202 gubernatorial elections that took place in Russia between May 1991 and June 2002, the incumbent governor received a second term at the polls only 67 percent of the time (Akhmedov, Ravichev, & Zhuravskaya, 2002).[8] Traditional political competition theories of judicial independence would predict that regional incumbents will have an interest in providing independent courts to minimize the risks associated with electoral uncertainty. The strategic pressure theory, on the other hand, predicts that while Russian judicial output would be independent from the electorally secure federal center, it would systematically reflect the preferences of electorally insecure regional authorities.

The data again offer evidence in favor of the strategic pressure theory. As the logit model presented earlier indicates and Figure 5.5 illustrates, an association with the regional administration has a significant and substantial effect on defamation trial outcomes. Protégés of the regional administration have a significantly higher probability of court victory than all other plaintiffs. The

---

[7] Whereas no law provides a formal role for the FSB in the selection or appointment of judges, Putin's former colleagues are involved in the process at the presidential approval stage. Since the president signs all decrees for judicial appointments, the FSB reportedly runs a check on all candidates before the decree goes to the president for signing (Skuratov, 2004; Solov'ev, 2006).

[8] By contrast, U.S. governors had a 76 percent reelection rate and U.S. senators had an 85 percent reelection rate between 1980 and 1992 (Squire & Fastnow, 1994, p. 707).

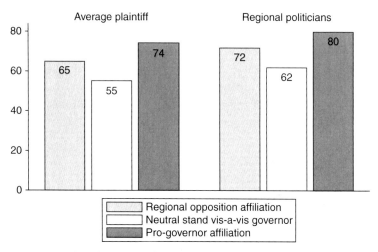

FIGURE 5.5. Predicted win-rates for different types of Russian plaintiffs according to relationship with the regional administration.

data also suggest that regional oppositionists might have a slightly higher win-rate than neutral plaintiffs. While the opposition advantage is not statistically significant, it might exist, because often times regional oppositionists have the federal center behind them. In the Red Belt regions and some of the authoritarian ethnic republics, the oppositionists are associated with the incumbent regime in Moscow. For example, in Kursk and in Voronezh, the main opposition to the communist governors were former FSB generals who had strong support from the Kremlin.

To report the uncertainty associated with these estimates, I simulated the first differences between the predicted probability of court victory for each plaintiff group and the modal plaintiff. Protégés of the regional administration, regardless of whether they hold elected office or not, have a significantly higher probability of winning a defamation lawsuit. Both regional incumbents and other plaintiffs close to the regional administration have a 20 percent higher probability of winning in court than other plaintiffs. The 95 percent confidence interval for this estimate is between 2 and 39 percent (in the case of regional incumbents) and 3 and 37 percent (in the case of other plaintiffs close to the regional government), so the difference is statistically significant.

## CONCLUSION

This systematic analysis of defamation trial outcomes and moral damage awards in Russia and Ukraine goes beyond the examination of suggestive high-profile cases. It also challenges the prediction of traditional political competition theories of judicial independence, which posit that intense competition between incumbents and opposition creates a strong incentive for the regime to provide and respect judicial independence. Certainly Russia's politics in the late 1990s through early 2000s were already less competitive than Ukraine's, yet Russian judicial output appeared to be less dependent on the preferences of politically powerful actors. Incumbent Russian politicians won the defamation lawsuits that they filed much less often than their Ukrainian colleagues did. In addition, in Russia victorious progovernment plaintiffs did not receive larger-than-average moral damage awards, whereas in Ukraine they enjoyed a huge advantage over opposition-affiliated plaintiffs.

These seemingly paradoxical results provide additional empirical support for the strategic pressure theory. In Ukraine where the Kuchma regime was quite vulnerable for the entire period, 1998–2003, winning a defamation lawsuit against an opposition-leaning media outlet became a high-stake affair. The regime sought victory in every case not just to muzzle its critics but also to signal its strength to its opponents in the Rada. By contrast, in Russia, where the Putin regime was feeling increasingly secure after 1999, defamation lawsuits gradually became mundane and routine and the Kremlin did not deem it necessary to interfere in each and every case. Since regional politics remained competitive longer, incumbent governors and their entourage took more interest in defamation cases and exerted pressure on judges in order to rein in critical media.

# 6

# Politicians' Capacity to Pressure the Courts

Institutional theories of judicial independence offer the same prediction for the relative difference in judicial independence in Russia and Ukraine during the late 1990s and 2000s, as the strategic pressure theory. They anticipate that Russia would have a higher level of independent judicial output than Ukraine because it has a more structurally insulated judiciary. The mechanism through which this result is expected to come about is very different, however. The structural insulation theories would claim that institutions constrained Russia's incumbents and made it harder for them to exert pressure on the courts, whereas Ukrainian incumbents were still free to continue in their Soviet ways.

This chapter presents qualitative evidence that the formal institutional structure of the judiciary does not truly constrain Russian politicians. Rather, despite the institutional difference that we observe during the 1990s and 2000s, the actual relationships both within the judicial hierarchy and between the judiciary and the political branches of government are surprisingly similar in Russia and Ukraine. Informal practices, which are a carryover from the Soviet period, appear to be durable and resilient to the challenge of new formal institutions. The chapter describes four interrelated informal mechanisms through which *both* Russian and Ukrainian politicians could impose their preferences on judicial output if they wanted to: (1) the widespread and acceptable practice of ex parte communication; (2) telephone law; (3) the high level of internal dependence within the judiciary; (4) the cozy relationship between the leadership of the judiciary and the Presidential Administration; and (5) the widespread perception among judges that officials in the agencies assigned to provide administrative and technical support for the courts supervise, rather than serve them.

## EX PARTE COMMUNICATION

The formal institutions may have been different in Russia and Ukraine as Chapter 3 argued, but the exact same informal mechanisms for exerting pressure on judges were available to both Russian and Ukrainian incumbents during the late 1990s through early 2000s. The first such mechanism is the practice among judges, lawyers, and prosecutors to engage in ex parte communication (i.e., discussion of cases outside the courtroom). As a result, even though most politicians would probably profess support for judicial independence, they also feel free to talk to judges about individual cases. The more the specifics of a case are discussed outside the courtroom, the more the case is actually decided outside the courtroom. In other words, ex parte communication is a conduit for extrajudicial interference in judicial decision making.

Ex parte communication is a standard practice with long history both in Russia and in Ukraine. Russian and Ukrainian judges readily discuss the specifics of individual cases with litigants or other people with a stake in the outcome of the case. They often do not see this practice as problematic, but as a legitimate information-gathering technique and a service to the population. At a conference sponsored by the Canadian International Development Agency (CIDA) in Shklo, Ukraine, seventy-nine Ukrainian district court chairs, appellate court chairs, arbitrazh court chairs, and regional heads of Union of Judges chapters discussed ways to improve the functioning of courts of general jurisdiction. One presenter's exposé on the importance of minimizing ex parte communication was met with a barrage of criticism from his fellow judges. Judge after judge stood up to protest. A few opposed the proposal on the principled position that they reject any counterproductive attempt to transplant "Western" or common law legal principles in a post-Soviet, civil law environment. Many, however, emphasized that even though they welcomed outside advice on judicial reform, they thought that limiting ex parte communication was neither feasible nor desirable. Judges in Ukraine (as in Russia) were used to holding regular "office hours" during which they would meet with litigants and answer questions (i.e., engage in ex parte communication). Judges felt that these office hours were an essential service that they provided to the community. They emphasized how they save people money routinely by instructing them whether their case has any merit. Once a case had been filed, judges often used the office hours to, in effect, pursue mediation between the sides. And, of course, they would welcome valuable information about a case from any source, as it would help them establish the truth. And establishing the truth is the crux of a judge's mission within the civil law legal tradition, to which both Russia and Ukraine belong (Merryman, 1969).[1]

Evidence of ex parte communication between judges and litigants in specific cases came out of several of the interviews that I conducted in both Russia and Ukraine with SMD candidates who participated in electoral registration lawsuits. The first example is from an interview with S. K., a Communist Party of Ukraine candidate from Crimea. Nine days before the election were to take place, the District Election Commission deregistered S. K. for failing to disclose all his properties. S. K. appealed the DEC decision to the Central Election Commission and filed a petition in a Kyiv district court asking the court to declare explicitly that S. K. did not have possession of the building that the DEC alleged that he owned. The CEC rejected the complaint, so S. K. appealed the CEC decision at the Supreme Court. Just one day before the elections, the Supreme Court of Ukraine denied his appeal. Having exhausted all appeal venues, S. K. could not run in the March 31 election. After the election, when his ownership of the unfortunate building was no longer relevant, the Crimean district court satisfied his petition and declared the sale contract null and void. I asked S. K. why he decided to take his case to the CEC and a Kyiv court, rather than to the Crimean courts first. S. K. explained that he himself and his lawyers consulted numerous times with judges both in Crimea and in Kyiv about the best way to maximize his chances for restoring his registration and acted upon the judges' recommendations (S. K., 2003).

In Russia, a Moscow SMD candidate who unsuccessfully sued to try to deregister a United Russia nominee also reported discussing the particulars of the case with the judge who heard it. S. R. was an ambitious youth organization leader who did not have any ideological disagreement with the party of power, but rather was looking for a way to make a political career. Oddly enough, taking the party of power nominee to court was S. R.'s chosen way of getting noticed and getting political credibility, not with voters, but with party organizers. S. R.'s strategy is reminiscent of the strategy of a software start-up positioning themselves as challengers to Microsoft, when their ultimate goal is to get bought by Microsoft. S. R.'s argument in the lawsuit that he filed with

---

[1]  It bears noting that during the mid-late 2000s, the judicial leaderships in both countries took steps to reduce ex parte communication. The office hours practice has been discontinued in both countries since the mid 2000s, at the urging of international donors pursuing judicial reform projects. In Russia, judicial assistants are now in charge of holding office hours for the populace. Lawyers and members of the public were quite apprehensive about these changes because they feared that only the judge could give them adequate legal advice. Court chairs, however, continue to hold office hours, during which they hear complaints from litigants and lawyers against judges on their court (Solomon, 2010, p. 444).

Moscow City Court was that the UR nominee should be deregistered because many of the advertising materials distributed on his behalf, were not paid for by his election fund. Moscow City Court rejected S. R.'s claim with the motivation that these materials were printed by the party, rather than ordered by the candidate himself and the candidate was, hence, not responsible for what the party did. S. R. did not stop there. His lawyers found some documentation that showed that the UR nominee's signature appeared on an order form for campaign materials. S. R. even found someone from the party, willing to testify to this effect in court, so he planned to appeal the Moscow City Court decision to the Supreme Court. S. R. said that the Moscow City Court judge explained to him and his legal team that the appeal would be rejected on a technicality. The explanation was that the court would not be willing to set a scandalous precedent, which would open the floodgates to similar claims about all UR SMD nominees in districts around the country. Unlike S. K. in Ukraine, S. R. did not follow the judge's recommendations and, nevertheless, filed the appeal. And, as the judge had predicted, the Supreme Court indeed rejected it by refusing to accept additional evidence.

## TELEPHONE LAW

Discussing the particulars of a case outside the courtroom always opens the door to some potential extrajudicial interference in judicial decision making, but once a politician and a judge start discussing the particulars of cases, we may start crossing the line into telephone law. *Telephone law* or *telephone justice* is a channel for politicians to communicate their preferences about the outcome of individual cases to the judges who hear them. Arkadii Vaksberg has claimed to have coined the "telephone law" term in 1986 to describe a supposedly ubiquitous Soviet practice, where Communist Party officials simply called in decisions in individual cases (Leneneva, 2008). Vaksberg actually thinks that the situation has only exacerbated during the post-Soviet period and telephone law has given way to something even more sinister – *Basmannoe pravosudie* (named after Basmannyi district court in Moscow, which decided some of the Khodorkovsky-Yukos cases).

Vaksberg was likely overstating the Soviet case somewhat because such crude and direct extrajudicial interference in judicial decision making as calling judges to tell them how to rule in a specific case does not seem to have been standard practice (Solomon 1996; Huskey, 1992;). Stalin's Soviet Constitution from 1936 contained a guarantee for judicial independence, and, in fact, it was considered improper for Communist Party officials to call judges and offer an opinion on specific cases (Solomon, 1996, p. 291). Thus, the influence of

Communist Party officials on judges was informal and slightly more subtle. It flowed through ex parte communication between local government and party officials and judges, which was seen as completely legitimate. It was legitimate because judges were supposed to be embedded within the local government institutions rather than in a separate branch. Ex parte communication about specific cases was part of the symbiotic relationship between the judiciary and the other branches. It purportedly increased the efficiency of the judiciary in tackling crime and resolving other disputes because it provided judges with "local knowledge," which supposedly helped them reach "the right" decisions (Solomon, 1996, p. 290–7).

The practice of routine ex parte communication between judges and representatives of the other branches of government has survived the collapse of communism and the state, as well as the judicial reform programs that independent Russia and Ukraine both pursued during the 1990s. An incident that took place at a confirmation hearing for judges eligible for life tenure appointments at a meeting of the Rada Committee on Legal Affairs illustrates the subtler manifestations of the close informal relationship between judges and politicians and how it continues to undermine judicial independence today. During the confirmation of a Kyiv district court judge, Nasha Ukraina MP and the current mayor of Kyiv, Leonid Chernovetskii, urged his fellow MPs to think twice before granting this judge life tenure because the judge was purportedly rude and irresponsible. Chernovetskii justified his recommendation by explaining that a couple of years earlier he had left a message for this particular judge asking him to call back so Chernovetskii could explain some circumstances of a case, which would help the judge reach a fair decision. The judge did not return Chernovetskii's call, which both surprised and disappointed the opposition MP. The MP described his disillusionment at the realization that this particular judge was not interested in hearing all sides to a story and thus could not possibly deliver just and well-informed decisions. Chernovetskii has a PhD in law from Ukraine's most prestigious law academy and used to be a law professor at Kyiv's Shevchenko University, so his position hardly stemmed from a low level of legal expertise. Moreover, many of his fellow MPs nodded in agreement or looked indifferent. The one MP who disagreed vociferously with Chernovetskii was Serhii Holovaty, a politician who is well-known for his pro-Western positions.

I do not have systematic data on the frequency of such "courtesy calls" by politicians either for Russia or for Ukraine. Ledeneva (2008) reports 2006 survey data, according to which the majority of Russian judges think that the telephone law is widespread and has a strong influence on judicial decision making. I did, however, use the Chernovetskii story as a vignette in my semi-structured interviews with jurists in both Russia and Ukraine, and everyone expressed confidence that the Soviet-era practice of open ex parte communication about specific cases between judges and politicians endures. Many thought Chernovetskii's call was acceptable insofar as he did not intend to instruct the judge on how to rule, but simply wanted to provide useful information. In other words, even though telephone law is perceived as improper, ex parte communication is perceived as an acceptable practice, even when it involves judges and politicians.

Even if it is perceived as improper, however, telephone law is not shocking, but quite real to both Russian and Ukrainian judges, which suggests that it may be a common practice. For example, Judge Yurii Vasilenko from Kyiv Appellate Court, who opened a criminal case against incumbent President Leonid Kuchma in October 2002, reported receiving many direct calls from politicians. He claimed that Presidential Administration head, Viktor Medvedchuk, called him immediately after hearing of the case to yell at him. So did a member of the Supreme Council of Justice (SCJ) who was the president of the Union of Jurists, and was firmly within Kuchma's political circle. By Vasilenko's account, both callers "warned" him privately that he would likely face criminal prosecution soon (Vasilenko, 2003).

Judge Mykola Zamkovenko, a Kyiv judge who made headlines when he released opposition leader Yuliya Tymoshenko from pretrial detention in April 2001, also echoed Judge Vasilenko's experience. Before he ruled in the Tymoshenko case, he also received warnings in the form of "friendly advice" by friends and acquaintances who were positioned within the Kuchma regime. Although Judge Zamkovenko was not as specific as Judge Vasilenko in naming the sources of telephone law, he did bring up PA head Medvedchuk. Zamkovenko emphasized that he knew Medvedchuk from their law school days together at Kyiv State University and stated that he believed that Medvedchuk had "set him up" by getting him involved in the Tymoshenko case, when he wanted to stay away from it and not take a side (Zamkovenko, 2004). The discussion suggested the participation of high-ranking members of the incumbent regime in individual cases through informal, rather than formal channels.

In Russia, the best example of the telephone law that I heard of involved Mayor Luzhkov's administration. Even though the evidence is more indirect than the Ukrainian one, it also suggests that the lines of communication between judges and politicians about specific cases are wide open. Andrei

Buzin, a Yabloko member of the Moscow City Election Commission (MCEC), told the following story. During the 2001 election campaign for the Moscow City Duma, a vice-mayor of Moscow showed up at a meeting of MCEC unannounced, took the podium, and spoke about why two candidates should be deregistered. The next day, a Moscow City Court judge ruled to take down these same candidates' registration using virtually the same language in explaining the motives. After the campaign was over and Mayor Luzhkov's faction captured a 33/35 majority in the city Duma, the Moscow City Election Commission dominated by Luzhkov supporters demonstrated the mayor's appreciation for the role that Moscow courts played in the race by awarding Moscow City Court chair Ol'ga Egorova with an honorary badge "For Active Contribution to the Elections," first rank (Buzin, 2002)!

## INTERNAL DEPENDENCE IN THE RUSSIAN AND UKRAINIAN JUDICIARIES: HOW SUPERIOR COURT JUDGES INFLUENCE LOWER COURT JUDGES

Communication between politicians and judges about specific cases can be an efficient vehicle for influence or indirect pressure. The practice of providing judges with housing, vacations, and other perks for the duration of their tenure is an even more powerful tool for influencing judicial output. Judges who deliver rulings that anger incumbent politicians can suddenly face eviction or a transfer to another apartment, which in the best-case scenario is a huge hassle. In a diabolical, but admittedly quite ingenious, worst-case scenario that I heard about, a prickly Ukrainian judge found himself living in the same apartment building as a recently released violent criminal whom the judge had put in jail years before (M. V., 2003). Other judges may simply be told that they have to wait for an apartment vacancy and that wait may extend to several years, during which these judges may preside over hundreds of cases in which the regional authorities who provide the housing have a strong interest. For example, Judge Zadorozhnaya in Moscow and Judge Vasilenko in Kyiv both had to sue in order to receive housing. A Moscow judge cited the fact that she owned her apartment as an important determinant of her independent adjudication of cases (Kudeshkina, 2004). In Ukraine, during hearings to recommend candidates for the about-to-be-created administrative court hierarchy, one MP asked each candidate whether he or she owned an apartment in Kyiv. When virtually all candidates said that they did not, the MP expressed concern about their future independence (Legal Affairs Committee Meeting, 2003).

In addition, independent judicial output is severely compromised by the very high level of internal judicial dependence within both the Russian and the Ukrainian judiciary. By internal judicial dependence, I mean the dependence of lower court judges on their superiors within the judiciary's ranks – court chairs and higher courts. Alternatively, the strong hierarchical relationship between lower and higher court judges has been called bureaucratic account-ability – like bureaucrats, judges are not independent decision makers, but are strongly bound by the guidelines and outright interference in their decision making by superiors within the same institution (see, e.g., Di Federico, 1976; Piana, 2010; Solomon, 2010).

The Qualification Commission (QC) hierarchy and the regional chapters of the Union of Judges (i.e., the formal institutions purportedly created to keep control over judicial careers within the judiciary) exemplify the inter-nal dependence phenomenon. Instead of giving rank-and-file judges a voice in the recruitment, appointment, promotion, disciplining, and dismissal of fellow judges, the Qualification Commissions actually serve as monitors for the federal executive of judicial behavior at the district court level. The com-missions do not foster debate but rather implement mandates from higher-ups in the judicial hierarchy. Whereas QCs do not always reach decisions unani-mously, if there is any dissent, it is usually a power struggle between two pow-erful fractions, not debate. The newly elected members take their cue from the more experienced members and vote accordingly.

QCs and Union of Judges chapters are vehicles for vertical accountability and dependence within the judiciary because the process of staffing them is de facto uncompetitive. Judges in both countries reported that court chairs handpick candidates to run for a seat at the qualification commissions and present the lists at the conference where all judges vote. The nominees do not campaign, and there is no debate on the candidacies. Individual judges usually have never heard of the nominees. Rank-and-file judges also virtually never throw their hats in the race. Even if an ordinary judge gets nominated by a colleague, they usually recuse themselves if they do not have their chair's backing. While there is the odd challenger from time to time, such insur-gency candidates never get a majority to vote for them against the candidate picked by the chairs.[2]

That is because court chairs wield great power over the judges on their courts. Chairs control the assignment of cases and distribution of bonuses to individual judges and panels of judges. If they want to harass a judge who does not take orders well they have a variety of options at their disposal. The list of

---

[2]  Interviews with O.K., S. P, V.R. in Russia; V. S., Y. V., M. Z., A. D., V. G. in Ukraine.

options cited by Russian judges is virtually identical to the examples given by Ukrainian judges.

Judges from Moscow City Court talked about the chair's discretion over bonuses, case assignment, and threats with disciplinary measures. Budget proposals contain a certain sum of money for bonuses based on the number of judges who work in the court. In Moscow City Court, for example, there are 150 judges. However, during a given year, maybe 90 of these judges work throughout the year, while the others are on sick leave, maternity leave, or accumulated vacation. This means that their bonuses, which are built into the estimate and thus get appropriated to the court, have to be redistributed among the other judges. The chair has full discretion over how to redistribute this additional bonus and the difference could be quite significant – some judges may receive 12,000 rubles and others can get 70,000 rubles. The court chair also decides who will hear which case and the practice is to give the cases that potentially bring good money in bribes to his or her favorite and most "reliable" judges. Finally, chairs can exert pressure indirectly through off-hand remarks, such as "You are acquitting an awful lot of people lately; are you taking bribes?" or "Why are other people hearing more cases per month than you? Maybe you are wasting too much time granting motions for the defense" (Pashin, 2004; Kudeshkina, 2004).

Several Ukrainian judges cited the same mechanisms for ensuring internal judicial dependence. Court chairs had wide discretion in assigning cases to judges on their court. In addition, court chairs can put a problem judge in panels with two other judges who have personal or ideological differences with the problem judge to neutralize the "trouble maker." Basically in every ruling the problem judge would be the one dissenting opinion, and thus he or she would be voiceless. The chair can use his or her case assignment power to make other judges isolate the trouble maker socially. The chair also determines the size of bonuses and can punish individual judges by giving them smaller bonuses (Vasilenko, 2003; Zamkovenko, 2004).

Just as in Russia, in Ukraine the court chair can also give problem judges smaller bonuses and or even withhold their entire salary. For example, Andrii Fedur, who represented the thirty-seven judges from Donetsk appellate court, reported that the entire criminal chamber simply did not receive salaries for eight months. The official explanation was that the entire budget had been spent on judges traveling around the region, but Fedur was convinced that the wage arrears were collective punishment for the chamber's decision to uphold a politically controversial lower court ruling. In 2002, Slavyansk district court judge Ivan Korchistii acquitted Yurii Veredyuk in the murder of investigative journalist Igor' Aleksandrov. Many believed that the homeless Veredyuk was used to cover up the involvement of the Donetsk regional authorities in the opposition journalist's slaying (Fedur, 2003).

Court chairs comply with directives from higher-ranking judges because they owe their appointment to a higher-standing Qualification Commission, which is in turn staffed with members loyal to the chairs of the higher court level. This well-oiled machine results in a high level of internal dependence within both the Russian and the Ukrainian judiciaries.

Some Russian judges I interviewed claimed that when a case appears sensitive, judges themselves approach the court chair and ask for "guidance" on how to decide the case. If the chair is uncertain about what the "politically correct" decision may be, he or she would discuss the issue higher up the hierarchy (Pashin, 2004; Kudeshkina, 2004). For example, former Prosecutor General Yurii Skuratov, who attempted a run for the Duma in his native Buryatiya, reported that when he appealed the district election commission's refusal to register him in the SMD, the chair of the Supreme Court of Buryatiya traveled all the way to Moscow to consult on how his court was supposed to rule in the case (Skuratov, 2004).

In Ukraine, judges reported that in politically sensitive cases, they usually "receive advice" from their court chair or from procurators or lawyers they know, about how to rule (A. D., 2003). S. K., an SMD candidate in Ukraine claimed that a Crimean judge who was supposed to hear his appeal against a decision of the District Election Commission informed him that he had "received word" directly from Kyiv that S. K. had to be taken out of the race in his Crimea district. Hence, the judge said that it is not "worth" ruling in his favor at the district court level because the decision would be reversed at the next instance (S. K, 2003).

The strong concern that lower court judges have about their decisions being reversed at the higher instance comes from the fact that reversal rates are one of the components of a judge's professional evaluation criteria. Each reversal is considered an "error" by the lower court judge, rather than a disagreement about the interpretation of the law or the facts of the case by two jurists. Thus, high reversal rates are considered a blemish on a judge's record and consequently can hurt a judge's promotion prospects or even get him/her fired.

This is true both in Russia and in Ukraine. For example, Sergei Pashin, one of the main forces behind Russia's judicial reform efforts in the early 1990s, was heavily criticized by his court chair at Moscow City Court for handing out too many acquittals in criminal cases, which were then reversed on appeal by the Supreme Court. His high reversal rate reflected badly on the court (Pashin, 2004; Kudeshkina, 2004). Judge Kudeshkina from Moscow City Court also claimed that if the court chair wants to punish a judge, she can

give the most complicated cases, which increases the likelihood that any decision delivered in such a case would be overturned on appeal. A high reversal
rate makes a judge vulnerable to disciplinary action by the QCs (Kudeshkina,
2004). In Ukraine, Judge Yurii Vasilenko made the same argument almost
word for word. A higher and more complex workload, Vasilenko explained,
increased the likelihood that he would "make a mistake" in one of them.
When I asked how one would know whether any given decision is a mistake or
not, his answer was that it was rather simple – if the decision was reversed on
appeal, it is a mistake. And if a judge makes many mistakes, this is grounds for
disciplinary action by the Qualification Commission (Vasilenko, 2003).

I observed first-hand how important reversal rates are as a component of
the evaluation of judges' professional competence. I attended meetings of the
Rada Committee on Legal Affairs, during which MPs examined judges who
had completed their initial trial term and were now up for confirmation. If
the MPs recommended them for confirmation, the judges would receive life
tenure. The process appeared very different from a U.S. Supreme Court confirmation hearing in the Senate. The process appeared nonpoliticized and
aimed at ascertaining whether the candidate has the necessary qualification
to be a judge. The MPs did not ask any questions that would allow them (or
anyone) to identify the political or ideological positions of the judges. Instead,
the questioning session had the feel of an oral examination of candidates to
the bar. For example, MP Holovaty asked each judge the same question –
he described a hypothetical case and asked the judge which article of the
European Convention on Human Rights was violated in this instance. Another
routine question focused on the judge's reversal rate on appeal. This appeared
to be a central component of a judge's record, because the MPs cited specific
numbers in their questions and repeatedly asked judges with high reversal
rates to explain why they allowed this to happen. The line of questioning and
the answers that the judges gave made it abundantly clear that a high reversal
rate is not a sign of a creative judicial mind or an "activist" judge, but instead
a sign of simple incompetence and lack of professionalism. The only judge
who did not receive confirmation during the hearings that I attended (which,
in effect, means that the Rada committee recommended his removal from the
bench) had two strikes against him: (1) He could not point to any justification
of his high reversal rate, and (2) he had delivered decisions in Russian, rather
than Ukrainian, even though he is required by law to do the latter.

A strong judicial hierarchy and the low internal independence within the
judiciary that comes with it are not unique to Russia and Ukraine. Arguably,
the Russian and Ukrainian experience in this regard is in line with the general
civil law legal tradition to which Russia and Ukraine belong. Studies of other

civil law judiciaries have made similar claims about the low independence of lower court judges from their superiors within the judiciary (see, e.g., Merryman, 1987; Guarnieri & Pederzoli, 2001; Hilbink, 2007).

However, unlike some other civil law judiciaries, which purportedly have a strong professional culture and tradition of being apolitical (see, e.g., Hilbink's book about the Chilean judiciary), both the Russian and the Ukrainian judiciaries are sprouts of the Soviet judiciary, which was hardly apolitical. In fact, Soviet judges' professional mandate was highly political – they were supposed to aid the Communist Party and its subordinate state institutions in the implementation of policies and the creation of the "Soviet man" (Solomon, 1996). Thus, the Ukrainian and Russian post-Soviet judiciaries still operate with an organizational culture that emphasizes a symbiotic relationship with the other branches of government. This heritage facilitates the easy transfer of political goals and mandates from incumbent politicians to the leadership of the judiciary, which then delegates the implementation of these goals down the hierarchy to the lower court judges.

## LINKS BETWEEN THE JUDICIARY'S LEADERSHIP AND THE PRESIDENTIAL ADMINISTRATION

Another piece of the informal institutional puzzle, in addition to the informal practices that facilitate internal dependence within the judiciary, was the existence of various cryptic departments within the Presidential Administration. These departments had a low public profile and no formal mandate but wielded significant influence over judicial careers through the informal connections between them and the highest echelons of the judicial hierarchy.[3] Kuchma's PA had a Department of Interior Policy, a Legal Department, and a Department of Judicial Reform Issues and Relations with the Procuracy and the Judiciary.[4] Interestingly enough, there was virtually no public information about the existence and activities of these departments. The structure of the Presidential Administration is not described in any law, and only Rada MPs, ministers, PA employees, and their assistants have access to a database listing all constituent departments of the PA. According to Ukraine's Minister of Justice in 2003, Aleksandr Lavrinovich, these departments were responsible

---

[3] Actually, the Presidential Administration itself has no formal mandate either in Russia or in Ukraine. It is not mentioned in either Constitution, and no laws have been passed to define its prerogatives, structure, or formal powers. Despite the absence of a legislative framework, the Presidential Administrations in both countries have been very powerful.

[4] In Russian and Ukrainian: *Upravlenie vnutrennoi politiki, Pravovoe upravlenie*, and *Upravlinne z pitan' sudovoi reformi ta z'vyazkiv z organami prokuraturi ta yustitsii.*

for analyzing legislation proposed as part of judicial reforms, advising the president about his position on such issues, and drafting presidential decrees in accordance with the existing laws (Lavrinovich, 2003).

According to former Prosecutor General, and former High Council of Justice member, Viktor Shishkin and others, however, the nontransparent PA departments were actually involved in closely monitoring judicial output and identifying "problem judges" who ruled against the president's interests (Shishkin, 2004). Judge Mykola Zamkovenko also talked about a PA department as a source of telephone law and an institution that generally "keeps an eye" on judicial behavior. In addition, Judge Zamkovenko reported that PA head, Viktor Medvedchuk, actually could influence the allocation of cases to different courts. Judge Zamkovenko believed that Medvedchuk had "set him up" by giving his court the hot potato criminal prosecution of opposition leader and former deputy premier Yuliya Tymoshenko (Zamkovenko, 2004). And, finally, election expert Volodymir Kovtunets argued that a PA department carefully monitored judicial output in electoral disputes (Kovtunets, 2004).

In addition, there were strong informal links between the higher echelons of the judiciary and the Presidential Administration. For example, the circumstances of the November 11, 2002, election of Judge Malyarenko to the position of chairman of the Supreme Court of Ukraine, which I heard unprompted in several interviews (including from a direct participant in the election) illustrate the informal influence that political incumbents seem to exercise in judicial affairs. President Kuchma and the head of his Presidential Administration, Viktor Medvedchuk, reportedly showed up personally to the session, during which the judges were scheduled to elect a new chair. They attended the session even though the president, let alone the head of his administration, did not have any formal role in the Supreme Court chair election. According to Article 128 of the Constitution of Ukraine and Article 42 of the Law of Ukraine on the Court System and the Status of Judges, which were in force at the time, the chair of the Supreme Court is elected through a secret (as opposed to open) vote by the Plenum of the Supreme Court (Constitution of Ukraine, 1995; Law of Ukraine on the Court System and the Status of Judges, 2002). There are, however, no formal rules that prevent the holders of these political offices from physically attending any Supreme Court session. Medvedchuk and Kuchma allegedly asked judges to vote for a specific candidate, Judge Malyarenko, and extolled his suitability for the job. They also, reportedly made two promises – first, not to pursue any measures to decrease the number of Supreme Court judges, and second, to propose to the Rada to raise the salaries of Supreme Court judges. Even though there had been supposedly a different front-runner for the Supreme Court chair position, the judges promptly elected Kuchma and Medvedchuk's proposed candidate, Judge Malyarenko (Y. V., 2003; V. S., 2004; A. V., 2004).

Putin's first Presidential Administration had several analogous components, all created by presidential decree – a State-Legal Department, a Department on Cadres and State Awards, a Commission on the Evaluation of Nominees for Judicial Posts at Federal Courts, a Council on Justice Enhancement Issues, and a vaguely named Department of Affairs, which provides the financial and organizational capacity for all constituent parts of the PA.[5] These institutions ran background checks on all nominees for judicial posts, analyzed legislation that might affect the functioning of the judiciary, and even collected statistics on judicial output, especially on electoral disputes. Although information on the number of employees at the PA departments was not readily available, the institutions seemed to run a massive operation. Judges reported that as part of the PA background check, their employers and even their spouses' and adult children's employers received personal visits by representatives checking for any compromising facts and general "reliability." These individual background checks were allegedly performed by FSB employees, but the information gathered was relayed back to the PA departments (O. K., 2004). It is hard to decide whether to treat this activity as the PA "outsourcing" tasks to the FSB or to interpret it as evidence that the Putin PA was basically run by the FSB. The head of the PA Commission on the Evaluation of Nominees for Judicial Posts at Federal Courts, Viktor Ivanov, was a former deputy head of the FSB in charge of economic security, which further blurred the distinction (President of Russia, 2006).

Regardless of the exact relationship between the PA and the FSB, it appears that these PA departments performed some tasks, which were supposedly at the crux of the mandate of the Qualification Commission system and the Court Department at the Supreme Court system (CDSC). If the PA indeed routinely performed its own fact-finding missions, then it, at best, doubled the work performed by the QCs. At worst, however, the PA departments served as a monitor of the QCs, which would suggest that the QCs were informally dependent on the executive. Even if we do not observe many (or any) cases, in which judicial nominees recommended for appointment by the QCs would be rejected following a PA-conducted background check, this might mean that QCs apprehensive about having their nominees rejected by the president

---

[5] In Russian, *Gosudarstveno-pravovoe upravlenie, Upravlenie po kadrovym voprosam i gosudarst-vennym nagradam, Komissiya po predvaritel'nomu rassmotreniyu kandidatur na dolzhnosti sudei federal'nykh sudov, Sovet po voprosam sovershenstvovaniya pravosudiya,* and *Upravlenie delami.* Information about the make-up and mandate of each institution is available on the President's site: http://president.kremlin.ru.

would try to select only candidates that would be acceptable to the PA. In addition, by collecting court statistics, which, as I have already discussed, are the main method for evaluating judges, the PA departments doubled the work performed by the Court Department hierarchy. As a result, the PA would informally check the work of one more judicial institution and would possess data, which it could then use to trigger disciplinary proceedings against judges, whose judicial records appear to deviate from what is expected. Thus, the PA would be well positioned as an important player in judicial careers, despite the formal structural insulation of the judiciary from the executive.[6]

In addition, the PA departments provide opportunity for informal interaction and ex parte communication about cases between the executive and the judiciary's leadership. The list of members of PA-affiliated commissions read like a "who's who" of the country's top judges and administrators. The chairs of the Supreme Court and the Supreme Arbitrazh Court, the director of the Court Department, and the chairs of the Supreme Qualification Commission and the Union of Judges all sit on these commissions together with the first deputy director of the FSB, the president's representative in the Duma, a member of the Federation Council, and the directors of several other departments within the PA structure.

Yurii Skuratov's registration travails during the 2003 Duma campaign illustrate the prevalence of ex parte communication and the cozy relationship between the Presidential Administration and the Supreme Court leadership. Besides attempting a run in Buryatiya's SMD, Skuratov also registered as a candidate on the federal list of the Party of Pensioners. However, after he was denied registration in Buryatiya for failing to disclose that besides being a department chair at a Moscow university, he was also a professor, Skuratov was also kicked off the federal list. Party of Pensioners Bloc chair Vladimir Kishenin petitioned the Supreme Court to cancel Skuratov's federal list registration because his lies about his employment status purportedly hurt the party's electoral chances. Skuratov argued that Kishenin is "an FSB man," so he was simply following orders by the Presidential Administration. Skuratov's claim seems to be corroborated by Kishenin's other pro-Kremlin and anti-KPRF actions during the 2003 campaign. The focus of the Pensioners' Party

---

[6] Note that this account is based solely on impressionistic evidence that I gathered from interviews with Russian and Ukrainian judges and others involved in judicial affairs. To fully back up these claims, one would need systematic data on the instances of QCs engaging in self-censorship and prematurely dropping nominees who may potentially fail a PA background check or on the instances of PA-initiated attacks on sitting judges that later resulted in formal disciplinary procedures against these judges. Even during the fairly open late 1990s through early 2000s, I could not gain access to this information, even if a paper trail of it existed.

campaign was to allege that KPRF leader Zyuganov had financial ties to exiled oligarch Boris Berezovskii, as well as expose Berezovskii's alleged financing of Chechen terrorists (Skuratov, 2004). Skuratov argued that the Kishenin petition should not have been heard at all because it had procedural errors (the law requires that an authorized person, rather than the chair of the party file any petitions). In fact, according to Skuratov, his sources at the Supreme Court had told him that the judge who was assigned to the case was going to dismiss it without a hearing. However, those same sources later informed Skuratov that Presidential Administration deputy head Vladislav Surkov spoke personally to Supreme Court chairman Vyacheslav Lebedev about the need to keep Skuratov out of the Duma race. The next day, Judge Lebedev reassigned the case to a close friend, Judge Nikolai Romanenkov, and Romanenkov not only decided to hear the case, but also ruled in favor of Kishenin and against Skuratov. A panel of three judges later upheld Romanenkov's decision at the cassation stage (Skuratov, 2004).

There are, of course, two sides to every story. I also interviewed one of the Supreme Court judges who had heard Skuratov's case. The judge argued that Skuratov had indeed lied to the voters. In the judge's recollection, Skuratov had misled voters that he was a full-time professor, while in reality he was a part-time adjunct professor. In addition, the judge argued that Skuratov had an inflated ego and believed that the Presidential Administration was out to get him, when in reality the president could care less whether Skuratov had a Duma seat or not. Therefore, the judge rejected Skuratov's claims that the Presidential Administration interfered in this case (Anonymous, 2006). The judge may well be right that Skuratov's application was technically in violation of electoral registration application guidelines. He may even be right that Skuratov may have had an inflated image of his own importance. Both of these issues are beside the point, however. What I think is striking in the judge's account of the Skuratov case was the argument that Skuratov was not worthy of a PA intervention. The judge did not reject outright the proposition that the PA intervenes in Supreme Court cases or whether it makes its position known to Supreme Court judges. Why would a Supreme Court judge know whether the PA had an opinion about an individual litigant and what it was?

## SUPPORTING AGENCIES AS SUPERVISORS, RATHER THAN ASSISTANTS

Finally, judicial independence may have been compromised in both countries by the very agencies assigned to provide administrative and technical support for the courts. Qualitative data that I gathered through semistructured interviews with Russian and Ukrainian judges, as well as participant observation provides evidence that, informally, both agencies used carrots and sticks to maximize judicial compliance. The majority of Russian and Ukrainian judges that I interviewed said they perceived the role of the two administrative and technical support institutions (called the Court Department of the Supreme Court in Russia and the State Court Administration in Ukraine) more as supervisory, than as supporting. Those who did not use the word "supervisory" still reported that the supporting agency officials could help or hurt judges if they wanted to.[7]

The Russian CDSC was established in 1999 as the institution in charge of securing the day-to-day operations of the courts. Its responsibilities include (1) drawing up the lists of candidates for judges; (2) organizing and providing logistical help to the judicial examination commissions; (3) keeping court statistics and archives; (4) dealing with the financing of the courts and the various judicial organizations (i.e., QCs, Union of Judges, etc.); (5) organizing procurement for the courts (e.g., supplying judges with everything from pen and paper to computers to light bulbs); (6) facilitating the provision of all services that judges are entitled to – housing, vacations, medical coverage, etc; (7) managing and disbursing the judiciary's budget (Sudebnyi Departament pri Verkhovnom Sude Rossiiskoi Federatsii, 2010). The CDSC is firmly situated within the judiciary as its director is appointed and dismissed by the Chairman of the Supreme Court with the consent of the Council of Judges (Law of the Russian Federation on the Judicial System, Art. 31.2; Law of the Russian Federation on the Court Department at the Supreme Court, Art. 8.1). He reports on the activities of the CDSC to the Congress of Judges, a meeting of all judges held every four years (Gusev, 2008). Thus, on paper, the CDSC and its chapters in the regions serve judges.

It appears, however, that the CDSC structure also provided another institutional mechanism, through which the higher echelons of the Russian judiciary can relay pressure to the lower echelons. It can play the role of a conduit for the flow of influence from top to bottom. In Russia, I arranged a meeting at the CDSC to obtain statistical information about defamation and electoral disputes. I was invited to wait for the head of the statistical department in the office of the director of the international cooperation department. As I arrived, a court chair from Kaluga region was wrapping up his visit. Both the judge and I had brought gifts for the director. However, while I gave my host a

---

[7]  I interviewed nineteen judges from sixteen different Ukrainian provinces and six judges from three provinces in Russia.

three-dollar university seal pen, the judge had brought a hand-woven tapestry portrait of the director in a procurator's uniform!

In Ukraine, the Kuchma administration established the State Court Administration ostensibly to provide technical and administrative support to the courts. Unlike the Russian CDSC, however, the SCA was part of the executive, rather than the judiciary. As a result, it was perhaps an even more straightforward conduit of influence from politicians to judges. The SCA could influence district court judges through their control over budget disbursement and logistics. A Ukrainian court chair described the following mechanisms. First, the SCA developed the cadre plans for each district court and the chair was unhappy that the local SCA chapter had decided to allocate money for hiring eight cleaners, when the court really needed a computer tech support specialist. The chair called the SCA and demanded that they amend the plan to better reflect the court's needs. Instead of implementing the judge's suggestion, the SCA leadership decided to show who was in charge and started sabotaging the chair's requests. For example, when the chair asked for toner, it took the SCA three weeks to wire over the money. During these three weeks, the price of toner had changed slightly, so the SCA asked the chair to file a new application for funds. The chair reported feeling like a beggar every time he had to approach the SCA for funds. Finally, besides being in charge of organizational logistics at the courts, both the CDSC and the SCA controlled such perks as trips abroad, subsidized vacations, access to rehabilitation centers, and conference travel (A. D., 2003).

At the Canadian-sponsored conference, which I attended at a mountain retreat managed by SCA, the head of the SCA, Volodymir Karaban', carried himself as the highest-ranked official, even though the group of judges included Supreme Court and Supreme Economic Court justices and the chairs of all appellate and appellate economic courts in the country. Karaban's air of superiority became particularly obvious when he chaired a discussion that followed a presentation by the director of the court administration at an Edmonton court. The judges asked a couple of questions about judicial salaries, but then interest in the speaker waned. A few judges began to talk softly to each other and soon the room was buzzing with various conversations. It looked like everybody was ready for an early coffee break. Visibly embarrassed that the foreign guest would be offended by the lack of interest, Karaban' scolded the judges with a tone usually reserved for students. After his remark, several judges eagerly raised their hands and asked perfunctory questions. During the coffee break, my roommate – a court chair and the head of her region's chapter of the Union of Judges – worried that Karaban' would be unhappy with the judges' performance during the conference. I asked her why she cared. She gave me a puzzled look and then mumbled something about a different set of judges being invited to the next event, also to be held at a beautiful retreat.

## IMPLICATIONS FOR JUDICIAL INDEPENDENCE THEORIES

The qualitative evidence discussed in this chapter suggests that despite the introduction of formal institutions aimed at protecting the Russian and Ukrainian judiciaries from outside interference in their affairs, politicians in both countries could still influence judicial output. Through various informal practices, motivated politicians could interfere in individual court cases and punish judges for delivering decisions not to their liking. In Russia, the Kremlin could impose its preferences on individual case outcomes through the following informal mechanism – the Kremlin's position would be communicated to the higher echelons of the judiciary through the close informal ties between politicians and the judiciary's leadership, then these preferences would get passed down to the lower courts through the highly effective hierarchical relationship within the judiciary. In Ukraine, incumbent politicians had the same tools at their disposal and, additionally, could provide carrots and sticks to judges directly through the SCA, which was part of the executive. In short, both Russian and Ukrainian politicians had the capacity to subordinate the courts and judges in both countries were aware of this reality.

This finding suggests that the institutional theories of judicial independence have a hard time explaining the realities of judicial-executive relations in Russia and Ukraine. The formal institutions adopted during the 1990s to try to separate the judiciary from the other branches of government are undermined by the continuation of informal practices. Motivated politicians can easily circumvent the structural insulation measures. In addition, the small differences that we observed in the level of independent judicial output in Russia and Ukraine cannot be attributed to the higher structural insulation of the judiciary in Russia. The formal concentration of the power to manage judicial careers within the judiciary, which distinguished Russia from Ukraine, has not made it significantly harder for Russian politicians to lean on the courts.

These findings suggest that judicial independence is unlikely to come about through institutional engineering, especially in the short term. Independence-fostering formal institutions may trigger the expected response in behavior if they are introduced in a brand new system, but they virtually never are. Even in new states, like Russia and Ukraine in 1991, the new judicial institutions that were adopted, were superimposed on a rich and long legal tradition.

The Soviet judicial experience was not erased with the collapse of the Soviet Union. In fact, most of the judges sitting on the bench in independent Russia and Ukraine during the 1990s and 2000s were educated and socialized within the ranks of the Soviet judiciary. Hence, the survival of the informal institutions and practices described in this chapter.

The interview data reported in this chapter also shows that neither Ukrainian, nor Russian judges felt particularly independent from politicians. They knew that incumbent politicians had a whole set of levers of influence. The question is how often these levers were activated and under what circumstances. When did politicians choose to actively lean on the courts, and when did they simply lurk in the background and leave the judiciary to its own devices? The next chapter deals with this question.

# 7

## Politicians' Willingness to Pressure the Courts, 1998–2004 and Beyond

The *strategic pressure theory* predicts that Russian incumbents would pressure the courts less often than Ukrainian incumbents, and Chapters 4 and 5 provide quantitative evidence that bears out the prediction. Chapter 6 argued that the Russian-Ukrainian difference cannot be attributed to the slightly more insulated Russian judiciary. The question that this chapter tackles is whether the difference can be attributed specifically to the higher level of political competition in Ukraine during the period under study – 1998–2004. The chapter provides qualitative data from semistructured interviews with judges, lawyers, and litigants that illustrate the theoretical mechanisms of the strategic pressure theory.

I argue that during the period under study, the electorally secure Russian incumbents could afford to (and did) let some lower-profile cases go against their preferences. Ukrainian incumbents, on the other hand, were apprehensive about the effect of court losses on their chances of retaining power, so they interfered forcefully even in lower-profile cases. I describe examples of similar situations, in which Russian and Ukrainian politicians reacted differently – the former with indifference, the latter with swift revenge. This contrast showcases the higher level of politicization of justice in Ukraine. Finally, I briefly discuss judicial politics developments after 2004 and their implications for testing the predictions of the strategic pressure theory.

### A TALE OF TWO MUNICIPAL ELECTIONS

The first comparison focuses on two municipal council elections – in Moscow in March 2004 and in Kharkiv in April 2002. It is important to note that the contexts in which the two municipal elections took place were very different. Ukrainian politics in 2002 were highly competitive, and the municipal election coincided with the hotly contested Rada election. By contrast, the level of political competition both at the federal level and at the regional level in Moscow in March–April 2004, was very low. Putin had just scored a resounding reelection victory in the March 2004 presidential election and Mayor Luzhkov's political machine was just as dominant at the regional level in Moscow.

In both elections, predictably, some opposition candidates went to court to defend their electoral rights. The strategic pressure theory suggests that the different levels of political competition would produce different levels of politicization of these cases and ultimately different levels of independent judicial output. Here, however, I focus not on the systematic analysis of the outcomes of the court cases but on the judicial decision-making process that produces these outcomes, as well as the ramifications of the outcomes for judge's careers. I look specifically at cases associated with each election where the opposition candidates achieved victory in court. How was this victory achieved? What was the incumbent regime's position and behavior in each case? The goal is to determine whether the higher level of political competition in Ukraine produced a higher level of politicization of the judicial decision-making process – whether the incumbent regime attempted to intervene in these cases and how judges responded.

The Moscow cases stem from the March 2004 multimandate elections for the city's municipal councils. Candidates backed by United Russia and Mayor Luzhkov's administration swept to victory in most districts. In several districts, however, opposition candidates successfully used the courts to defend their electoral rights. Several unsuccessful opposition candidates charged that the vote had been falsified and petitioned the courts to overturn the results. In Strogino's district #5, the third-place vote-getter – a KPRF candidate named V. Yu. Molochkov – filed a complaint that he, rather than his rival T. S. Piryazeva had come in second in the race. Strogino's district #5 had two mandates, which meant that the top two vote-getters would receive seats on the municipal council. Molochkov had obtained copies of the official vote tally from all Polling Station Election Commissions (PSECs) in the district, tabulated the results of these documents, and compared them to the official vote tally published by the Territorial Election Commission (TEC). The TEC results showed him in third place, but the PSEC results showed him in second place. Further investigation into the discrepancy suggested that two of the PSEC protocols were falsified at the TEC. Thus, the KPRF candidate, Molochkov, went to court to seek the overturn of the election results and victory in court would translate into a municipal seat for the KPRF. Even though both the procurator and the TEC representatives argued that the case should be dismissed, on March 29 Judge Ol'ga Grigor'eva from Khoroshevskii district court, ruled in favor of the plaintiff and canceled the results in district #5 (Buzin, 2005, p. 55). Over the next few months, two more Moscow district court judges sided with opposition candidates and overturned election results. In May, Judge Inga Smotrichenko from Kuntsevskii district court overturned the results in Krylatskoe district #4, satisfying a complaint by independent opposition candidate A. Tutov (p. 62). Finally, in July 2004, Khoroshevskii district court Judge Lyudmila Saltykova overturned the results in Strogino's district #4. In that case, the court established that in one of the voting stations, the votes that had been cast "against all" were divided up among two candidates (p. 56).

In each of these three cases, the judge delivered a ruling that went against interests of a litigant associated with the incumbent political regime. I actually learned about these rulings from Andrei Buzin, a leading electoral law expert from Yabloko, who has been involved in hundreds of electoral disputes around the country (Buzin, 2002; 2004). His position, based on his experiences as an election dispute consultant (as opposed to a systematic analysis of case outcomes), is that the level of judicial independence in Russia is very low. In April 2004, I sat down with him for a third interview, and we talked about the Moscow municipal elections, which had just taken place. He was working as a consultant on a number of electoral disputes, and he was very discouraged by what he was observing. He reported that in several cases, judges ignored solid evidence by opposition candidates and dismissed their complaints. Buzin eventually described this evidence in a book that he published in 2005 (Buzin, 2005). In April 2004, however, he had just observed Judge Grigor'eva rule in favor of the KPRF candidate, and I asked him how he can account for this particular decision – was Judge Grigor'eva an ardent KPRF supporter or a quixotic figure who decided to defend Russian citizens' electoral rights? In Buzin's view, Judge Grigor'eva was none of these things – she was simply taken by surprise by the solid evidence presented by the oppositionist litigants. She had no time to consult with higher-ups, and she apparently had not been forewarned by the court chair about the sensitivity of the case. Absent any guidance or signal that political incumbents care about the outcome of this particular case, the judge decided it on the merits. In fact, this is what Buzin thought explained most decisions in favor of opposition candidates in electoral dispute cases. Judges in those cases did not rule against the stated preferences of the incumbent regime.[1] Rather, they ruled on the merits of the case as they perceived them only when they thought the regime was indifferent about the

---

[1]  In Buzin's view, the powerful actor against whose preferences judges almost never rule is not necessarily United Russia, but "чиновничество" or "the bureaucracy."

outcome of the case (Buzin, 2002; 2004). In his book, Buzin offers more context specifically about the 2004 Moscow municipal election. He claims that the Luzhkov administration had opted for a hands-off approach and minimal interference. They purportedly wanted to check how effective each district's leadership would be in managing the elections. The "less experienced" district leaderships, such as Krylatskoe's leadership, dropped the ball and allowed some opposition victories (Buzin, 2005, p. 8). Buzin's logic made perfect sense to the Russian judges I did interview (S. P. and O. K., 2004).

What happened to the Moscow judges after they chose to deliver rulings that went against the interests of the incumbents? All judges survived professionally in the short term. Andrei Buzin argues that Judge Grigor'eva "paid dearly" for her independent behavior, but only states that she no longer works at the court. He does not provide more information, however, and I know of no evidence to link her leaving to the municipal election decisions (Buzin, 2005). Judge Saltykova, on the other hand, has moved up the judicial career ladder and is currently an appellate judge in Moscow City Court's civil collegium (Moskovskii Gorodskoi Sud, 2010). This is a very significant step up in the judicial hierarchy, which is by no means a seniority-driven appointment, as the majority of Russian judges serve their entire careers in one court. Clearly, Judge Saltykova's decision in the Strogino election has not affected her judicial career. I have no information about the professional trajectory of the third judge.[2] It appears, however, that neither judge suffered any professional repercussions immediately following the municipal election results. The municipal election court disputes do not seem to have been highly politicized.

[2] I know of no studies on judges' turnover rate in the Russian courts, and I do not know whether it is high or low and what the probability should be to find a judge at the same court at which they worked six years earlier. However, I checked the professional status of all judges that Buzin mentions in his 2005 book – both those who ruled against the incumbents and those who ruled for the incumbents. The goal was to look for some indirect evidence that would suggest whether ruling against the incumbents has been detrimental to a judge's career or not, or, alternatively, to check whether ruling for the incumbents might have carried professional rewards. Of the three judges that delivered "oppositionist" rulings, two no longer work at the courts where they delivered these decisions (Judge Grigor'eva and Judge Smotrichenko), but there is no information about how they left the bench. One has moved up the career ladder to Moscow City Court (Judge Saltykova). Of the four judges that delivered "pro-incumbent" rulings, two no longer work at the courts where they delivered these decisions, and two remain at their 2004 position. Judge Dedneva from Khamovnicheski district court has moved up the career ladder to Moscow City Court. Judge Petrenko from Zamoskvoretskii district court was deputy chair of the court in 2004, but no longer works there in 2010. Two judges still work at the same courts, but have not climbed the judicial career ladder – Judge Mareeva at Kuntsevskii district court and Judge Dolgova at Gagarisnkii district court. Thus, it does not appear that the 2004 municipal elections have had any demonstrable effect on the careers of the judges who heard electoral disputes.

By contrast, electoral cases associated with the spring 2002 municipal elections in Ukraine, were highly politicized. In April 2002, Kharkiv businessman Aleksandr Davtyan was running for a municipal council seat. Davtyan was in opposition to the incumbent Kharkiv governor, Evgenii Kushnarev, who was in turn a central figure in the Kuchma political coalition. Although Davtyan was neither a member nor a nominee of the opposition *Nasha Ukraina*, it was common knowledge in Kharkiv that he was an oppositionist. It is also important to note that the municipal council deputy position that Davtyan was running for was not particularly powerful. Karkiv's municipal council has ninety-nine members (www.city.kharkov.ua), and municipal deputies do not enjoy immunity (Zadorozhnii, 2004, p. 62).[3] Moreover, in 2002, Kharkiv was politically quite firmly in Kuchma's camp. In other words, although certainly more politically competitive than Moscow, Kharkiv was not about to fall into the hands of Kuchma's opposition. Thus, it does not seem immediately obvious that the municipal election would be such a high-stakes political affair that the center would interfere forcefully in it. But, as the evidence suggests, it did.

On March 7, a fellow municipal candidate named Karen Davtyan petitioned Kievskii district court to deregister Aleksandr Davtyan for providing inaccurate information on his electoral registration application. Given the rarity of the name Davtyan in Kharkiv, it is safe to assume that Karen Davtyan was a "clone" candidate whose sole purpose in running in the municipal elections was to take away votes from "the real" Davtyan. On March 12, the court satisfied the petition and deregistered Aleksandr Davtyan. He immediately appealed the decision both at the higher instance court (the Appellate Court of Kharkiv oblast) and filed a petition of his own for reinstatement at another district court in Kharkiv (Dzerzhinskii district court). On April 25, Judge Mikhail Borodin from the appellate court reversed the lower court's decision and reinstated Davtyan. On April 26, Davtyan won his Dzerzhinski district court case, which was heard by Judge Valerii Fedosenko (Barabash, 2003, pp. 395–9). Aleksandr Davtyan went on to win a seat on the municipal council in the elections held a week later.

What happened to the two judges right after the election illustrates the high level of politicization of the judicial decision-making process. In contrast to the electorally secure Russian incumbents, the electorally insecure

---

[3]  I bring up the issue of deputy immunity because for many Ukrainian and Russian business-people, the main motivation of running for a parliamentary seat was the immunity from prosecution that comes with it. Municipal council deputies do not enjoy such immunity, which makes their position relatively less desirable and powerful.

Ukrainian incumbents were anything but indifferent to the outcomes of the seemingly inconsequential municipal electoral disputes. Almost immediately after Borodin and Fedosenko delivered the rulings, three MPs from Za Edu – Mikhail Dobkin, Dmitrii Svyatash, and Oleg Karatumanov – petitioned the High Council of Justice (HCJ) to investigate the two judges' records. By the end of November, the HCJ completed its inquiry and found that both judges had violated electoral laws and provisions of the civil procedural code and had even falsified court documentation (Goncharenko, 2003). Then in March 2003, the HCJ voted to recommend that the judges be dismissed for violating the judicial oath (Goncharenko, 2003). In April 2003, both judges were fired from their administrative positions by a presidential decree.

The merits of the cases against Judge Borodin and Judge Fedosenko are difficult to assess. The judges may have been corrupt, or they may have been clean. There is reason to believe, however, that both cases would not have been initiated in the first place had Borodin and Fedosenko not committed a political transgression. Judge Borodin certainly was convinced that he was the victim of a political vendetta. He took Anatolii Selivanov, the HCJ member who presented the case for his dismissal, to court arguing that Selivanov had defamed him in press interviews that detailed the judge's alleged document crimes.[4] Borodin's legal counsel in the defamation case was also convinced that Borodin's troubles were directly tied to the municipal election trial and worked pro bono because she was convinced she was standing up against political persecution. According to the lawyer, Judge Borodin had been warned that the repercussions of ruling in favor of Davtyan would be swift and serious (Borodin's counsel, 2004).

Former HCJ member Viktor Shishkin also believed that Borodin was investigated for political reasons. Shishkin explained that during Kuchma's second term the HCJ received thousands of complaints from citizens and groups every year, but only politically salient complaints received serious consideration. If the judge had political protection from the president's circle, proceedings against him or her usually wrapped up without disciplinary action even if HCJ analysts found significant evidence that the allegations against the judge had merit. If, on the other hand, there was a clear signal from the Presidential Administration that a judge should be punished, his or her fate was sealed, regardless of the strength of the allegations (Shishkin, 2004).

---

4    Borodin lost the defamation trial.

Finally, the political nature of the disciplinary action against Judge Borodin was underscored by the fact that on January 29, 2005, a mere week after Yushchenko's presidential inauguration, Mikhail Borodin was reinstated to his post as deputy court chair by a decision of Kyiv's appellate court. The Kyiv judges overturned both Kuchma's presidential decree and the HCJ decision to recommend that Judge Borodin be impeached by the Rada for violating the judicial oath ("Stolichnye sud'i otmenili...," 2005). Later, Judge Borodin was appointed chair of the Khar'kiv Appellate Court by presidential decree issued by President Yushchenko, the leader of Nasha Ukraina, whose candidates Judge Borodin had helped back in 2002 (Vechernii Khar'kov, 2006). Judge Fedosenko has also been reinstated to his position at Dzerzhinskii district court (Vechernii Khar'kov, 2006).

Let us go back to the questions that motivated this focused comparison. How was the opposition victory achieved? What was the incumbent regime's position and behavior in each case? It seems that, in Russia, the judges presiding over the electoral cases calculated that in the absence of an instruction from above, they should decide on the merits. The incumbent regime appeared to have no strong position on the outcome of the Russian cases or, at least, there is no evidence that the regime tried to communicate any preferences to the presiding judges. In other words, in Russia, the opposition scored these victories primarily due to the indifference of the political incumbents. The level of politicization of these electoral cases was low.

By contrast, in Ukraine, the judges presiding over the electoral cases appear to have received unambiguous messages from the regime that they should rule against the opposition-supported candidate. The incumbent regime seems to have had a very strong preference about the outcome of this case. The judges disregarded these signals and ruled for the opposition at their own peril. The level of politicization of these electoral cases was high. In fact, my semistructured interviews with Ukrainian judges confirmed that electoral cases were highly politicized throughout Ukraine during the highly competitive early 2000s. I asked six judges from various Ukrainian provinces whether they had presided over electoral disputes. Four had and two had not (V. G., O. K, V. G., O. M., P. G., A. P, 2003). The four who had experience with these disputes talked about their high political sensitivity, the position of the presiding judge between a rock and a hard place, and the multiple levers of pressure applied on judges who hear such cases. One of the judges, who had not presided over any electoral cases, noted that he consciously avoided them by always timing his annual vacation to coincide with the critical period of the election campaign (P. G., 2003).

## A TALE OF TWO LAWYERS FOR THE OPPOSITION

A similar contrast between Russia and Ukraine emerges when we consider the experiences of two lawyers – Genri Reznik and Andryi Fedur – who represented opposition figures. It appears that in Russia, the incumbent regime was secure enough to allow some lawyers for the opposition to practice generally free of harassment.[5] In Ukraine, the Kuchma regime's attempts to keep its slipping grip on power meant that not only opposition politicians, but their lawyers felt the heat.

Leading Moscow lawyer Genri Reznik is a member of the Moscow Helsinki Group and has represented many human rights activists (*pravozashchitniki*). He has also represented many Russian oppositionists, including Boris Berezovskii, Vladimir Gusinskii, Anatolii Chubais, and Egor Gaidar. Reznik defended Liberal Russia's leader Mikhail Kodanev, who in March 2004 was convicted for the murder of Duma deputy and fellow Liberal Russia leader, Sergei Yushenkov. Liberal Russia, which was Boris Berezovskii's attempt to retain (or regain?) a foothold in Russian politics, was as oppositionist vis-à-vis the Kremlin as Russian parties got. In 2002, the Ministry of Justice refused to register the party on account of its platform being unacceptable, even though the authors had actually lifted sections of United Russia's platform word for word (Korsunskii, 2004). Finally, although Reznik did not represent the Kremlin's number one enemy, Mikhail Khodorkovsky, he represented Khodorkovsky's close friend and associate, Leonid Nevzlin, in his murder trial (Simakin, 2004).

More importantly, Reznik has gone on the record numerous times with sharp criticism for how the Yukos cases were handled by the investigation, the procuracy, and the courts. He denounced two investigators from the infamous pretrial detention facility "Matrosskaya Tishina" for harassing Khodorkovsky's lawyer Ol'ga Artyukhova (Skrobot, 2004). He blasted the General Procuracy for violating various procedures in the Khodorkovsky case (Boldyrev & Reznik, 2003). He decried the fact that Basmannyi District Court, which heard Yukos-related cases, and Moscow City Court, which heard all appeals against Basmannyi Court decisions, have satisfied every single motion brought forth by the General Procuracy and denied virtually every motion brought forth by the defense. Finally, he explicitly put into words what most critics of the Putin regime thought as the Yukos cases were unfolding:

---

[5]  This discussion is limited to the period until 2005. After Khodorkovsky's conviction in 2005, opposition lawyers (though not Reznik, specifically) and *pravozashchitniki* have suffered serious repercussions.

I posit that the [Nevzlin] case, in principle, has very little to do with law. In this instance, a political task is carried out through criminal law means. Criminal law is being transformed from a means to defend citizens from crimes into a political instrument, a way of governing the country.

Я полагаю, что это дело в принципе к праву имеет отдаленное отношение. В данном случае уголовно-правовыми средствами решается политическая задача. Уголовное право из средства защиты граждан от преступлений превращается в инструмент политики, управления страной. (Sas, 2004)

Yet, when I met with Genri Reznik in 2004, he did not really fit the image of what you would expect from a lawyer for the opposition, practicing in an increasingly closed regime. He had a thriving practice and headed the Moscow City Lawyers College (he still did in 2011). He reported that he had won 105 of the 106 defamation lawsuits that he had litigated (Reznik, 2004). He mingled with the president as a member of the Presidential Administration's Council on Justice Enhancement Issues.

Ukrainian lawyer Andrii Fedur represented a motley group of high-profile clients, all united by one common denominator – a fierce anti-Kuchma stance. Fedur represented former PM and later Kuchma arch-rival, Pavlo Lazarenko who was charged and tried in absentia for fraud. Fedur also represented Georgii Gongadze's mother, Lesya Gongadze. Georgii Gongadze was the editor of an oppositionist online newspaper, *Ukrainska Pravda*, who in 2000 was kidnapped and murdered, most likely for his opposition activities. Gongadze's death motivated the "Ukraine Without Kuchma" movement, which unsuccessfully pressed for Kuchma's resignation. Later on a secret service officer named Mykola Mel'nichenko leaked a series of tapes, which linked Kuchma to Gongadze's murder. Fedur served as Mel'nichenko's lawyer as well.

Fedur also represented Boris Fel'dman, a deputy director of Slavyanskii Bank, who was charged with tax evasion and other fraud charges in 2000 and spent four years in pretrial detention. Fel'dman and Slavyanskii Bank were also known as Yuliya Tymoshenko's bankers, and many believed that their association with Kuchma's major political opponent accounted for the selective prosecution. Fedur appealed Fel'dman's unlawful pretrial detention all the way to the European Court for Human Rights. After the Orange Revolution, Fel'dman finally won his case at the Supreme Court (Ageyev & Fedur, 2011). Fedur also represented Fel'dman as a plaintiff in several civil cases, such as a civil action against the National Tax Administration and against its head Mykola Azarov (currently Ukraine's PM and in the early 2000s a central figure in the Kuchmist camp). Finally, Fedur represented judge Mykola Zamkovenko who was indicted for abuse of office in 2001. More about the Tymoshenko case and Judge Zamkovenko later (Fedur 2003; 2004).

Fedur did not manage to win anything more than a few motions for these clients while Kuchma was president. Moreover, Fedur reported that he received frequent warnings and veiled threats from procurators and politicians that there would be consequences to him personally and professionally from taking on these cases. For example, after he took on the Gongadze case, Fedur received warnings that the procuracy would find a way to open a criminal case against him. In 2002, the admonishers were proven right – Fedur was arrested for driving a stolen car. When he presented documents that he owned the car, the procuracy opened a criminal case, charging Fedur with falsifying the notarized documents that showed that he bought and did not steal his own car. In the course of the trial, Fedur got the investigator to admit on the stand that the documents in question appear to be authentic and that they have been drafted according to all the laws that were in force in 1998 when the car was bought. However, the procuracy refused to close the case, thus making it possible for Procurator General Svyatoslav Piskun to claim in interviews that Fedur was still under investigation and the case against him was stalled simply for lack of sufficient evidence. Fedur sued Piskun for defamation but lost the case in Pecherskii district court, the court formerly chaired by his client Mykola Zamkovenko (Fedur, 2003).

In short, Andrii Fedur's experience with high-profile cases is very different from Genri Reznik's. It seems that the politicization of justice was so high in Ukraine during the early-mid 2000s that the regime monitored and interfered in the professional activity, not only of judges, but also of lawyers. Each case with political ramifications was perceived as important and consequential for the power balance between the opposition and the regime. As a result, the regime intervened forcefully, using all informal mechanisms, inherited from the Soviet period, to circumvent the new formal institutions, established in the post-Soviet period. In other words, Ukraine's higher level of political competition seems to have produced an incentive for politicians to limit independent judicial output as the strategic pressure theory predicts, rather than an incentive for politicians to bolster judicial independence, as the traditional political competition theories posit.

## TALES OF MAVERICK JUDGES

Finally, I discuss three high-profile cases, in which Ukrainian judges appeared to stand up to the incumbent Kuchma regime and demonstrate independence, in contrast to their Russian colleagues. Before the December 3, 2004,

Supreme Court ruling, which effectively ended the Orange Revolution in a resounding victory for the opposition Orange coalition, two Ukrainian lower court judges famously ruled against the preferences of the Kuchma regime. In the spring of 2001, Judge Mykola Zamkovenko, then the chair of Kyiv's Pecherskii district court, became a household name when he presided over the criminal prosecution against former deputy premier, opposition leader, and "gas princess" Yuliya Tymoshenko (Rudenko, 2001). Tymoshenko was arrested in the spring of 2001 and charged with embezzlement and facilitating the contraband of Russian gas. She was put in a provincial pretrial detention facility, which, she later said, was a horrifying experience. This move by the Kuchma regime was widely interpreted as the Ukrainian president taking cue from Putin's "handling" of the Russian oligarchs (Berezovskii and Gusinskii) in order to sideline them from politics (Mostovaya, 2001). However, Kuchma failed to destroy his political opponent through the courts. Yuliya Tymoshenko spent only forty-two days in pretrial detention and on April 7, 2001, Judge Zamkovenko delivered a decision to release her from pretrial detention. Once she was out of jail, the case against her dragged on but ultimately unraveled. On October 14, 2002, another Kyiv judge, Judge Yurii Vasilenko from Kyiv Appellate Court, tried to deliver an even more direct blow to the Kuchma regime. He opened a criminal investigation against incumbent President Kuchma on some very serious charges, including abuse of office, embezzlement, wasteful spending of government funds, bribe-taking, contraband, forceful confinement of a person, kidnapping, attempted murder, and illegal use of wiretapping. The most serious charges carried a fifteen-year prison sentence (Rudenko, 2002). The majority of the charges stemmed from the information contained on the notorious Mel'nichenko tapes.[6] Even though the case was dismissed by the Supreme Court within a couple of months, the very fact that Judge Vasilenko opened the case may be seen as a sign of judicial independence. But is it?

---

[6]  It is important to note that what Judge Vasilenko did was rather unorthodox. He started a criminal case by issuing a statement (*postanovlenie*) that opens a criminal investigation. This is the very first stage of a criminal case, but it is usually taken by the procuracy after it receives enough evidence of wrong doing. The evidence in this case was contained in a petition (*zayavlenie*) filed by several opposition MPs. In effect, the judge opened a criminal case without the consent of the procuracy, which is supposed to prosecute the case. Vasilenko explained that his decision was based on Article 97 of the Criminal Code of Ukraine, which distinguishes between the court as an actor and the individual judge as an official (*dolzhnostnoe litso*). Vasilenko interpreted Article 97 as requiring any official (including a judge) to open a criminal case when faced with evidence of criminal activity. This appears to be a somewhat tenuous justification, which effectively extends the power to open criminal cases beyond the procuracy and to the court.

Rather than boost his sense of personal independence, the intense political rivalry between the opposition and the regime, Zamkovenko reported, put him between a rock and a hard place and made him very vulnerable. Rather than pull back from the judicial process, both the opposition and the regime tried to mobilize all resources available to them to exert pressure on the judge presiding in the case in order to force him to take their side. The opposition accused him in his own courtroom of propresidential bias, Tymoshenko's counsel yelled at him during hearings, and they used the opposition media (Kontinent newspaper and Radio Liberty) to lob ad hominem attacks against him. The regime, on the other hand, sent ample off-the-record warnings to Zamkovenko that releasing Tymoshenko from pretrial detention would be the end of his judicial career (Zamkovenko, 2004).

The Tymoshenko case indeed proved to be fateful for Judge Zamkovenko. The judge expected retribution by the regime; however, the swiftness and force of the regime's reaction took him by surprise. In fact, in later media interviews, Zamkovenko has openly said that he regrets taking the decision that he did as his life would have been much simpler had he not released Tymoshenko from jail (Kovalskii, 2007). Within a couple of months of the ruling, Zamkovenko went from a court chair and a leading jurist[7] to being unemployed and indicted on criminal charges. Zamkovenko claimed that once the Kuchma regime decided to pounce on him, there was very little he could do to defend himself. He just watched helplessly as his former colleagues, themselves under immense informal pressure, scurried to provide the Supreme Council of Justice (SCJ) with the made-up evidence and motives it needed in order to fire him (Zamkovenko, 2004). Indeed, immediately after the Tymoshenko case ruling, the SCJ started disciplinary proceedings against Judge Zamkovenko for "actions that violated the judicial oath of office." In June 2001, the SCJ sent its recommendation to the president and on July 24, President Kuchma issued a decree that removed Judge Zamkovenko both from his position as court chair and from the bench altogether.[8] Moreover, on

---

[7]  Zamkovenko pointed out in my interview with him that he was only one of twenty-five people in Ukraine to hold the honorary title of Distinguished Jurist (*zasluzhennyi yurist*) (Zamkovenko, 2004).

[8]  Zamkovenko argued that the presidential decree was illegal, at least partially. The president can indeed fire judges from their administrative positions (i.e., as court chairs) through decree, albeit only after a recommendation from the SJC. However, the president cannot remove judges from the bench, even with an SJC recommendation. This is the prerogative of the Rada, rather than the president. Zamkovenko appears to be correct, as per Article 14.2 of the Law of Ukraine on the Status of Judges (Zamkovenko, 2004).

May 29, the Kyiv procuracy opened a criminal case against Zamkovenko for abuse of office (Ukrainskaya Pravda, 2002).

Yurii Vasilenko's story of intense pressure from the Kuchma regime is quite similar to Zamkovenko's. Judge Vasilenko became famous in the fall of 2002, when he opened a criminal case against President Kuchma, under eleven articles of the Criminal Code of Ukraine. The criminal case did not go very far. Deputy Procurator General Kudryavtsev swiftly filed a complaint at the Supreme Court that Vasilenko is violating the law and is overstepping his powers by opening a criminal case. Before the Supreme Court held any hearings on the case, however, the legal merits of Judge Vasilenko's decision were discussed in detail in the media. A long list of pro-Kuchma politicians and people in leadership positions within the judiciary openly attacked the judge and slammed him as an opposition hack and an incompetent jurist and even made veiled threats. In addition to Medvedchuk and Evdokimov (whom Judge Vasilenko said called him directly), President Kuchma himself, his representative in the Rada Oleksandr Zadorozhnii, Rada Speaker Volodymir Litvyn, Minister of Justice Aleksandr Lavrinovich, Procurator General Svyatoslav Piskun, the chairman of the Rada Committee on Legal Affairs Yurii Karamzin, Rada deputy Aleksandr Bandurko, and other MPs freely doled out legal commentary in the progovernment media on the judge's actions and motivations (Gazeta.ru, 2002). Medvedchuk, rather ironically, called Vasilenko's actions a symptom of *legal nihilism* – a tradition of denying the importance of law. Legal nihilism is commonly bemoaned both in Russia and in Ukraine as a major obstacle to the development of the rule of law, so Medvedchuk's criticism of Vasilenko was damning. Lavrinovich characterized Vasilenko's actions as having no proper justification in the law. Procurator General Piskun perhaps went the farthest in his remarks to the media and came close to openly threatening Vasilenko with retribution. Piskun said that the best-case scenario would be if the judge simply "made a mistake" by opening the case, but if Vasilenko pursued the case intentionally, he would be "held accountable" for his actions (Borovikov, 2002). On December 27, 2002, the Supreme Court, in record speed according to Vasilenko, heard the Procuracy's complaint. The Supreme Court decided to grant the appeal and declare that Vasilenko indeed had overstepped his powers by opening a criminal case (Vasilenko, 2003). A year later, on December 10, 2003, the Constitutional Court decided that the president had immunity from prosecution, so, in fact, no one could open a criminal case against him (Constitutional Court of Ukraine, Decision 19-rp).

Whether or not Judge Vasilenko was on solid legal ground is an important, but perhaps unresolvable, question. It is possible that his interpretation of the Criminal Code was a stretch. It may be fully warranted that the case was so quickly dismissed. Even the SCJ investigation of Judge Vasilenko's record that followed and the push to fire him for violating the judicial oath of office could be seen as a justifiable reaction against a judge overstepping his powers. However, the reaction of the regime to Judge Vasilenko's actions suggests that the Kuchma regime wanted to demonstrate that it can dominate the judiciary. If the criminal case was indeed weak and the Constitution indeed guaranteed the president's immunity from prosecution, then the president had nothing to worry about. Why was it then necessary to rush the appeal through the Supreme Court and to start disciplinary proceedings against the judge almost immediately after he took the decision? It appears that the electorally insecure Kuchma regime did not try to signal a commitment to judicial independence, but rushed to demonstrate that it could still muster the strength to subordinate the judiciary.

## JUDICIAL (IN)DEPENDENCE IN RUSSIA AND UKRAINE, POST-2004

Both the quantitative and the systematic qualitative data analyzed in this book cover the 1998–2004 period, and therefore all the conclusions and arguments that I have made apply specifically to this period and should not be extrapolated into claims about the current situation either in Russia or in Ukraine. While in the late 1990s through early 2000s, Russia and Ukraine appeared to be a more competitive and a less competitive version of the same political regime, in 2011, they may appear to be representatives of two distinct regime types. I argue that in 2011, Ukraine continues to be an emerging democracy and thus the strategic pressure theory can still help us understand the relationship between judges and politicians. Russia, on the other hand, seemed to revert back to authoritarianism around 2004, so the strategic pressure theory may not be applicable anymore. We may need to start looking at judicial politics in today's Russia through the lens of the rule by law literature about the role of courts in authoritarian settings. In this section, I briefly examine the relationship between judges and politicians in both countries since 2004 and the implications of recent developments for the strategic pressure theory that I proposed in this book.

### *Continued Politicization of Justice in Post-Orange Ukraine*

For a while after the Orange Revolution, Ukraine appeared to be moving toward democratic consolidation. Political and civil rights improved significantly. Freedom of the press appeared to flourish, although there was still concern that powerful business interests dominated the media market (Dyczok & Gaman-Golutvina, 2009). Elections between 2006 and 2010 were held without the manipulation and use of administrative resources that characterized previous campaigns (Orenstein & Kalandadze, 2008; Hale, 2010). Indeed, in the late 2000s, observers were optimistic that Ukraine had firmly found a place among the world's democracies (see, e.g., McFaul, 2007; Aslund, 2009; Sasse, 2010). It became the first post-Soviet country outside the Baltics to be ever classified as fully "free" by Freedom House (Freedom House, 2008).

Ukrainian democracy has proven to be fragile, however. Since Viktor Yanukovych's February 2010 election to the presidency, observers have noted significant backsliding in democratic gains (see, e.g., Copsey & Shapovalova, 2010; O'Brien, 2010; Kuzio, 2010, 2011; Haran, 2011). Barely two months after Yanukovych's election, the president's party muscled its way to a parliamentary majority by changing laws and by allegedly pressuring the Constitutional Court into allowing the amendments. Parliamentary procedure laws in place since 2005 prohibited individual MPs from entering a governing coalition. In 2008, the Constitutional Court had upheld the constitutionality of the prohibition, but in April 2010, it in effect reversed itself and allowed the Party of Regions to change the law with the help of deputies elected on other parties' tickets. The Yanukovych administration has also undermined media freedom by appointing oligarchs close to the president to head state institutions that regulate or are major players in the media market, such as the National Television Company of Ukraine. Finally, the Yanukovych administration changed the local election laws in ways that it through would benefit the president's Party of Regions. Yanukovych also moved the scheduled 2010 local elections by several months to give his supporters more time to prepare for them and, it appears, that administrative resources have made a comeback. While Yanukovych still faces vociferous opposition, some have started wondering whether he could emerge as Ukraine's Putin (Haran, 2011). In its 2011 rating of freedom around the world, Freedom House took Ukraine out of the "free" category and put it back into the "partly free" category where it had been before the gains of the Orange Revolution (Puddington, 2011).

Although more research needs to be conducted to back these arguments, it is clear that post-2004 Ukrainian politics have been characterized by great institutional fluidity – the Constitution has been changed several times in very important parts. Ukraine has gone back and forth between presidential and parliamentary forms of government and changes to the electoral system have been frequent and multidirectional. Authoritarian informal practices may or may not have waned some during Yushchenko's term in office, but they appear to be alive and well under the Yanukovych's administration. Ukraine in 2011 gives a sense of déjà vu of the early 2000s that have been the focus of this book's analysis.

Therefore, the strategic pressure theory should continue to be a useful tool for understanding judicial politics in Ukraine today. According to the strategic pressure theory, the intense political competition between the Yanukovych, Tymoshenko, and Yushchenko camps that has characterized the post-2004 era should translate into political pressure on the courts from all sides and a continued high level of politicization of justice. Rather than observing restraint vis-à-vis the courts by politicians who realize that their hold is tenuous, the strategic pressure theory predicts that the insecure incumbents would be mobilizing all their resources to try to use the courts as instruments against political opponents.

And indeed, recent studies report evidence that backs up the predictions of this book's theory. Alexei Trochev (2010) has examined the effects of intense political competition on judicial independence during the Orange period, 2005–2010. He argues, following the strategic pressure theory, that Ukrainian politicians have been leaning on the courts and judicial decision making is highly politicized. Much like their maligned predecessor Leonid Kuchma, incumbent president Viktor Yushchenko and his Orange Coalition ally, Yuliya Tymoshenko, pursued a strategy of engineering the election of friendly judges to leadership positions within both the Constitutional Court and the ordinary judiciary. In 2006, the chairs of both the Constitutional Court and the Supreme Court were close allies of the president and the prime minister (Trochev, 2010, p. 133). Lower court judges who delivered rulings that went against the preferences of powerful political actors suffered swift consequences – they faced disciplinary investigations and summary dismissal, even their entire courts were abolished (Trochev, 2010, p. 134–5). By contrast, lower court judges who had aided the Orange politicians during their oppositionist days appeared to receive significant career boosts during Yushchenko's presidential term. For example, in December 2006, Judge Borodin, the Khar'kiv district court judge who had suffered serious repercussions for ruling in favor of a Nasha Ukraina municipal candidate, was appointed chair of the Khar'kiv Appellate Court by presidential decree (Vechernii Khar'kov, December 16, 2006).

There is even reason to suspect that political interference in the workings of the lower courts intensified, rather than eased up during the Orange period, in comparison to the Kuchma period. A survey of 1024 Ukrainian judges from lower and appellate courts, conducted by the Center of Court Studies in Kyiv, reveal that in 2007, the majority of judges felt that their independence decreased during the Orange period. The retrospective assessment of judicial independence during different periods in Ukraine's post-Soviet development shows that 60 percent perceived their level of independence in 1996–2002 as "satisfactory" and 33 percent thought it was "unsatisfactory." The figures for 2007 are basically reversed – only 35 percent of judges perceived their level of independence as "satisfactory," whereas 57 percent perceived the level as "unsatisfactory" (Alexeeva, 2007, p. 57). The survey was repeated again in 2008 using the same questions. This time the researchers received 1,072 of the 1,200 surveys back – a very high 89 percent response rate (Alexeeva, 2008, p. 47). The results were slightly more nuanced but still reflect the same clear trend – the majority of judges believed that their independence has decreased over time. The "unsatisfactory" assessment increased steadily from 39 percent in 1996–2002 to 51 percent in 2008 and the "satisfactory" assessment decreased steadily from 49 percent in 1996–2002 to 37 percent in 2008 (Alexeeva, 2008, p. 53).

The politicization of justice appears to be reaching new heights under the Yanukovych administration. The prosecution reopened old criminal cases and started new ones against several political opponents. Former Deputy Minister of Justice, Evhen Korniichuk was arrested in December 2010 and charged with abuse of office (Ukraine Investigates, 2010). Former Minister of the Economy, Bohdan Danylyshyn is also under criminal investigation for abuse of office, but has left Ukraine, so the case against him has stalled (Wanted by Police, 2010). Former Minister of the Interior, Yurii Lutsenko, an ardent Yanukovych opponent, has been in jail since December 2010, awaiting trial on charges of abuse of office and embezzlement (Ukraine ex-Interior Minister, 2010). Lutsenko's case, in particular, has raised serious concerns about the politicization of Ukrainian justice. He has been on a hunger strike and in May 2011 the European Court of Human Rights (ECHR) announced that it will start considering Lutsenko's complaint, which is a rather swift decision for the ECHR (European Court, 2011). In June 2011, the European Parliament passed a resolution, which censures the Ukrainian government for apparently using criminal law to achieve political goals (European Parliament, 2011). Finally, as this book goes to press, ex-prime minister Tymoshenko has been convicted on abuse of office charges and sentenced to seven years in prison after what has widely been perceived both within Ukraine and abroad as a highly politicized trial.

More systematic research is necessary to examine the level of judicial independence in post-2004 Ukraine and to verify its level in comparison to previous periods. Even this anecdotal evidence, however, significantly undermines the claim of the traditional political competition theories of judicial independence that politicians who face a realistic chance of electoral defeat would refrain from pressuring the courts. Instead, it bolsters the strategic pressure theory, which predicts that in emerging democracies electoral uncertainty and intense political competition create strong incentives for politicians to try to use the courts as instruments in their struggle for political survival.

### *Russia's Authoritarian Reversal and the Courts: Looking beyond the Khodorkovsky/Yukos Cases*

In contrast to Ukraine, which provides useful ground for further tests of the strategic pressure theory, Russia may no longer be a good test case because it seems to have exited the group of regimes that hover between consolidated authoritarianism and consolidated democracy. There is growing scholarly consensus that, under the second Putin presidential administration and the Medvedev/Putin tandem leadership since 2008, Russia has consolidated an authoritarian regime (see, e.g., McFaul & Stoner-Weiss, 2008; Silitski, 2009; Freedom House, 2010; etc.). Thus, even though current data on politically salient disputes could be collected and some of the analysis presented in this book could be replicated, it is uncertain whether the results and conclusions would provide a systematic test of the strategic pressure theory.

It is hard to pinpoint exactly when Russia's struggling democracy of the 1990s and early 2000s slid back into authoritarianism (Silitski, 2009). Scholars have identified several cornerstones on this path. McFaul and Stoner-Weiss (2008) point to the gradual and incremental weakening of all institutions that could provide a check to the presidency – opposition parties in parliament, regional governments, the independent media, and civil society. This process started with Putin's attack on media oligarchs Boris Berezovsky and Vladimir Gusinsky in 2000, but it was arguably not complete until the mid-late 2000s. Regional government elections were abolished in February 2005. The party law amendments that resulted in the obliteration of the democratic opposition (Yabloko and SPS) were passed in 2005–6 and United Russia took absolute control of parliament in 2007 (Smyth, Lowry, & Wilkening, 2007; Reuter & Remington, 2009). The harassment of NGOs and other civil society organizations also intensified in the mid2000s (Verkhovskii, 2006).

One of the most often cited pieces of evidence that Russia reverted to authoritarianism, used in even the briefest accounts of the process, is the conviction of Russia's richest man, oil oligarch Mikhail Khodorkovsky, in May 2005 and then again in December 2010. Certainly, the Khodorkovsky convictions unambiguously demonstrate the capacity of Russian incumbents to lean on the courts and obtain favorable rulings in cases they care about. However, Khodorkovsky and the dozen or so former Yukos employees who were criminally prosecuted during the mid-late 2000s seem to be the exception, rather than the rule. Boisterous, yet ultimately marginal, oppositionists like Gary Kasparov (and perhaps Boris Nemtsov) have not become subject to serious criminal prosecution, even though the regime could probably put them behind bars if it wanted to. I would argue that the reason for the relative marginalization of the courts as a tool of political competition is that during Putin's second term in office and during the Medvedev-Putin tandem term, the Kremlin has been able to neutralize and sideline political opponents through means other than politicized justice. Yabloko, SPS, and the KPRF have been immobilized by changing electoral and party laws, and regional governors were emasculated by the conversion of their office from elected to appointed. In short, incumbents in Russia's authoritarian regime simply do not need to resort to using the courts to achieve their goals. This incumbent complacency can change very quickly, however. If the protests following the December 4th, 2011 Duma elections turn out to be a harbinger of increased political competition in Russia, the strategic pressure theory predicts that Russia's incumbents will start using the courts more often and the level of politicization of the Russian judiciary would increase.

In routine, lower-profile cases, recent research suggests that Russian courts continue to have some wiggle room. For example, Trochev (2010) shows that citizens who sue state agencies continue to have high win-rates in court and the number of cases keeps increasing exponentially. When Putin took office in 2000, the courts awarded a total of 2.43 billion rubles in damages to individual plaintiffs who sued the state. By 2008, this figure had increased over ten times to 33.2 billion rubles in only two types of cases – wrongful actions committed by state officials and failure of the state to meet contractual obligations (Trochev, 2010, p.1). Hendley (2009) seeks to understand civil case court statistics, which show that Russians use the courts in ever-increasing numbers to resolve disputes. What she finds through focused semistructured interviews with ordinary Russian citizens is the impression that when the state appears to not have an interest in the case, Russian courts can be used as credible tools for resolving disputes, despite other problems such as judicial corruption. According to Hendley, Russian citizens perceive the courts as a necessary evil, rather than an institution to be always avoided and feared (Hendley, 2009, p. 248).

## CONCLUSION

This chapter provided qualitative evidence that electorally secure Russian incumbents did not always use the informal channels for pressuring the judiciary that were available to them during the late-1990s through early 2000s. Electorally vulnerable Ukrainian incumbents, by contrast, took full advantage of the informal opportunities for exerting influence. The qualitative examples complement the quantitative results presented in Chapters 4 and 5 and add empirical support to the strategic pressure theory of judicial independence. They also undermine the conventional wisdom that holds that intense political competition boosts judicial independence.

Anecdotal evidence and recent research on judicial independence in Ukraine confirm the predictions of the strategic pressure theory. Ukraine's sustained intense political competition has resulted in continued willingness on the part of incumbent politicians to lean on the judiciary and attempt to use it as a political weapon. Even if competitive politics produce judicial independence in the long run, it appears that the mechanism is not the one that political insurance theories of judicial independence propose. Rather than reducing politicians' willingness to pressure the courts, sustained politician competition may eventually start eroding politicians' capacity to impose their preferences on the courts. This capacity is likely to erode through increasing levels of strategic defection by judges, rather than by any formal changes in the institutional structure of the judiciary.

# Conclusion: Politicized Justice in Russia, Ukraine, and Beyond

This book examined the variation in judicial independence in Russia and Ukraine during the late 1990s and early 2000s. Since the establishment of the rule of law is the normative beacon for this project, I chose a conceptualization of judicial independence, which is most closely related to the principle of equal protection and responsibility under the law. I defined decisional judicial independence as judicial output that does not systematically reflect the preferences of nonjudicial actors.

The scope of the project was delineated through several analytical choices. The first choice involved focusing on decisional judicial independence from a specific potential principal, namely incumbent politicians. Not only do incumbent politicians boast ample resources through which they can impose their preferences on judicial output, but also their doing so seems unambiguously undesirable. Effective incumbent control of judicial decision making severely undermines the rule of law, which in turn stunts economic growth and enhances injustice. In addition, if courts do not constrain state action by implementing the laws on the books consistently, government accountability declines, and good governance becomes an ephemeral goal.

The second decision was to assess the level of judicial independence in two legal issue areas that are both analytically useful and substantively important. Electoral registration disputes and defamation lawsuits against media outlets are both potentially highly salient to politicians, so by looking specifically at these two types of cases, one can gauge the capacity or willingness of politicians to provide independent courts. Interference should be most tempting in cases where the stakes for incumbent politicians are high (at least potentially). Both types of cases are also central to the functioning and consolidation of democratic regimes as they are at the core of two basic democratic political rights – the right to contest an election and the right to free speech.

The third decision involved moving away from analyses of Supreme Court output that dominate the judicial studies literature and investigating the output of lower courts. The objective was not simply to fill a gap in the literature, but to study the track record of the institutional component of the judiciary that adjudicates the overwhelming number of disputes. The independence of the lower courts is perhaps more important to the majority of societal actors than the independence of the Supreme Court, because relatively few individuals and organizations have the resources to take a case all the way to the highest court. Moreover, supreme courts are usually more political than judicial institutions as a result of the high-profile cases they hear, whereas the lower courts are the main dispute resolution venue. Thus, the output of the lower courts might to be more consequential to the level of the rule of law than is the output of the Supreme Court.

The fourth analytical choice was to examine the lower courts' decisional independence from politicians in emerging democracies. By emerging democracies I mean polities that hold elections to select the incumbents in the executive and the legislative branches of government, but have yet to consolidate a democratic regime. Emerging democracies combine democratic institutions with remnants of authoritarian practices and display high levels of uncertainty about whether the institutional landscape would persist or even whether democracy will be sustained in the long run. The rationale for narrowing the scope of study to emerging democracies is that, following the recent waves of democratization, the majority of regimes around the world fit in this category. If we want to understand the process of generating and sustaining independent courts, we need to delve into the experience of emerging democracies.

I argued that in emerging democracies, incumbents benefit less than their counterparts in consolidated democracies from judicial independence because they often cannot be sure that they would be in politics for the long haul. As a result, future policy control may be worthless, while the current policy control that stems from pressuring the courts may be very valuable. In addition, incumbents willing to leave politics after losing an election can negotiate immunity for themselves and thus minimize the risk of legal harassments through means other than respecting judicial independence. The costs of pressuring the courts are also lower in emerging democracies due to lower institutionalization, a public more accepting of subservient courts, immature free media, and recent, authoritarian-era "know how" on how to circumvent institutional guarantees against meddling. Finally, the benefits of politically subservient courts are higher for incumbents in emerging democracies because these regimes usually provide a "window of opportunity" for amassing power and resources and thus holding on to power is more important to incumbents.

The combination of these factors accounts for the fact that in emerging democracies independent courts are usually the exception rather than the norm. To explain variation within this particular set of regimes, I proposed a new political competition theory of judicial independence. In contrast to traditional judicial independence theories, the strategic pressure theory posited that in emerging democracies political competition hinders rather than promotes judicial independence.

The first reason for this inverse relationship is that weak incumbents in emerging democracies have a stronger incentive to lean on the courts because subservient courts can provide a greater boost to their reelection chances. This is because in contrast to consolidated democracies, emerging democracies have weakly institutionalized party systems by definition. When parties lack well-developed grass-roots organizations, stable financing, and a party label that transcends the name recognition of the leader, a few court decisions can do a whole lot of damage.

The second reason for the negative impact of political competition on the level of judicial independence in emerging democracies is that the costs of applying pressure on the courts seem unrelated to the amount of electoral uncertainty. Informal channels for influencing judicial decision making do not require institutional capacity, which weak incumbents may be short on. In addition, while political competition may increase transparency, it does not necessarily lead to more significant public backlash against meddling incumbents. Rather, the media wars that usually accompany intense rivalry between the incumbents and the opposition often have the inverse effect of reducing popular trust both in the media and the judiciary.

Finally, in emerging democracies, greater political competition fosters a wider trend toward the "politicization of justice." Weak incumbents care about the outcomes of a larger set of cases than strong incumbents because they are more sensitive about small power shifts between them and the opposition. Given the incentive to interfere in every case where they have a stake, this expanded interest motivates incumbents to impose their preferences on a much larger set of disputes. The increase in both the rate and intensity of pressure creates a collective action problem for lower court judges who may wish to resist. The end result is that a larger portion of judicial output systematically reflects the incumbents' preferences. Decisional judicial independence decreases.

The first test of the strategic pressure theory against traditional political competition theories of judicial independence focused on two postcommunist countries, Russia and Ukraine, which were emerging democratic regimes during the late 1990s through early 2000s.[1] The two countries share a very similar historical, legal, economic, and institutional trajectory since the ninth century. Yet they differed significantly when it comes to the two crucial independent variables identified in the judicial independence literature – structural insulation of the judiciary and political competition. Even though Russia went further than Ukraine in establishing institutional safeguards against outside interference in judicial decision making, Ukraine had consistently higher levels of political competition. Traditional political competition theories thus predict a higher level of judicial independence in Ukraine than in Russia. The "strategic pressure" theory and structural insulation theories predict more independent judicial output in Russia than in Ukraine.

To assess the level of decisional judicial independence from politicians in Russia and Ukraine, I proposed a new quantitative measure that is both more reliable and more directly tied to the rule of law than existing measures. The multistage win-rate analysis of decisions is based on comparing the probability of going to court and the probability of winning for different types of plaintiffs according to their political affiliation. This is a rather labor-intensive exercise as it requires collecting extensive background information on individual litigants, but it has significant advantages. Unlike institutional indicators and reputational indices, this measure directly estimates the degree to which politicians succeed in imposing their preferences on judicial output. Moreover, the measure directly captures the equality of litigants under the law, which is a central tenet of the rule-of-law doctrine. Unlike measures based on the government's batting average in court, the multistage measure corrects for the selection bias associated with looking only at trial outcomes, which are not a random sample of the entire universe of disputes in a given legal issue area.

The application of the multistage win-rate analysis measure to electoral registration disputes and defamation disputes suggests that in both legal issue areas Ukrainian judicial output is more reflective of the preferences of incumbent politicians than Russian judicial output. In the run-up to the 2002 Rada election, candidates with a realistic chance of winning a parliamentary seat who were close to the incumbent Kuchma regime were 27 percent more likely to win an electoral registration dispute than opposition-affiliated plaintiffs, ceteris paribus. By contrast, during the 2003 Duma election campaign, viable

---

[1] Obviously, it is important to conduct empirical testing of the strategic pressure theory beyond the Russian and Ukrainian cases. The first results of large-*n* quantitative studies confirm the theory's prediction that intense political competition hinders the rule of law in emerging democracies (Popova, 2010).

Kremlin-backed candidates had a much smaller advantage in court compared to opposition-affiliated plaintiffs – 12 percentage points. The fact that Russian incumbents reportedly used administrative resources as much as Ukrainian incumbents did suggests that the Russian courts also failed to act as watchdogs for electoral rights as they did not punish progovernment candidates for this clear violation of electoral laws.

The analysis of defamation rulings involving media outlets also confirms the predictions of the strategic pressure theory of judicial independence. Russian incumbents and their protégés won the defamation lawsuits that they filed less often than their Ukrainian counterparts did. Russian incumbents lost about 40 percent of the time, but Ukrainian incumbents basically never lost – their predicted win-rate was at 99 percent! In addition, in Russia, victorious progovernment plaintiffs did not receive larger-than-average moral damage awards. Like opposition-affiliated plaintiffs, pro-Kremlin plaintiffs received a paltry median award of US$200. In Ukraine, by contrast, progovernment plaintiffs won three times as much money as opposition-affiliated plaintiffs. At close to US$10,000, the average damage award in Ukraine was a significant constraint for the cash-strapped media.

I also tried to disentangle the strategic pressure theory from the structural insulation theory, which also predicts that Russian judicial output would be less reflective of incumbent politicians' preferences than Ukrainian judicial output. I argue that Russian judicial independence is due more to politicians' indifference toward the courts than to their inability to interfere. Interviews with Russian and Ukrainian judges, litigants, and court administrators reveal that virtually identical informal channels for influencing the judiciary are open to both sets of incumbent politicians. However, the electorally secure Putin administration tended to use them less often than the weak Kuchma regime did.

## PATHWAYS TO INDEPENDENT COURTS?

To conclude, let me go back to the questions with which I started this book: (1) why has the rule of law proven so hard to establish in postauthoritarian settings, despite what appears to be near universal consensus that it is the most desirable legal arrangement? (2) Why are independent courts such a rarity outside of the old consolidated democracies of Western Europe, North America, and Asia? (3) What factors promote the development of independent courts, and what factors undermine this process?

First, legacies matter, but they are not the main factor that explains the rarity of independent courts in emerging democracies. To paraphrase a popular saying, it might be possible to teach an old dog new tricks, but it is hard to make him forget the old ones. Informal practices of telephone law, open and frequent ex parte communication between judges and nonjudicial actors about ongoing cases, and a legacy of low levels of institutional prestige for the judiciary all stay around long after a state has introduced basic democratic political institutions, such as competitive elections and a free press. Thus, even if most people see independent courts and the rule of law as desirable, rational politicians will continue resorting to informal channels for interfering in judicial decision making whenever they have a strong incentive to try to obtain favorable rulings. Legacies, however, do leave room for variation in outcomes. As this book demonstrated, the differences in the level of independent judicial output in Russia and Ukraine are not trivial. While the two states share a common legal legacy and culture, the courts were significantly more politicized and their output significantly less independent in Ukraine than in Russia during the late 1990s and early 2000s.

Second, a strong and independent judiciary cannot be created through institutional engineering. Chapter 6 presented evidence that politicians both in Russia and in Ukraine can easily impose their preferences on the judiciary despite the introduction of best-practices institutions. Both Russia and Ukraine have taken important steps to insulate the judiciary from the other branches of government and, thus, have introduced de jure (or structural) independence. However judges in both countries do not enjoy de facto (or decisional) independence to render decisions without considering and bowing down to the preferences of powerful political actors. This finding adds to the growing literature that is skeptical that there is a simple and straightforward relationship between judicial institutions and judicial behavior. In other words, the rule of law is rare outside the old consolidated democracies, but not because emerging democracies have been reluctant to adopt the necessary laws and institutions that guarantee judicial independence.

Third, the thrust of this book's argument is that in emerging democracies political competition eggs on, rather than restrains, power-hungry politicians. By showing that political competition can have a negative effect on the rule of law, I certainly do not mean to suggest that a country needs to sacrifice democracy in order to attain the rule of law. On the contrary, the implication of this book's argument is that in order for the rule of law to thrive, a country needs more than competitive, unpredictable elections. I caution against the assumption that as long as different political factions compete and cannot wipe each other out, the effects of this struggle for the rule of law will be positive. Political competition alone does not in itself help the establishment of the rule of law. Only in a consolidated democracy will political competition bolster the rule of law.

This brings me to the final practical question of rule-of-law promotion. A particularly successful rule of law promotion strategy has zeroed in on the task of closing some of the informal channels of communication between politicians and judges, which facilitate the continuation of telephone law that seriously undermines judicial independence. Efforts by the Canadian International Development Agency to reduce and "phase out" ex parte communication have had positive impact (Solomon, 2010). However, many of the programs aimed at strengthening the judiciary through budgetary independence and life tenure guarantees are unlikely to have a profound impact on judicial independence. As I attempted to demonstrate in this book, motivated politicians in the institutionally fluid environment of emerging democracies have ample opportunity and capacity to circumvent formal guarantees of judicial independence.

The strategic pressure theory suggests that rule-of-law promoters should aim to reduce the willingness of politicians to lean on the courts rather than to engage in ultimately futile attempts to wipe out their capacity to interfere in judicial decision making. Thus, rather than focus on institutional building within the judiciary, rule-of-law promoters should turn their attention to the development of important democratic institutions, such as an institutionalized party system and a free and independent press. Bolstering these institutions will reduce the level of uncertainty for all political actors and will thus reduce the incentives for incumbents to use the courts as political instruments. As democracies become more entrenched and consolidated, political competition may start bolstering the rule of law, and a virtuous circle may finally materialize.

# Bibliography

267 Spisok kandidatov v deputaty Gosudarstvennoi Dumy Federal'nogo Sobraniia Rossiiskoi Federatsii (2003, December 1). *Novaya Gazeta*. Retrieved 2011 from http://zoom.cikrf.ru/zoom/EdFields.asp?nqr=1&ndoc=2&npg=-1

ABA/CEELI. (2002a). *Judicial Reform Index for Bulgaria*. Sofia: ABA/CEELI.

(2002b). *Judicial Reform Index for Ukraine*. Kyiv: ABA/CEELI.

Abdullaev, N. (2002a, March 19). Novaya Gazeta Facing the Wall. *The St Petersburg Times*.

(2002b, March 19). Novaya Gazeta Fined $1.5 Million for Defamation. *The Moscow Times*.

A. D. (2003). Personal interview.

Ageyev & Fedur, Attorneys at Law. (2011). Delo B. Fel`dmana i Banka Slavyanskii. Retrieved October 21, 2011 from: http://ageyev-fedur.net/mediawiki/index.php

Akhmedov, A., Ravichev, A., & Zhuravskaya, E. (2002). Regional Political Cycles in Russia: New Economic School. Retrieved from http://www.nes.ru/NES10/cd/materials/Zhuravskaya.pdf

Alekseeva, A. (2007). *Monitoryng Nezalezhnosti Suddiv v Ukraini*. Kyiv-Tsentr Suddivskikh Studii.

(2008). *Monitoryng Nezalezhnosti Suddiv v Ukraini*. Kyiv-Poligraf Ekspress.

Amayreh, K. (1999). Domesticating Dissent. *Middle East International*, 597, 22.

Anonymous (2006). Interview with author. Toronto, Canada.

A. P. (2003). Personal Interview.

Appelyatsionnii sud Khar`kovskoi oblasti vozglavil Mikhail Borodin. (2006, December 15). *Vechernii Khar'kov*. Retrieved October 21, 2011 from http://vecherniy.kharkov.ua/news/7984

Artemenkov, I. (2004). Interview with author, April 11. Moscow, Russia.

Aslund, A. (1995). *How Russia Became a Market Economy*. Washington, DC: Brookings Institution.

(2004). The Misguided Blame Game. *Transition Newsletter*, 14/15, 25–6.

(2009). *How Ukraine Became a Market Economy and Democracy*. Washington, DC: Peter Peterson Institute for International Economics.

A. V. (2004). Personal interview.

Barabash, O. (2003). Zbirnyk sudovykh rishen' u spravakh z vyborchyh sporiv na vyborakh 2002 roku deputativ mistsevykh rad ta sil'skykh, selyshtnykh, mis'kykh goliv. Kyiv: Proekt Vybory ta Politychni Protsesy.

175

Barry, D. (Ed.) (1992). *Towards the Rule of Law in Russia?* Armonk, NY, and London: M. E. Sharpe.

Becker, T. (1970). *Comparative Judicial Politics: The Political Functionings of Courts.* Chicago: Rand McNally.

Bergara, M. E., Henisz, W. J., & Spiller, P. T. (1997). Political Institutions and Electric Utility Investment: A Cross-Nation Analysis. *California Management Review*, 40(2), 18–35.

Berine, P. (Ed.). (1992). *Revolution in Law, Contributions to the Development of Soviet Legal Theory, 1917–1938.* Armonk, NY: M. E. Sharpe.

Berman, H. (1963). *Justice in the USSR: An Interpretation of Soviet Law.* Cambridge, MA: Harvard University Press.

Black, B. S., & Tarassova, A. S. (2002). Institutional Reform in Transition: A Case Study of Russia. *Stanford Law School Working Paper*, Stanford Law School.

Bogdanov, V. (2002, March 6). Vashington Uchit Kiev Plyasat' Gopaka. *Rossiiskaya Gazeta.*

Boldyrev, Y., & Reznik, G. (2003, October 26). Litsom k litsu: Svobodnaya Tema. *Radio Svoboda.* Retrieved April 28, 2006, from http://www.svoboda.org/programs/ftf/2003/ftf.102603.asp

Boone, P., & Rodionov, D. (2002). *Rent Seeking in Russia and the CIS.* Moscow: Brunswick UBS Warburg.

Booth, E., & Robbins, J. (2010, September 7). Assessing the impact of campaign finance on party system institutionalization. *Party Politics*, 16 (5), 629–50.

Borodin counsel. (2004). Interview with author, April 28. Kyiv.

Borovikov, S. (2002, October 24). Sud Nad Kuchnioi Ne Budet. *Press Obozrenie.* Retrieved June 24, 2010, from http://press.try.md/item.php?id=21376

Braguinsky, S., & Myerson, R. (2003). Oligarchic Property Rights and Investment. SUNY – Buffalo, University of Chicago.

Brutus. (1787–1788). Anti-Federalist Papers. *New York Journal.*

Bunce. (1993). Uncertainty in Transition: Post-Communist Hungary. *East European Politics and Society*, 7(2), 240–75.

Bunce, V. (1995). Should Transitologists be Grounded? *Slavic Review*, 54(1), 111–27.

Burbank, S. B., & Friedman, B. (Eds.). (2002). *Judicial Independence at the Crossroads: An Interdisciplinary Approach.* Thousand Oaks, CA: Sage Publications.

Burrett, T. (2011). *Television and Presidential Power in Putin's Russia.* New York: Routledge Publishers.

Buzin, A. (2002). Interview with author, August 3. Moscow, Russia.

(2004). Interview with author, April 9. Moscow, Russia.

(2005). Moskovskie munitsipal'nye vqbory 2004 goda: istoriya fal'sifikatsii. Moscow: RDP "Yabloko".

Cabinet of Ministers of Ukraine. (2006). State Court Administration of Ukraine. *Government Portal.* Retrieved May 8, 2006, from http://www.kmu.gov.ua/control/en/publish/article?art_id=16905896&cat_id=73048

Carothers, T. (2002). The End of the Transition Paradigm. *Journal of Democracy*, 13(1), 5–21.

Caslon Analytics. (2005, September). Caslon Analytics Profile: Defamation and the Net. Retrieved April 29, 2006, from http://www.caslon.com.au/defamationprofile11.htm

Cashu, I., & Orenstein, M. (2001). The Pensioners' Court Campaign: Making Law Matter in Russia. *East European Constitutional Review*, 10(4), 67–72.

Chavez, R. B. (2004). The Evolution of Judicial Autonomy in Argentina: Establishing the Rule of Law in an Ultrapresidential System. *Journal of Latin American Studies*, 36, 451–78.

Chernaya, O. (2001, December 22–28). Nablyudatel'. *Zerkalo Nedeli*, 50.

Chua, Y. T. (2002). Democrats and Dictators: Southeast Asia's Uneven Information Landscape. *Development Dialogue*, 1, 22–36.

Civil Chamber of the Supreme Court of Ukraine. Vozmeshchenie Moral'nogo Ushcherba. *Byulleten' Zakonodatel'stvo i Praktika Sredstv Massovoi Informatsii*, 7(9). Retrieved from http://medialaw.ru/publications/zip/national/ua/09/kievo9_13.html

Clark, D. S. (1975). Judicial Protection of the Constitution in Latin America. *Hastings Constitutional Law Quarterly*, 2, 405–42.

Clark, T. D., & Wittrock, J. N. (2005). Presidentialism and the Effect of Electoral Law in Postcommunist Systems: Regime Type Matters. *Comparative Political Studies*, 38(2), 171–88.

Collier, D., & Levitsky, S. (1997). Research Note: Democracy with Adjectives: Conceptual Innovation in Comparative Research. *World Politics*, 49(3), 430–51.

Colton, T. (2000). *Transitional Citizens: Voters and What Influences Them in the New Russia*. Cambridge, MA: Harvard University Press.

Committee of Voters of Ukraine. (2002). Long Term Observation Report on the 2002 Parliamentary Elections March 1 –March 25, 2002. Kyiv: Committee of Voters of Ukraine.

Constitution of the Russian Federation, (1993).

Constitution of Ukraine, (1996).

Constitutional Court of Ukraine, Decision 19-rp. (2003, December 10). Retrieved October 21, 2011, from http://www.ccu.gov.ua/ru/doccatalog/list?currDir=12475

Cooter, R. D., & Ginsburg, T. (1996). Comparative Judicial Discretion: An Empirical Test of Economic Models. *International Review of Law and Economics*, 16(3), 295–313.

Copsey, N., & Shapovalova, N. (2010). The Ukrainian Presidential Election of 2010. *Representation*, 46(2), 211–25.

Council of Europe/Directorate General of Human Rights/Media Division. (2003). Legal Provisions Concerning Defamation, Defamation and Insult: Brief Overview of Related Legislation in Selected European Countries. Strasbourg: Council of Europe.

Crescenzi, M. (1999). Violence and Uncertainty in Transition. *Journal of Conflict Resolution*, 43(2), 192–212.

D'Anieri, P. (2003). Leonid Kuchma and the Personalization of the Ukrainian Presidency. *Problems of Post-Communism*, 50(5), 58–65.

Darden, K. (2001). Blackmail as a Tool of State Domination: Ukraine under Kuchma. *East European Constitutional Review*, 10, 67–72.

Diamond, L. (1996). Is the Third Wave Over? *Journal of Democracy*, 7(3), 20–37.

(2002). Thinking About Hybrid Regimes. *Journal of Democracy*, 13(2), 21–35.

Diamond, L., & Morlino, L. (2004). An Overview. *Journal of Democracy*, 15(4), 20–31.

Di Federico, G. (1976). The Italian Judicial Profession and Its Bureaucratic Setting. *Juridical Review, 21*, 40–55.

Dix, S. (2005). *Breaking with Deference: Supreme Court Politics in Argentina.* Unpublished Book, Yale University, New Haven, CT.

Domingo, P. (2000). Judicial Independence. *Journal of Latin American Studies, 32*, 705–35.

Dyczok, M. (2005). Breaking Through the Information Blockade: Election and Revolution in Ukraine, 2004. *Canadian Slavonic Papers, 47*(3), 241–64.

Dyczok, M., & Gaman-Golutvina, O. (2009). *Media, Democracy, and Freedom: The Post-Communist Experience.* Bern, Switzerland: Peter Land Academic Publishers.

Easter, G. (1997). Preference for Presidentialism: Postcommunist Regime Change in Russia and the NIS. *World Politics, 49*(2), 184–211.

Economist Intelligence Unit. (2002). *Country Report Italy June 2002 Updater.* London.

Elections Canada (2011). How to Become a Candidate. Retrieved October 20, 2011, from http://www.elections.ca/content.aspx?section=vot&dir=yth/inv/can&document=index&lang=e

Eremin, I. (2000). *The Media and the Presidential Elections in Russia 2000.* Moscow, Russia: Human Rights Publishers

ESPN SoccerNet. (2009). Shevchenko Ponders Return to Dynamo Kyiv. Retrieved October 21, 2011, from http://soccernet.espn.go.com/news/story?id=658903&sec=transfers&cc=5901

European Court starts considering Lutesnko's complaint. (2011, May 6). *Kyiv Post.* Retrieved 2011 from http://www.kyivpost.com/news/politics/detail/103776/

European Institute for the Media. (1998). Monitoring Report of the Media Coverage of the March 1998 Parliamentary Elections in Ukraine. *Post-Soviet Media Law and Policy Newsletter.* Retrieved May 1, 2006, from http://www.vii.org/monroe/issue51/election.html

European Parliament Censors Ukraine over Selective Justice. (2011, June 10). *Radio Free Europe/ Radio Liberty.* Retrieved 2011 from http://www.rferl.org/content/european_parliament_censures_ukraine_over_selective_justice/24230781.htm

Fedur, A. (2003). Interview with author, December 12. Kyiv, Ukraine.

(2004). Interview with author, April 17. Kyiv, Ukraine.

Feld, L. P., & Voigt, S. (2003). Economic Growth and Judicial Independence: Cross-Country Evidence Using a New Set of Indicators. *European Journal of Political Economy, 19*(3), 497–527.

Ferejohn, J. (1999). Independent Judges, Dependent Judiciary: Explaining Judicial Independence. *Southern California Law Review, 72*(353), 353–84.

Finkel, J. (2004). Judicial Reform in Argentina in the 1990s: How Electoral Incentives Shape Institutional Change. *Latin American Research Review, 39*(3), 56–80.

(2005). Judicial Reform as Insurance Policy: Mexico in the 1990s. *Latin American Politics and Society, 47*(1), 87–113.

(2008). *Judicial reform as political insurance: Argentina, Peru, and Mexico in the 1990s.* Notre Dame, IN: University of Notre Dame Press.

Fish, S. M. (1997). The Pitfalls of Russian Superpresidentialism. *Current History, 96*(612), 326.

(2005) *Democracy Derailed in Russia: the Failure of Open Politics.* New York: Cambridge University Press.

(2006). Stronger Legislatures, Stronger Democracies. *Journal of Democracy,* 17(1), 5–20.

Fiss, O. M. (1993). The Limits of Judicial Independence. *Inter-American Law Review,* 25(1), 57–76.

Fond Zashchity Glasnosti. (1998). *Ukraina.* Moscow: Fond Zashchity Glasnosti.

Fossato, F. (2001). The Russian Media: From Popularity to Distrust. *Current History,* 100, 343–8.

Freedom House. (2008). *Freedom in the World 2008: The Annual Survey of Political Rights and Civil Liberties.* PA: Rowman & Littlefield Publishers, Inc.

(2010). *Freedom in the World 2010: The Annual Survey of Political Rights and Civil Liberties.* PA: Rowman & Littlefield Publishers, Inc.

Gazeta.ru. (2002, October 17). Kuchma – Eto Dyra v Ukrainskikh Zakonakh. Retrieved June 23, 2010, from http://4vlada.net/vlast/kuchma-eto-dyra-v-ukrainskikh-zakonakh

Gely, R., & Spiller, P. T. (1990). Congressional Control or Judicial Independence: The Determinants of U.S. Supreme Court Labor Relations Decisions, 1949–1988, *International Review of Law and Economics* (Vol. 12): Chicago – Center for Study of Economy and State, University of Chicago – George G. Stigler Center for Study of Economy and State, 1990.

(1992). The Political Economy of Supreme Court Constitutional Decisions: The Case of Roosevelt's Court Packing Plan. *International Review of Law and Economics,* 12(1), 45–67.

Ginsburg, T. (2003). *Judicial Review in New Democracies: Constitutional Courts in Asian Cases.* New York and Cambridge: Cambridge University Press.

Ginsburg, T., & Moustafa, T. (Eds.). (2008). *Rule by law: The Politics of Courts in Authoritarian Regimes.* Cambridge and New York: Cambridge University Press.

Golosov, G. (1999). From Adygeya to Yaroslavl: Factors of Party Development in the Regions of Russia, 1995–1998. *Europe-Asia Studies,* 51(8), 1333–65.

Goncharenko, T. (2003, March 25). Vysshii Sovet Yustitsii: Kadrovye peremeny. *Yuridicheskaya Praktika,* 1, 274–5.

González Casanova, P. (1970). *Democracy in Mexico* (2nd ed.). New York: Oxford University Press.

Gorobets, A. (2002, April 8). V Kirovograde i ryade drugikh gorodov Ukrainy prokhodyat mitingi protesta protiv rezul'tatov vyborov. *Pravda.ru.*

Gorodnichenko, Y., & Grygorenko, Y. (March 01, 2008). Are oligarchs productive? Theory and evidence. *Journal of Comparative Economics,* 36(1), 17–42.

Gotsuenko, E. (2002, June 22–27). Razdor v stane "zaedistov" startuet iz provintsii? *Zerkalo Nedeli,* 23.

Grankin.ru. (2004, March 15). Krasheninnikov Pavel Vladimirovich. *Grankin.ru.* Retrieved May 8, 2006, from http://www.grankin.ru/dosye/ru_bio30.htm

Grazhdanskii Kodeks Rossiiskoi Federatsii (izvlecheniya), (1996, 1997, 1999, 2001, 2002).

Grazhdanskii Kodeks Ukrainy, 2554–12 (1992).

Grinenko, A. (2003). Uzagal'nennya praktiki rozglyadu sudami pozoviv pro vidshkodu-vannya moral'noi shkodi (u tsivil'nomy ta kriminal'nomu provadzhennyakh) po spravakh, rozglyanutikh sudami v 2002 rotsi. Kyiv: Supreme Court of Ukraine.

Guarnieri, C. (2001). Judicial Independence in Latin Countries of Western Europe. In P. H. Russell & D. M. O'Brien (Eds.), *Judicial Independence in the Age of Democracy: Critical Perspectives from Around the World* (pp. 111–30). Charlottesville: University Press of Virginia.

Guarnieri, C., & Pederzoli, P. (2002). *The Power of Judges: A Comparative Study of Courts and Democracy*. Oxford: Oxford University Press.

Guriev, S., & Rachinsky, A. (2005). The Role of Oligarchs in Russian Capitalism. *Journal of Economic Perspectives*, 19(1), 133.

Gusev, A. V. (2008). Otchet General'nogo Direktora Sudebnogo Departamenta A. V. Guseva VII Vserossiiskomu S'ezdu Sudei o Deyatel'nosti Sudebnogo Departamenta pri Verkhovnom Sude Rossiiskoi Federatsii v 2005–2008 godakh. Retrieved June 11, 2010, from http://www.cdep.ru/index.php?id=49&item=148

Haggard, S., & Kaufman, R. R. (1995). *The Political Economy of Democratic Transitions*. Princeton, NJ: Princeton University Press.

Hale, H. E. (2006). *Why Not Parties in Russia? Democracy, Federalism, and the State*. Cambridge and New York: Cambridge University Press.

(2010). The Uses of Divided Power. *Journal of Democracy*, 21(3), 84–98.

Hall, D. J., Stromsen, J. M., & Hoffman, R. B. (2003). Professional Court Administration: The Key to Judicial Independence. *Gestion Judicial y Administration de Tribunales*. Retrieved May 1, 2006, from http://www.cejamericas.org/doc/documentos/daniel-hall5.pdf

Hanson, S. (2007). The Uncertain Future of Russia's Weak State Authoritarianism. *East European Politics & Societies* 21(1), 67–81.

Hanssen, F. A. (2004). Is There a Politically Optimal Level of Judicial Independence? *American Economic Review*, 94(3), 712–29.

Harvesting Heads and other Political Shenanigans Highlight Political Week. (2002, March 14). *Kyiv Post*. Retrieved 2011 from http://www.kyivpost.com/news/nation/detail/10701

Haran, O. (2011, April 1). From Viktor to Viktor: Democracy and Authoritarianism in Ukraine. *Demokratizatsiya*, 19(2), 93–110.

Hasen, R. (2005). Beyond the Margin of Litigation: Reforming U.S. Electoral Administration to Avoid Electoral Meltdown. *Washing and Lee Law Review*, 937, 956–7.

Hayek, F. A. v. (1975). *The Rule of Law*. Menlo Park, CA: Institute for Humane Studies.

Hayo, B., & Voigt, S. (January 01, 2007). Explaining de facto judicial independence. *International Review of Law and Economics*, 27, 3, 269.

Hellman, J. (1998). Winners Take All: The Politics of Partial Reform in Postcommunist Transitions. *World Politics* 50(2), 203–34.

Helmke, G. (2002). The Logic of Strategic Defection: Court-Executive Relations in Argentina under Dictatorship and Democracy. *American Political Science Revie*, 96(2), 291–303.

(2005). *Courts under constraints: judges, generals, and presidents in Argentina*. Cambridge, United Kingdom: Cambridge University Press.

Helmke, G., & Levitsky, S. (2004). Informal Institutions and Comparative Politics: A Research Agenda. *American Journal of Political Science*, 2(4), 725–40.

Helmke, G., & Rosenbluth, F. M. (2009). Regimes and the Rule of Law: Judicial Independence in Comparative Perspective. *Annual Review of Political Science*, 12, 345–366.

Hendley, K. (1996). *Trying to Make Law Matter: Legal Reform and Labor Law in the Soviet Union*. Ann Arbor: University of Michigan Press.

(1997) Legal Development in Post Soviet Russia. *Post-Soviet Affairs* 13(3), 228–251.

(1999). Rewriting the Rules of the Game in Russia: The Neglected Issue of the Demand for Law. *East European Constitutional Review*, 8(4), 89–96.

(2001). "Demand" for Law in Russia: A Mixed Picture. *East European Constitutional Review*, 10(4), 72–8.

(2004). Business Litigation in the Transition: a Portrait of Debt Collection in Russia. *Law and Society Review*, 38(2), 305–48.

(2009). 'Telephone Law' and the 'Rule of Law': The Russian Case. *Hague Journal on the Rule of Law*, 1(2), 241–62.

Herron, E. S. (2002). Mixed Electoral Rules and Party Strategies: Responses to Incentives by Ukraine's Rukh and Russia's Yabloko. *Party Politics*, 8(6), 719–33.

Herron, E. S., & Randazzo, K. A. (2003). The Relationship Between Independence and Judicial Review in Post-Communist Courts. *Journal of Politics*, 65(2), 422–38.

Hilbink, L. (2007). *Judges Beyond Politics in Democracy and Dictatorship: Lessons from Chile*. Cambridge: Cambridge University Press.

Hirschl, R. (2000). The Political Origins of Judicial Empowerment Through Constitutionalization: Lessons from Four Constitutional Revolutions. *Law and Social Inquiry*, 25(1), 91–149.

(2004). *Towards Juristocracy: The Origins and Consequences of the New Constitutionalism*. Cambridge, MA: Harvard University Press.

Hoff, K., & Stiglitz, J. E. (2002). After the Big Bang? Obstacles to the Emergence of the Rule of Law in Post-Communist Societies. *American Economic Review*, 94(3), 753–63.

Hoffman, D. E. (2003). *The Oligarchs: Wealth and Power in the New Russia*. New York: Public Affairs.

Holmes, S. (1993–1994). Superpresidentialism. *East European Constitutional Review*, 2, 123–6.

Howard, M. M. (2003). *The weakness of civil society in post-Communist Europe*. Cambridge: Cambridge University Press.

Howard, R. M., & Carey, H. F. (2004). Is an Independent Judiciary Necessary for Democracy? *Judicature*, 87(6), 284–90.

Hughes, S., & Lawson, C. (2005). The Barriers to Media Opening in Latin America. *Political Communication*, 22(1), 9–25.

Huskey, E. (1992). *Executive Power and Soviet Politics: The Rise and Decline of the Soviet State*. Armonk, NY: M. E. Sharpe.

(1999). *Presidential Power in Russia*. Armonk, NY: M. E. Sharpe.

Iaryczower, M., Spiller, P. T., & Tommasi, M. (2002). Judicial Independence in Unstable Environments, Argentina 1935–98. *American Journal of Political Science*, 46(4), 699–716.

Inclan, S. (2009). Judicial Reform in Mexico: Political Insurance or the Search for Political Legitimacy? *Political Research Quarterly*, 62(4), 753–66.

Institut Regional'nykh Problem. (2002). *Predvybornaya situatsiya v Odesse.* Odessa: Institut Regional'nykh Problem.

Ishchenko, R. (2004, January 16). Chto Budet s 'Rodinoi': Glaz'ev kak Novyi Proekt Kremlya. *Compromat.ru.* Retrieved May 8, 2006, from http://www.compromat.ru/main/glaziev/novproekt.htm

Ishiyama, J. T., & Kennedy, R. (2001). Superpresidentialism and Political Party Development in Russia, Ukraine, Armenia and Kyrgyzstan. *Europe-Asia Studies,* 53(8), 1177–91.

Kapiszewski, D. (2007). *Challenging Decisions: High Courts and Economic Governance in Argentina and Brazil.* Doctoral Dissertation, Political Science, UC Berkley.

Kaufman et al. (2010). The Worldwide Governance Indicators: Metholody and Analytical Issues. *World Bank Policy Research Working Paper No. 5430.*

Kaufman, I. R. (1980). The Essence of Judicial Independence. *Columbia Law Review,* 80(4), 671–701.

Kaufmann, D., Kraay, A., & Mastruzzi, M. (2005, May 2005). Governance Matters IV: Governance Indicators for 1996–2004. *Working Paper Series.* Retrieved May 6, 2006, from http://www.worldbank.org/wbi/governance/pdf/GovMatters_IV_main.pdf

Kaufmann, D., Kraay, A., & Zoido-Lobaton, P. (2000). Governance Matters from Measurement to Action. *Finance and Development,* 37(2), 10–13.

Kistiakovskii, B. (1916) *Sotsial'nyia Nauki i Pravo.* Moskva: Izdanie M. i. S. Sabashnikovyh.

Kitschelt, H. (1995) Formation of Party Cleavages in Post-Communist Democracies: Theoretical Propositions. *Party Politics, 1,* 447–72.

Khodorkovskii, M. (2004, March 29). Krisis Liberalizma v Rossii. *Vedomosti.*

Knack, S., & Keefer, P. (1995). Institutions and Economic Performance: Cross-Country Tests Using Alternative Institutional Measures. *Economics and Politics,* 7(3), 207–27.

Koltsova, O. (2006). *News, Media, and Power in Russia.* New York: Routledge Publishers.

Kornhauser, L. A. (2002). Is Judicial Independence a Useful Concept? In S. B. Burbank & B. Friedman (Eds.), *Judicial Independence at the Crossroads: An Interdisciplinary Approach* (pp. 45–55). Thousand Oaks, CA: Sage Publications.

Korsunskii, V. (2004, March 22). 'Putin vinoven v ubiistve Yushenkova. *Grani.ru.* Retrieved April 28, 2006, from http://www.grani.ru/Politics/Russia/Parties/m.64562.html

Kovalskii, V. (2007, July 31). Nikolai Zamkovenko: "Ne Vypustil by Yulyu na Volyu, Ne Bylo by Khaosa, a Zhil by Ogo-go!". *Stolichnye Novosti,* 27(464). Retrieved June 15, 2010, from http://cn.com.ua/N464/politics/interview/index.html

Kovtunets, V. (2004). Interview with author, April 18. Kyiv, Ukraine.

Krug, P. (1995). Civil Defamation Law and the Press in Russia: Private and Public Interests, the 1995 Civil Code, and the Constitution (Part One), *Cardozo Arts and Entertainment Law Journal,* 13, 847–79.

(1996) Civil Defamation Law and the Press in Russia: Private and Public Interests, the 1995 Civil Code, and the Constitution (Part Two). *Cardozo Arts and Entertainment Law Journal*, 14, 297–342.

Kudeshkina, O. (2004). Interview with author, April 9. Moscow, Russia.

Kuts, D. (2006). Email communication with author, February 11.

Kuzio, T. (2003). The 2002 parliamentary elections in Ukraine: Democratization or authoritarianism?. *The Journal of Communist Studies and Transition Politics*, 19 (2), 24–54.

(2010). Populism in Ukraine in a Comparative European Context. *Problems of Post-Communism*, 57(6), 3–18.

(2011). Political Culture and Democracy, Ukraine as an Immobile State. *East European Politics and Societies*, 25(1), 88–113.

Landes, W. M., & Posner, R. A. (1975). The Independent Judiciary in an Interest-Group Perspective. *Journal of Law and Economics*, 18(3), 875–901.

Larkins, C. M. (1996). Judicial Independence and Democratization: A Theoretical and Conceptual Analysis. *American Journal of Comparative Law*, 44(4), 605.

Lavrinovich, A. (2003). Interview with author, December 14. Kyiv, Ukraine.

Law of the Russian Federation on Mass Media, 2124–1 (1991).

Law of the Russian Federation on the Court Department at the Supreme Court, 7-FZ (1995).

Law of the Russian Federation on the Judicial System, 2869–1 (1992).

Law of the Russian Federation on the Status of Judges, (1993).

Law of Ukraine on the High Council of Justice, 22/98-BP (1998).

Law of Ukraine on the Judicial System, 3018-III (2002).

Law of Ukraine on the Qualifying Commissions, Qualifying Certification, and Responsibility of Judges of the Courts of Ukraine, 2536-III (2001).

Law of Ukraine on the Status of Judges, 2862-XII (1992).

Law on the Election of Deputies of the State Duma of the Federal Assembly of the Russian Federation, 175-FZ (2002).

Law on the Election of People's Deputies of Ukraine, 97-III (297–14) (2002).

Ledeneva, A. (2008). Telephone Justice in Russia. *Post-Soviet Affairs*, 24(4), 324–50.

Levada, Y. A. (2004). Russian Democracy in Eclipse: What the Polls Tell Us. *Journal of Democracy*, 15(3), 43–51.

Levitsky, S., & Way, L. A. (2010) *Competitive Authoritarianism: Hybrid Regimes After the Cold War*. New York: Cambridge University Press.

Linz, J. J., & Stepan, A. C. (1996). *Problems of Democratic Transition and Consolidation: Southern Europe, South America, And Post-Communist Europe*. Baltimore: Johns Hopkins University Press.

Logan, D. (2001). Libel Law in the Trenches: Reflections on Current Data on Libel Litigation. *Virginia Law Review*, 87(3), 503–29.

Lubarev, A. E. (Ed.). (2006).*Rossiiskie Vybory v Kontekste Mezhdunarodnykh Izbiratel'nykh Standartov*. Moscow: Aspect Press.

Lubenskii, A. (2002, July 15). Nikakikh vyborov tam net! Vmesto vyborov – absolyutnaya vakkhanaliya. *Pravda.ru*.

M. V. (2003). Personal interview.

Magalhães, P. C. (1999). The Politics of Judicial Reform in Eastern Europe. *Comparative Politics*, 32(1), 43–62.

Mainwaring, S., O'Donnell, G. A., & Valenzuela, J. S. (1992). *Issues in democratic consolidation: The new South American democracies in comparative perspective.* Notre Dame, IN: Published for the Helen Kellogg Institute for International Studies by University of Notre Dame Press.

Mainwaring, S., & Zoco, E. (2007). Political Sequences and the Stabilization of Interparty Competition. *Party Politics,* 13(2), 155–78.

Maitra, P., & Smyth, R. (2004). Judicial Independence, Judicial Promotion and the Enforcement of Legislative Wealth Transfers – An Empirical Study of the New Zealand High Court. *European Journal of Law and Economics,* 17(2), 209–35.

Marsh, C. (2000). Social Capital and Democracy in Russia. *Communist and Post-Communist Studies,* 33, 183–99.

Marsh, C., & Foese, P. (2004). The State of Freedom in Russia: A Regional Analysis of Freedom of Religion, Media and Markets. *Religion, State and Society,* 32(2), 137–49.

McCubbins, M. D., & Schwartz, T. (1984). Congressional oversight overlooked: police patrols versus fire alarms. *American Journal of Political Science,* 28(1), 165–79.

McFaul, M. (1999). Perils of a Protracted Transition. *Journal of Democracy,* 10(2), 4–18.

(2001). *Russia's Unfinished Revolution.* Ithaca, NY: Cornell University Press.

(2007). Ukraine Imports Democracy: External Influences on the Orange Revolution. *International Security,* 32(2), 45–83.

McFaul, M., & Petrov, N. (2004). Russian Democracy in Eclipse: What the Elections Tell Us. *Journal of Democracy,* 15(3), 20–31.

McFaul, M.,& Stoner-Weiss, K. (2008). Myth of the Authoritarian Model- How Putin's Crackdown Holds Russia Back. *Foreign Affairs,* 87(1), 68–84.

McMann, K., & Petrov, N. (2000). A Survey of Democracy in Russia's Regions. *Post Soviet Geography and Economics,* 41, 155–82.

Merryman, J. H. (1969). The Civil Law Tradition: An Introduction to the Legal Systems of Western Europe and Latin America. Stanford, CA: Stanford University Press.

Mereu, F. (2003, December) Yukos Takes a Bite out of Yabloko's Party List. *The Moscow Times.*

Messick, R. E. (1999, February). Judicial Reform and Economic Development: A Survey of the Issues. *World Bank Research Observer,* 14(1), 117–36.

Molinelli, N. G., Palanza, M. V., & Sin, G. (1999). *Congreso, presidencia y justicia en Argentina: materiales para su estudio* (1st ed.). Buenos Aires: Temas Grupo Editorial.

Moraski, B., & Reisinger, W. (2003). Explaining Electoral Competition across Russia's Regions. *Slavic Review,* 62(2), 278–301.

Moskovskii Gorodskoi Sud. (2010). Sudebnaya Kollegiya po Grazhdanskim Delam Kassatsionnoi Instantsii. Retrieved August 10, 2010, from http://www.mos-gorsud.ru/sud/chief/g2/

Mostovaya, Yu. (2001, April 8). Tymoshenko: V Tyur'me Raz v Sto Khuzhe, Chem Ya Dumala. *Zerkalo Nedeli.* Retrieved from http://korrespondent.net/ukraine/politics/16945-timoshenko-v-tyurme-raz-v-sto-huzhe-chem-ya-dumala

Moustafa, T. (2007). *The Struggle for Constitutional Power: Law, Politics, and Economic Development in Egypt.* New York: Cambridge University Press.

Mycio, M. (2003). Interview with author, November 30. IREX-Promedia, Kyiv, Ukraine.

North, D. C., & Weingast, B. R. (1989). Constitutions and Commitment: The Evolution of Institutions Governing Public Choice in Seventeenth-Century England. *Journal of Economic History*, 49(4), 803–32.

Novaya Gazeta Could Get a Reduced Fine. (2002, 9 April). *The Moscow Times*.

Oates, S. (2006). *Television, Democracy, and Elections in Russia*. New York: Routledge Publishers.

O'Brien, D. M., & Ohkoshi, Y. (2001). Stifling Judicial Independence from Within: The Japanese Judiciary. In P. H. Russell & D. M. O'Brien (Eds.), *Judicial Independence in the Age of Democracy: Critical Perspectives from Around the World* (p. 39). Charlottesville: University Press of Virginia.

O'Brien, T. (2010). Problems of political transition in Ukraine: leadership failure and democratic consolidation. *Contemporary Politics* 16(4), 355–67.

O'Donnell, G. (2004). Why the Rule of Law Matters. *Journal of Democracy*, 15(4), 32–46.

O'Donnell, G., & Schmitter, P. (1986). *Transitions from Authoritarian Rule: Tentative Conclusions about Uncertain Democracies*. Baltimore: Johns Hopkins University Press.

O. K. (2003). Personal interview.

O. K. (2004). Personal interview.

O. M. (2003). Personal interview.

Orenstein, M., & Kalandadze, K. (2009). Electoral Protest and Democratisation Beyond the Colour Revolutions. *Comparative Political Studies*, 42(11), 1403–25.

Open Society Institute. (2001). *Judicial Independence in the Czech Republic*. Budapest: Open Society Institute.

OSCE/ODIHR (2001). Ukraine: Review of the Law on Elections of People's Deputies, 26 November 2001. Warsaw: OSCE/ODIHR.

OSCE/ODIHR. (2002). Ukraine Parliamentary Elections, 31 March 2002, Final Report. Warsaw: OSCE/ODIHR.

(2004). Russian Federation Elections to the State Duma, 7 December 2003 Election Observation Mission Report. Warsaw: OSCE/ODIHR.

Parkhomchuk, T. (2002). Osobennosti Provintsial'nogo Oprotestovyvaniya. *Zerkalo Nedeli 14*.

Partiya "Yabluko" na s'ezde ob'yavila o perekhode v zhestkuyu oppozitsiyu k vlasti. (2002, March 25). *UNIAN*.

Pashin, S. (2004). Interview with author, April 7. Moscow, Russia.

Pedersen, M. (1983). Changing Patterns of Electoral Volatility in European Party Systems, 1948–1977: Explorations in Explanation. In H. Daalder & P. Mair (Eds.), *West European Party Systems: Continuity and Change* (pp. 29–66). Beverly Hills, CA: Sage Publications.

P. G. (2003). Personal interview.

Piana, D. (2010). *Judicial Accountabilities in New Europe: From Rule of Law to Quality of Justice*. Farnham, England: Ashgate.

Popova, M. (2010). Political Competition and Judicial Independence in Electoral Democracies: An Empirical Test of the Strategic Pressure Theory, Laws Locations:

The Textures of Legality in Developing and Transitional Societies, University of Wisconsin Law School.

Priest, G., & Klein, B. (1984). The Selection of Disputes for Litigation. *The Journal of Legal Studies*, XIII, 1–55.

Protsyk, O. (2004). Ruling with Decrees: Presidential Decree Making in Russia and Ukraine. *Europe-Asia Studies*, 56(5), 637–60.

Protsyk, O., & Wilson, A. (2003). Centre Politics in Russia and Ukraine: Patronage, Power and Virtuality. *Party Politics*, 9(6), 703–27.

Puddington, A. (2011). Democracy Under Duress. *Journal of Democracy* 22(2), 18–31.

Ramseyer, J. M. (1994). The Puzzling (In)dependence of Courts: A Comparative Approach. *Journal of Legal Studies*, 23(2), 721–47.

Ramseyer, J. (1997). Judicial Independence in a Civil Law Regime: The Evidence from Japan. *Oxford Journal of Law, Economics, and Organisation*, 13(2), 259–86.

Ramseyer, J. M., & Rasmusen, E. B. (1997). Judicial Independence in a Civil Law Regime: The Evidence from Japan. *Journal of Law, Economics, and Organization*, 13(2), 259–86.

(2001a). Why Are Japanese Judges So Conservative in Politically Charged Cases? *American Political Science Review*, 95(5), 331–44.

(2001b). Why Is the Japanese Conviction Rate So High? *Journal of Legal Studies*, 30(1), 53–88.

(2003). *Measuring Judicial Independence: The Political Economy of Judging in Japan.* Chicago: University of Chicago Press.

Ramseyer, M. J., & Rosenbluth, F. M. (1993). *Japan's Political Marketplace*, Cambridge, MA: Harvard University Press

Raz, J. (1990). The Politics of the Rule of Law. *Ratio Juris*, 3(3), 330–45.

Razumkov Centre. (2001). Factors Leading to the Escalation of Threats to Ukraine's Information Security, 1 (13). Kyiv.

Reuter, O., & Remington, T. (2009). Dominant Party Regimes and the Commitment Problem: The Case of United Russia. *Comparative Political Studies*, 42(4), 501–26.

Reznik, G. (2004). Interview with author, April 5. Moscow, Russia.

Rios Figueroa, J. (2006). Institutional Determinants of the Judicialisation of Policy in Brazil and Mexico. *Journal of Latin American Studies*, 38(4), 739–66.

Rodan, G. (1998). Asia and the International Press: Political Significance of Expanding Markets. *Democratization*, 5(2), 125–54.

Rose, R. (2001). A diverging Europe. *Journal of Democracy*, 12(1), 93–106.

Rosenberg, G. N. (1992). Judicial Independence and the Reality of Political Power. *The Review of Politics*, 54(3), 369–88.

Rosenn, K. (1987). The Protection of Judicial Independence in Latin America. *University of Miami Inter-American Law Review*, 19 (1), 1–35

Ross, C. (2000). Federalism and Democratization in Russia. *Communist and Post-Communist Studies*, 33(4), 403–20.

Rudenko, G. (2001, August 10). V Kieve Osvobodili Muzha Yulii Tymoshenko. *Kommersant.* Retrieved June 28, 2010, from http://www.kommersant.ru/doc.aspx?DocsID=278001

(2002, October 16). Prezident i ego Delo: Leonid Kuchma Poshel po 11 Stat'yam Ugolovnogo Kodeksa. *Kommersant.* Retrieved June 28, 2010, from http://www.compromat.ru/page_12342.htm

Russell, P. H., & O'Brien, D. M. (Eds.). (2001). *Judicial Independence in the Age of Democracy: Critical Perspectives from Around the World*. Charlottesville: University Press of Virginia.

Russell, P. H., & Malleson, K. (2006). *Appointing judges in an age of judicial power: Critical perspectives from around the world*. Toronto: University of Toronto Press.

Sagareva, O. (2004, October 22). 'Rodina' v Kol'tse Druzei. *Moskovskie Novosti*.

Salzberger, E. M. (1993). A Positive Analysis of the Doctrine of Separation of Powers, or: Why Do We Have an Independent Judiciary? *International Review of Law and Economics, 13*(4), 349–79.

Salzberger, E. M., & Fenn, P. (1999). Judicial Independence: Some Evidence from the English Court of Appeal. *Journal of Law and Economics, 42*( 2), 831–47.

Sartori, A. (2003). An Estimator for Some Binary-Outcome Selection Models Without Exclusion Restrictions. *Political Analysis, 11*, 111–38.

Sas, I. (2004, September 15). Ugolovnoe Pravo Prevrashchaetsya v Instrument Politiki, *Nezavisimaya Gazeta*. Retrieved June 12, 2007, from http://www.ng.ru/events/2004–09–15/6_reznik.html

Sasse, G. (2010). The Role of Regionalism. *Journal of Democracy, 21*(3), 99–106.

Schedler, A. (1998). What Is Democratic Consolidation? *Journal of Democracy, 9*(2), 91–107.

Scheppele, K. L. (1999). The New Hungarian Constitutional Court. *East European Constitutional Review, 8*(4), 81–8.

(2002). Declarations of Independence: Judicial Reactions to Political Pressure. In S. B. Burbank & B. Friedman (Eds.), *Judicial Independence at the Crossroads: An Interdisciplinary Approach* (pp. 227–79). Thousand Oaks, CA.: Sage Publications.

Schmitter, P. (1994). Dangers and Dilemmas of Democracy. *Journal of Democracy, 5*(2), 57–74.

Schwarz, C. (1973). Judges Under the Shadow: Judicial Independence in the United States and Mexico. *California Western International Law Journal, 3*, 260–332.

(1977). Rights and Remedies in the Federal District Courts of Mexico and the United States. *Hastings Constitutional Law Quarterly, 4*, 60–95.

Segal, J. A., & Spaeth, H. J. (1993). *The Supreme Court and the Attitudinal Model*. Cambridge and New York: Cambridge University Press.

Selznick, P. (1996). Social Justice: A Communitarian Perspective. *Responsive Community, 6*(4), 13–25.

Shapiro, M. M. (1981). *Courts, a Comparative and Political Analysis*. Chicago: University of Chicago Press.

Sharafutdinova, G. (2006). When Do Elites Compete? The Determinants of Political Competition in Russian Regions. *Comparative Politics, 38*(3), 273–93.

Shetreet, S. (1984). Judicial Independence and Accountability in Israel. *International and Comparative Law Quarterly, 33*(4), 979–1012.

Shevchenko, T. (2003). Novye Sredstva Sudebnoi Zashchity v Delakh Protiv SMI i Zhurnalistov v Ukraine. In *Sbornik analiticheskikh dokladov po sovremennomu sostoyaniyu zakonodatel'stva o SMI v stranakh SNG I Pribaltiki*. Moscow: Institut Problem Informatsionnogo Prava. Retrieved from http://medialaw.ru/publications/books/sng/08.html

Shevel, O. S. (2011). *Migration, Refugee Policy, and State Building in Postcommunist Europe*. New York: Cambridge University Press.

Shishkin, V. (2004). Interview with author, April 26. Kyiv, Ukraine.

Shklar, J. N. (1986). *Legalism: Law, Morals, And Political Trials.* Cambridge, MA: Harvard University Press.

Silitski. V. (2009). What Are We Trying to Explain? *Journal of Democracy,* 20(1), 86–9.

Simakin, D. (2004, January 23). Nevzlina Zashchitit Reznik, *Nezavisimaya Gazeta.* Retrieved June 15, 2007, from http://www.ng.ru/events/2004–01–23/6_nevzlin. html

Simon, R. (2004). Media, Myth and Reality in Russia's State-Managed Democracy. *Parliamentary Affairs,* 57(1), 169–84.

S. K. (2003, November). Personal interview.

Skaar, E. (2003). *Judicial Independence: A Key to Justice. An Analysis of Latin America in the 1990s.* Los Angeles: University of California, Los Angeles.

Skrobot, (2004, June 11). Vykhodit Vse Zhe Sharili?. *Nezavisimaya Gazeta.* Retrieved June 12, 2007, from http://www.ng.ru/events/2004–06–11/7_reznik.html

Skuratov, Y. (2004). Interview with author, April 5. Moscow, Russia.

Smithey, S. I., & Ishiyama, J. (2000). Judicious Choices: Designing Courts in Post-Communist Politics. *Communist and Post-Communist Studies,* 33(2), 163–82.

Smyth, R., Lowry, A., & Wilkening, B. (2007). Engineering Victory: Institutional Reform, Informal Institutions, and the Formation of a Hegemonic Party Regime in the Russian Federation. *Post- Soviet Affairs,* 23(2), 118–37.

Sokolov, M. (2003). Rossiya Odnomandatnaya: ot Moskvy do Vladivostoka. *Radio Svoboda.* Retrieved May 8, 2006, from http://www.svoboda.org/programs/el/2003/ el.101603.asp

Solomon Jr., P. H. (1996). *Soviet Criminal Justice Under Stalin.* New York: Cambridge University Press.

(2002). Putin's Judicial Reform: Making Judges Accountable as well as Independent. *East European Constitutional Review,*1 (1/2), 117–24.

(2004). Judicial Power in Russia: Through the Prism of Administrative Justice. *Law and Society Review* 38(3), 549–82.

(2010). Improving Russian Justice with Foreign Assistance: Model Courts and the Tactical Approach. *Governance: An International Journal of Policy, Administration, and Institutions,* 23(3), 437–62.

Solomon Jr., P. H., & Foglesong, T. S. (2000). *Courts and Transition in Russia: The Challenge of Judicial Reform.* Boulder, CO: Westview Press.

S. P. (2004, April). Interview with author.

Spiller, P. T., & Gely, R. (1990). A Rational Choice Theory of Supreme Court Statutory Decisions with Applications to the State Farm and Grove City Cases. *Journal of Law, Economics and Organization,* 6(2), 263–300.

Spitzer, M. L., & Cohen, L. R. (2000). The Government Litigant Advantage: Implications for the Law. *Florida State University Law Review,* 28(1), 391–425.

Squire, P., & Fastnow, C. (1994). Comparing Gubernatorial and Senatorial Elections. *Political Research Quarterly,* 47(3), 705–20.

Stephenson, M. (2003). When the Devil Turns…: The Political Foundations of Independent Judicial Review. *Journal of Legal Studies,* 32, 59–89.

Stiglitz, J. E. (1999). Whither Reform? Ten Years of the Transition. Paper presented at the Annual World Bank Conference on Development Economics. Retrieved May

8, 2006. from http://www2.gsb.columbia.edu/faculty/jstiglitz/download/1999_4_ Wither_Reform.pdf

(2002). *Globalization and Its Discontents.* New York: W. W. Norton.

Stolichnye sud'i otmenili ukaz Prezidenta ob uvol'nenii khar'kovskogo sud'i Mikhaila Borodina. (2005). *Ves' Khar'kov.* Retrieved May 1, 2006, from http://www.all. kharkov.ua/news/news/2005–01–29/_p4.html

Stone Sweet, A. (2000). *Governing with Judges: Constitutional Politics in Europe.* Oxford: Oxford University Press.

Storozhenko, A. (2001, December 26). Omelchenko Announced Jihad to His Opponents. *Part.org.ua.* Retrieved May 6, 2006, from http://part.org.ua/eng/index. php?art=32839763

Stromback, J., & Kaid, l. (2008). *The Handbook of Election News Coverage around the World.* New York: Routledge Publishers.

Sudebnyi Departament pri Vekhovnom Sude RF. (2000). Rabota Sudov Obshchei Yurisdiktsii v 1999 godu, *Rossiiskaya yustitsiya, 7,* 57–60.

Sudebnyi Departament pri Vekhovnom Sude Rossiiskoi Federatsii. Sistema Sudebnogo Departamenta. Retrieved November 10, 2010, from http://www.cdep.ru/index. php?id=34&item=144

Tate, N. C., & Vallinder, T. (Eds.). (1995). *The Global Expansion of Judicial Power.* New York: New York University Press.

Timoshenko, B. (2002). Interview with author, August 3. Moscow, Russia.

(2004). Interview with author, April 10. Moscow, Russia.

Trochev, A. (2004). Less Democracy, More Courts: A Puzzle of Judicial Review in Russia. *Law & Society Review, 38*(3), 513–48.

(2006). Judicial Selection in Russia: Towards Accountability and Centralization. In K. Malleson & P. H. Russell (Eds.), *Appointing Judges in an Age of Judicial Power: Critical Perspectives from Around the World.* Toronto: University of Toronto Press.

(2008). *Judging Russia: Constitutional Court in Russian Politics, 1990–2006.* Cambridge: Cambridge University Press.

(April 01, 2010). Meddling with justice: Competitive politics, impunity, and distrusted courts in post-orange Ukraine. *Demokratizatsiya, 18,* 2, 122–47.

(2010). Suing Putin: Patterns of Anti-Government Litigation in Russia, 2000–2008. *Univ. of Wisconsin Legal Studies Research Paper No. 1134.*

Tselobanova, R. (2003, December 3). Pochemu Gubernator Podderzhivaet Vyacheslava Shporta: Interv'yu s Viktorom Ivanovichev Ishaevym. *Amurskaya Zarya.*

Tsentral'na Viborcha Komisiya. (2002). Zbirnik Rishen' Sudiv Za Rezul'tatami Rozglyadu Skarg Sub'ektiv Vyborchogo Protsesu Po Vyborakh Narodnykh Depitativ Ukrainy V 2002 Rotsi. Kyiv: Tsentral'na Viborcha Komisiya.

Tsetsura, K. (2009). An Explanatory Study of Media Transparency in Ukraine. *Public Relations Journal* 3(2), Retrieved October 21, 2011, from http:// www.prsa.org/SearchResults/download/6D-030205/0/An_Exploratory_ Study_of_the_Media_Transparency_in

Tucker, J. A. (2006). *Regional Economic Voting: Russia, Poland, Hungary, Slovakia and the Czech Republic, 1990–1999.* Cambridge and New York: Cambridge University Press.

Ukraine ex-Interior Minister Yuri Lutsenko arrested. (2010, December 28). *BBC News.* Retrieved from http://www.bbc.co.uk/news/world-europe-12085959

Ukraine Investigates another Tymoshenko Minister. (2010, December 24). *Spero News*. Retrieved 2011 from http://www.speroforum.com/a/45654/Ukraine-investigates-another-tymoshenko-minister

Vanberg, G. (2001). Legislative-Judicial Relations: A Game-Theoretic Approach to Constitutional Review. *American Journal of Political Science*, 42(2), 346–62.

Vasilenko, Y. (2003). Interview with author, November 27. Kyiv, Ukraine.

Verkhovnii Sud Ukraini. (2004). Analiz Roboty Sudiv Zagal'noi Yurisdiktsii v 2004 r. Retrieved October 20, 2011, from http://www.scourt.gov.ua/clients/vs.nsf/o/D990 C6B449593AACC3257019002411C9?OpenDocument&CollapseView&RestrictT oCategory=D990C6B449593AACC3257019002411C9&Count=500&

Verkhovskii, A. (2006). *Demokratiya Vertikali*. Moscow: Sova.

V. G. (2003). Personal Interview.

V. S. (2004). Personal interview.

Wagner, W. (1997). Civil Law, Individual Rights, and Judicial Activism in Late Imperial Russia, in Peter Solomon, Jr. (Ed.), *Reforming Justice in Russia, 1864–1996*. Armonk, NY and London: M. E. Sharpe.

Waisbord, S. (2002). The Challenges of Investigative Journalism. *University of Miami Law Review*, 56(2), 377–95.

Waldron, J. (1989). The Rule of Law in Contemporary Liberal Theory. *Ratio Juris*, 2(1), 79–96.

Walicki, A. (1979). *A History of Russian Thought: From the Enlightenment to Marxism*. Stanford, CA: Stanford University Press.

Wanted by Police: Former Economy Minister Bohdan Danylyshyn. (2010, August 26). *Kyiv Post*. Retrieved 2011 from http://www.kyivpost.com/news/nation/detail/79932

Way, L. A. (2005). Authorization State Building and the Sources of Regime Competitiveness in the Fourth Wave: The Cases of Belarus, Moldova, Russia, and Ukraine. *World Politics*, 57(2), 231–61.

Weingast, B. (1997). The Political Foundations of Democracy and the Rule of Law. *The American Political Science Review*, 91(2), 245–63.

White, S., Oates, S., & McAllister, I. (2005). Media Effects and Russian Elections, 1999–2000. *British Journal of Political Science*, 35(2), 191–208.

Whittington, K. (1999). *Constitutional Construction: Divided Powers and Constitutional Meaning*. Cambridge, MA: Harvard University Press.

Whittington, K. E. (2003). Legislative Sanctions and the Strategic Environment of Judicial Review. *International Journal of Constitutional Law*, 1(3), 446–74.

Widner, J. A. (2001). Building the Rule of Law: Francis Nyalali and the Road to Judicial Independence in Africa. *Journal of Democracy*, 12(4), 166–70.

Wikipedia. (2006). Andriy Shevchenko. Retrieved May 2, 2006, from http://en.wikipedia.org/wiki/Andriy_Shevchenko

Williams, K. (2007). The Growing Litigiousness of Czech Elections. *Europe-Asia Studies* 59(6), 937–59.

Wilson, A. (2002). Ukraine's 2002 Elections: Less Fraud, More Virtuality [Electronic Version]. *East European Constitutional Review*, 11. Retrieved from http://www.law.nyu.edu/eecr/vol11num3/focus/wilson.htm

Wilson, A., & Birch, S. (1999). Voting Stability, Political Gridlock: Ukraine's 1998 Parliamentary Elections. *Europe-Asia Studies*, 51, 1040–60.

Woods, P. J., & Hilbink, L. (2009). Comparative Sources of Judicial Empowerment: Ideas and Interests. *Political Research Quarterly*, 62(4), 745–52.

Wortman, R. (1976) *The Development of Russian Legal Consciousness*. Chicago: University of Chicago Press.

Wright, S. (2003). The French Conseil Constitutionnel in 2001 and 2002. *European Public Law*, 9(3), 315–22.

Yabloko Press Release. (2003, March 6). Judicial Reprisal Against Novaya Gazeta Newspaper Represents Another Stage of the Onslaught Against the Free Mass Media. Retrieved May 2, 2006, from http://www.eng.yabloko.ru/Press/2002/3/060302.html

Y. V. (2003). Personal interview.

Zadorozhnii, O. (2004). Deputats'ka nedotorkannist': suchasna parlaments'la ta sudova praktika: pravoviy analiz. Kyiv: Logos.

Zamkovenko, M. (2004). Interview with author, April 27. Kyiv, Ukraine.

Zamkovenko Uvolili Spravedlivo: Verkhovnyi Sud Ukrainy. (2002, June 6). *Ukrainskaya Pravda*. Retrieved June 6, 2007, from http://www.pravda.com.ua/rus/news/2002/06/6/4368047/

Zassoursky, A. (2004). *Iskusheniya Svobodoi: Rossiskaya Zhurnalistika 1990–2004*. Moscow, Russia: Moscow State University Press.

# Index